The Elements of Creativity and Giftedness in Mathematics

Edited by

Bharath Sriraman
The University of Montana, USA

Kyeong Hwa Lee
Seoul National University, Korea

SENSE PUBLISHERS
ROTTERDAM/BOSTON/TAIPEI

A C.I.P. record for this book is available from the Library of Congress.

ISBN: 978-94-6091-437-9 (paperback)
ISBN: 978-94-6091-438-6 (hardback)
ISBN: 978-94-6091-439-3 (e-book)

Published by: Sense Publishers,
P.O. Box 21858,
3001 AW Rotterdam,
The Netherlands
http://www.sensepublishers.com

Printed on acid-free paper

The Elements of Creativity and Giftedness in Mathematics

ADVANCES IN CREATIVITY AND GIFTEDNESS
Volume 1

TABLE OF CONTENTS

AIMS AND SCOPE

Advances in Creativity and Giftedness is the first internationally established book series that focuses exclusively on the constructs of creativity and giftedness as pertaining to the psychology, philosophy, pedagogy and ecology of talent development across the milieus of family, school, institutions, organizations and society. ACG strives to synthesize both domain specific and domain general efforts at developing creativity, giftedness and talent. The books in the series are international in scope and include the efforts of researchers, clinicians and practitioners across the globe.

BHARATH SRIRAMAN AND KYEONG HWA LEE

1. WHAT ARE THE ELEMENTS OF GIFTEDNESS AND CREATIVITY IN MATHEMATICS?

An Overview of the KMS-AMS Symposium and the Book

INTRODUCTION

The first joint meeting of the Korean Mathematical Society and the American Mathematical Society was held in Seoul, Korea from December 16 to 20, 2009. We organized a special session and posted the main theme "Creativity, Giftedness and Talent Development in Mathematics" for this meeting to share recent research results and perspectives on creativity and giftedness from the two countries. Three presentations from the United States and nine from Korea were invited for the meeting. Different settings, goals, trials, results, and implications for creativity development and gifted education from the two countries were actively discussed in the meeting. We first briefly summarize the papers presented at the meeting and then provide an overview of this book.

At the joint meeting discoveries and verifications by gifted elementary students were reported by Na from Korea. She focused on how mathematically gifted students collect and activate relevant knowledge and strategies to discover something new to them. Jung from Korea also reported how he developed a student-centred gifted education program using technology and what characteristics he identified from the students who experienced conjecturing and justification while partaking in the education program designed by him. Yi, Hong and Choi from Korea presented their trial to design and application of a reading program for mathematically gifted students. Lee, Oh and Lee from Korea discussed inclusion of ambiguity in creativity development. Their presentation provoked the audience to think about relevant teaching perspectives to meet the gifted in mathematics. Park from Korea detailed the comparison data between Korean gifted high school students in mathematics and science. Kim and Song shared what they observed on generalization and cognition of representation from Korean mathematically gifted students. Phillips, Phillips and Du from U.S. reported on the history, the kinds, and the use of Chinese abacus in gifted education. Suh, Seshaiyer and Fulginiti from U.S. presented their research result on educating gifted students from diverse populations while focusing on their efforts to develop mathematical potential of underrepresented groups. Kim, Lee, Park and Ko from Korea reported on gifted students' building their understandings on mathematical logic. Ko and Lee from Korea discussed if Korean mathematically gifted students are also good at statistical reasoning. Last but not least, Cho and Song presented how to use technology for facilitating spatial-visualization and mathematization.

B. Sriraman and K.H. Lee (eds.), The Elements of Creativity and Giftedness in Mathematics, 1–4.

The meeting was fruitful for all participants from the two countries to understand why creativity development is so crucial in gifted education though it became clear that the two countries face quite different needs or requests on gifted education from society, parents, and gifted students.

Being aware of the need to take cultural influences or background into consideration for any discussion of creativity and gifted development in mathematics, we were inspired to open up the book to incorporate and include current research on creativity and giftedness from other countries. We extended our invitation for contributions to the present book to countries where creativity and giftedness are finding an important voice in discussions of policy, school programs, university education, teacher training, and changing needs of society in countries like Sweden, Norway, Turkey, Israel, Iran, China and Canada. The different chapters highlighted each nation's context on gifted education and culture-laden interpretations on creativity or giftedness in mathematics.

In Chapter 2, Yuan & Sriraman report on a cross cultural study involving U.S and Chinese high school students exploring the construct of mathematical creativity from a problem posing point of view. Numerous quantitative batteries such as the Torrance Tests of Creative Thinking [TTCT] and problem posing tasks were used to discern similarities and differences in creative abilities of comparable groups of U.S and Chinese students. Among the findings reported in this chapter are a significant relationship between creativity and mathematical problem-posing abilities of high school students taking advanced courses in the Chinese group but not in the U.S. group.

Chapter 3 by Ko & Lee focuses on mathematically talented students' understanding of the concept of average, whether they have a greater understanding of average than non-talented students, and how mathematically talented students' ability in statistics, especially as it relates to average, can be improved.

Chapter 4 by Juter & Sriraman explores the complexity inherent in distilling the elements of creativity and giftedness by constructing seven hypothetical case studies based on the research literature. This chapter examines questions such as: What characterizes high achieving in mathematics? Does it require certain extraordinary skills, skills you are born with or skills you can acquire by hard work, i.e., can anyone become a high achiever? On the other hand, what does it mean to be gifted in mathematics? What does it mean to be creative in mathematics? What does it mean to be intelligent in mathematics? Is it enough to work hard from an average level of understanding to become gifted? What are the relations between gifted, high achieving, creative, intelligent? Are these terms synonyms? antonyms? Or is there more complexity to these terms and the need to understand the subtleties in their usage? These issues are discussed in Juter & Sriraman's chapter.

Scandinavian countries have traditionally emphasized egalitarianism in educational policy and curricula. However with the changing needs of society as a result of globalization, "the winds are changing" so to speak even in countries which have been staunchly socialistic and non-meritocratic in their sociopolitical orientation. Mattson & Bengmark in Chapter 5 provide a description of the status of gifted education in mathematics in Sweden by highlighting the development of four components - a) national policies, b) advocacy groups, c) research, teacher education and curriculum development, and d) implementation in schools.

In the Israeli context, Leikin & Stanger report on an ongoing study which discusses the opportunities that are available to students with high mathematical abilities in school mathematics. The focus of chapter 6 is on teaching mathematically able students (MAS) in heterogeneous mathematics classrooms. Based on individual interviews with teachers, these researchers describe images that teachers hold of mathematically gifted students. Through their analysis in Chapter 6, Leikin & Stanger suggest that mathematics teachers need special preparation for the education of MAS in each and every type of mathematics class.

In Chapter 7, Suh & Fulgniti report on a study conducted in the U.S, which explored strategies for developing mathematical potential and enhancing mathematics instruction for diverse learners from a low socio-economic population identified as "young scholars".

Chapters 8 (Karp) and 11 (Freiman) contain narratives from researchers with an intimate knowledge of models of talent development in the former Soviet Union, but who are now respectively situated in the U.S and Canadian contexts. They reflection on challenges and issues arising in implementing models that work elsewhere in other cultural and national contexts and provide food for thought to those that consider talent development to be culturally invariant. Freiman focuses on challenges encountered in ongoing projects in New Brunswick, Canada, while Karp gives a reflective narrative of his personal experiences.

Chapter 9 unpacks the notion of mathematical creativity by taking into account specific research findings from contemporary literature. Sriraman, Yaftian & Lee do not attempt a summative review or a meta-synthesis of what is known, but instead focus on findings related to what it means to solve a problem in mathematics, and unpack different constituent ideas in mathematical creativity, such as "incubation".

Cho, Song and Lee (Chapter 10) feature multi-dimensional considerations such as observation and performance assessment to evaluate students' abilities, and a teacher training program for the purpose of giving guidance for the selection process of gifted students.

In chapter 11, the results from an ambitious qualitative study on mathematical creativity in Turkey are reported. The authors (Kyymaz, Sriraman and Lee) extend current frameworks on mathematical creativity to determine the characteristics of creative thinking skills developed by secondary mathematics prospective teachers' during the process of mathematical problem-solving.

In the Norwegian context, Øystein is currently investigating high achieving students' mathematical reasoning when given unfamiliar mathematical tasks. In Chapter 13, high achieving students are given an unfamiliar trigonometric equation and through interpretive inquiry, Øystein found that the students' way of thinking is strongly linked with imitative reasoning and only when they received some form of guidance, are they able to display flexible and creative mathematical reasoning.

The book concludes with an aesthetically pleasing chapter from Israel in which pathways of creativity and the practice in creation and analysis of useful and mathematically meaningful artifacts are reported. In chapter 14, Massarwe, Verner & Bshouty followed the aforementioned creative pathway in the workshop "Geometry of Ornaments" conducted in 2008–2009 in one of the Israeli Arab teacher colleges.

Putting together this book has not been an easy task given the multitude of perspectives that needed to be considered to offer the reader the "constituent" elements of creativity and giftedness in mathematics. We thank the authors that are a part of this edited collection for their work, the editorial advisory board for their background support. Last but not least, we are grateful to Peter de Liefde, the founder of Sense Publishers for bringing educational human development in the forms of creativity and giftedness into the Sense fold by launching the new series *Advances in Creativity and Giftedness*, and for his valuable technical support in producing this book.

ACKNOWLEDGEMENT

The first editor (Sriraman) extends his sincere gratitude and appreciation to the second editor (KyeongHwa Lee) for co-ordinating the special sessions on creativity, giftedness and talent development at the first joint meeting of the Korean and American mathematical societies, and for providing continuous support in developing this book over the course of the last 10 months. Without this strong support, the book may never have materialized.

Bharath Sriraman
Dept of Mathematical Sciences
The University of Montana
USA

Kyeong Hwa Lee
Seoul National University
Korea

XIANWEI YUAN AND BHARATH SRIRAMAN

2. AN EXPLORATORY STUDY OF RELATIONSHIPS BETWEEN STUDENTS' CREATIVITY AND MATHEMATICAL PROBLEM-POSING ABILITIES

Comparing Chinese and U.S Students

INTRODUCTION

The literature is replete with statements alleging that people in the Western countries are more creative than people in the East Asian countries (Zhao, 2008; Rudowicz & Hui, 1998; Yue & Rudowicz, 2002; Lubart, 1990; Dunn, Zhang, & Ripple, 1988). A typical explanation for those statements is that, citizens of the Western cultures tend to be independent and to find meaning largely by reference to their own internal thoughts, feelings, and actions rather than by those of others; while citizens of the East tend to hold an interdependent perspective of the self in which meaning depends more on interpersonal relationships (Markus & Kitayama, 1991). In other words, in the Western countries, individuals often focus on discovering and expressing themselves and on accentuating differences from others, whereas East Asians tend to organize more into hierarchies in which individuals seek membership in larger communities (Zha, Walczyk, Grifffith-Ross, & Tobacyk, 2006).

In the domain of mathematics, it is widely accepted in China that U.S. students are more creative in mathematics than Chinese students (e.g., National Center for Education Development, 2000; Yang, 2007). According to Mathematics Curriculum Development Group of Basic Education of Education Department (2002), one of the most alleged prominent weaknesses is that Chinese students lack creativity in mathematics. In the professional world, it is said that the publishing activities of Chinese mathematicians in the world-class journals are far from enough (Ye, 2003). At the same time, many Chinese teachers and educators believe that U.S. teachers and educators hold the opinion that it is more important to develop students' creativity in mathematics than to teach students basic mathematical knowledge (Jia & Jiang, 2001). It is also well-known in China that, in the United States, mathematics teachers emphasize students' active involvement in the process of learning and that they also tend to use open problems and various activities in teaching mathematics–which are perceived to benefit students' development of creativity in mathematics (e.g., Bai, 2004; Zhu, Bai, & Qu, 2003).

Despite the fact that "mathematical creativity ensures the growth of the field of mathematics as a whole" (Sriraman, 2009, p. 13), there is a lack of an accepted definition of mathematical creativity (Mann, 2006). Sriraman (2005) pointed out that most of the extant definitions of mathematical creativity are vague or elusive.

B. Sriraman and K.H. Lee (eds.), The Elements of Creativity and Giftedness in Mathematics, 5–28.

For example, according to Sriraman, Hadamard and Poincaré defined mathematical creativity as the ability to discern, or choose; Birkhoff defined mathematical creativity as the ability to distinguish between acceptable and unacceptable patterns; to Ervynck, creativity is the ability to engage in nonalgorithmic decision-making. More recently, according to Chamberlin and Moon (as cited in Shriki, 2010), in the context of mathematics, creativity of students is defined as having "an unusual ability to generate novel and useful solutions to simulated or real applied problems using mathematical modeling". Sriraman (2009), however, argued that in the context of creativity in mathematics, "the results of creative work may not always have implications that are 'useful' in terms of applicability in the real world ... it is sufficient to define creativity as the ability to produce novel or original work" (p. 14–15).

In the mean time, there are claims that the ability of posing problems in mathematics is linked to creativity. For example, Jensen (1973) looked at students' ability to pose mathematical questions based on a given scenario as one measure of mathematical creativity. According to Jensen, for students to be creative in mathematics, they should be able to pose mathematical questions that extend and deepen the original problem as well as solve the problems in a variety of ways. Silver (1997) argued that inquiry-oriented mathematics instruction which includes problem-solving and problem-posing tasks and activities can assist students to develop more creative approaches to mathematics. It is claimed that through the use of such tasks and activities, teachers can increase their students' capacity with respect to the core dimensions of creativity, namely, fluency, flexibility, and originality (e.g., Presmeg, 1981; Torrance, 1988). English (1997a) claimed that in her study of a problem posing program, the activities had a strong emphasis on children being creative, divergent, and flexible in their thinking and students were encouraged to look beyond the basic meanings of mathematics with those activities.

In the United States, problem posing has been a goal of school mathematics since at least 1989. According to the National Council of Teachers of Mathematics [NCTM] (1989), students should be given opportunities to solve mathematical problems using multiple solution strategies and to formulate and create their own problems from given situations. In China, problem posing was added to the goals for school mathematics only in the year 2002. In a document entitled the Interpretation of Mathematics Curriculum (Trial Version) (Mathematics Curriculum Development Group of Basic Education of Education Department, 2002), it is pointed out that students' abilities in problem solving and problem posing should be emphasized and that students should learn to find problems and pose problems in and out of the context of mathematics.

At the same time, mathematical problem posing has emerged to be a heated topic (e.g., English a, b, c, 1997; Silver, 1994). Despite the fact that the achievements in mathematics of students in the United States are poorer than those of students in East Asian countries (Stevenson & Stigler, 1992; Stigler & Hilbert, 1999), studies have shown that when it comes to mathematical problem posing, it is not the case. For example, in Cai and Hwang's (2002) study, the Chinese sixth graders outperformed the U.S. sixth graders on computational tasks, whereas with regard to problem posing, the Chinese students did not outperform the U.S. students. At the college and graduate school level, ability in problem posing also has caught the attention of mathematicians. For example, the Harvard professor Shing-Tung Yau (Sun, 2004), who is the only Chinese-born mathematician to have won the Fields Medal, compared graduate students who studied under him and commented that students from China are very good in basic skills but, in comparison with U.S. students, often lack mathematical creativity and ability in posing research questions.

In sum, the discussion about creativity and mathematical problem-posing abilities suggests that students in the Western countries are more creative than students in the East Asian countries and that the former are better at problem posing in mathematics than the latter. These claims seem to indicate some correlation between creativity and mathematical problem-posing ability. Although there are findings that show the correlations between the two in other fields, such as art (Csikszentmihalyi & Getzels, 1971), there are researchers who claimed that there was an incomplete basis for asserting a relationship in the domain of mathematics (Haylock, 1987).

The present study into U.S. and Chinese students promises to provide a rich and rewarding context for the investigation of the relationship between creativity and mathematical problem-posing ability. Specifically, the following three questions will be addressed in this study:

1. Are there differences in students' mathematical problem-posing abilities in the comparable groups? If so, what are the differences?
2. Are there differences in their creativity? If so, what are the differences?
3. Is there a significant relationship between students' creativity and mathematical problem-posing abilities in the comparable groups?

CONCEPTUAL FRAMEWORK

Guilford's Structure of Intellect Model

In the year 1950, Guilford and his associates hypothesized that fluency, flexibility, and originality would be three important aspects of creativity (Guilford, 1959). Such traits were found in Guilford's well-known structure of intellect model. Guilford claimed that the intellectual factors fall into two major groups–thinking and memory factors—and the great majority of them can be regarded as thinking factors. Within this group, a threefold division appears—cognitive (discovery) factors, production factors, and evaluation factors. The production group can be significantly subdivided into a class of convergent thinking abilities and a class of divergent thinking abilities. Guilford defined divergent production as the generation of information from given information, where the emphasis is on variety of output from the same source (information, originality, unusual synthesis or perspective). Included in the divergent thinking category were the factors of fluency, flexibility, originality, and elaboration. Fluency in thinking refers to the quantity of output. Flexibility in thinking refers to a change of some kind: a change in the meaning, interpretation, or use of something, a change in understanding of the task, a change of strategy in doing the task, or a change in direction of thinking, which may mean a new interpretation of the goal. Originality in thinking means the production of unusual, far-fetched, remote, or clever responses. In addition, an original idea should be socially useful. Elaboration in thinking means the ability of a person to produce detailed steps to make

7

a plan work. Guilford saw creative thinking as clearly involving what he categorized as divergent production.

In the present study, *Torrance Tests of Creative Thinking* [TTCT] (Torrance, 1966), which are based on the four factors, namely, Fluency, Flexibility, Originality, and Elaboration, are used to measure participants' creativity. However, only the three factors, namely, Fluency, Flexibility, and Originality, are used to guide the design and data analysis of the whole study, including the mathematical problem-posing test. Elaboration is not used because, in the scoring manual provided by the test designer, the scoring procedure has been greatly streamlined by having the scorer estimate the number of details within the six sets of limits determined by normative data (Torrance, 2008a). In other words, the scoring of the Elaboration is at best an estimate and, therefore, will not provide accurate information on participants' Elaboration ability. Also, the analysis of the problem-posing test (discussed in the next section) will be guided by the three factors mentioned above, too.

Mathematical Problem-posing Framework

Stoyanova and Ellerton classified a problem-posing situation as free, semi-structured or structured. According to this framework, a problem-posing situation is free when students are asked to generate a problem from a given, contrived or naturalistic situation (see Task 1 below), semi-structured when students are given an open situation and are invited to explore the structure of that situation, and to complete it by applying knowledge, skills, concepts and relationships from their previous mathematical experiences (see Task 2 below), and structured when problem-posing activities are based on a specific problem (see Task 3 below). The first two tasks were adapted from Stoyanova's (1997) dissertation and the third task was adapted from Stoyanova's (1997) dissertation and Cai's (2000) research.

Task 1: There are 10 girls and 10 boys standing in a line. Make up as many problems as you can that use the information in some way.

Task 2: In the picture below, there is a triangle and its inscribed circle. Make up as many problems as you can that are in some way related to this picture.

Task 3: Last night there was a party at your cousin's house and the doorbell rang 10 times. The first time the doorbell rang only one guest arrived. Each time the doorbell rang, three more guests arrived than had arrived on the previous ring.

(a) How many guests will enter on the 10th ring? Explain how you found your answer.

(b) Ask as many questions as you can that are in some way related to this problem.

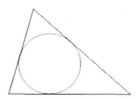

Figure 1. Figure for the semi-structured problem-posing situation example.

STUDY VARIABLES AND DEFINITION OF STUDY TERMS

Definition of Creativity

Although many researchers have attempted to define the concept of creativity, there is no universally accepted definition. However, Plucker and Beghetto (2004), in their literature review on creativity, argued that there are two key elements of creativity, specifically novelty (i.e., original, unique, new, fresh, different creations) and usefulness (i.e., specified, valuable, meaningful, relevant, appropriate, worthwhile creations). Plucker and Beghetto also pointed out that the combination of these two elements serves as the keystone of scholarly discussions and definitions of creativity. The production of something new is included in almost all of the definitions (Torrance, 1988), either explicitly or implicitly. According to Torrance, on the one hand, there are definitions maintaining that the product does not have to be new to the whole society but new to the person; On the other hand, there are definitions that emphasize the newness in terms of the society. In addition to novelty, the second defining component of creativity concerns the extent to which a proposed idea fits within boundaries imported by constraints. In other words, novel productions need to be useful in a given context to quality as being creative. According to Torrance, creativity is defined as the process of sensing difficulties, problems, gaps in information, missing elements, something askew; making guesses and formulating hypotheses about these deficiencies; evaluating and testing these guesses and hypotheses; possibly revising and retesting them; and finally communicating the results (Torrance, 1988, p. 47).

The creativity measurement in this study, *Torrance Tests of Creative Thinking* (Torrance, 1966), comprise test activities that are models of the creative process described in the definition of Torrance. Also, Torrance's definition is to some extent parallel to Polya's (1954) four principles on how to solve problems in mathematics, namely, understand the problem, devise a plan, carry out the plan, and look back/ Review/extend. Therefore, in this study, Torrance's definition are adopted.

Definition of Mathematical Problem Posing

There are different terms that are used in reference to problem posing, such as problem finding, problem sensing, problem formulating, creative problem-discovering, problematizing, problem creating, and problem envisaging (Dillon, 1982; Jay & Perkins, 1997). In the present study, mathematical problem posing will be defined as the process by which, on the basis of mathematical experience, students construct personal interpretations of concrete situations and from these situations formulate meaningful mathematical problems (Stoyanova & Ellerton, 1996). In the proposed study, mathematical problem-posing abilities will be measured by means of a mathematical problem-posing test. More details about the test were discussed in the Conceptual Framework section.

RESEARCH DESIGN

In this study, three tests were administered to the students. The first test is the *Torrance Tests of Creative Thinking* (Torrance, 1966). The second is a mathematical

9

problem-posing test, and the third, a mathematics content test. Medians of the first two tests were compared and correlations between the scores of the first two tests were used to explore relationships between creativity and mathematical problem-posing abilities. The third test, the mathematics content test was used to examine students' levels of mathematical knowledge.

Since this study is exploratory and the participants in this study were not randomly selected from well-defined populations, the results will only provide some major attributes of the groups studied so that the researchers will be able to place the study in a larger context in the future. In other words, the findings of this study will not be generalized to the whole high school student population in each county. For that reason, descriptive rather than inferential statistics were used (Vogt, 2007). Spearman correlation coefficients were computed to measure the relationship between the two variables, namely, creativity and mathematical problem-posing ability.

PARTICIPANTS

Participants from China were selected from Shandong province which has a strong root in Confucian culture in the north of China. Participants from the United States were selected from a mid-western town in the United States. In English's (1997b) framework of Key Elements of Problem Posing, students' knowledge and reasoning play an important role in students' problem posing. Therefore, this study selected students who were taking advanced mathematics courses as participants to make sure that the participants have the knowledge and reasoning abilities needed for the problem-posing activities.

Participants from China

Chinese students in this study were from a small city, Jiaozhou, in China. As of the 2008 census, Jiaozhou has an urban population of 450,000 and an area of 45 km^2. As its name indicates, the No.1 High School of Jiaozhou is one of the two best high schools of the five high schools in the city. It currently has 49 staff, 159 teachers and about 3600 students distributed in the 10th, 11th, and 12th grades. In Jiaozhou, high school students are divided into two strands, namely, a science strand and an art strand. Usually, after the first semester in high school, students choose a strand and are assigned to different classes. Science students take more advanced mathematics courses in high school than arts students. In the school in this study in Jiaozhou, in each grade, there are two art strand classes and ten science strand classes, two of which are express science strand classes. Students in these two express science strand classes were admitted according to their achievement (total score of five subjects, namely, mathematics, literature, English, physics, and chemistry) in the high school entrance examination of the city, which they took after the 9th grade immediately before they entered the high school. The class in this study is one of the two 12th grade express science strand classes. Therefore, the participants from Jiaozhou can be considered as advanced in mathematics.

Participants from the United States

Normal is an incorporated town in McLean County, Illinois, United States. As of the 2000 census, it had a population of 45,386. According to the United States Census Bureau, the town has a total area of 13.7 square miles (35.4 km^2). There are three high schools in town. One of them is the University High School, which is a laboratory school of the College of Education at Illinois State University. University High School has about 600 students in grades 9 through 12. The U.S. students in this study were from two Advanced Placement Calculus classes and two Pre-Calculus classes. Those students were in the 11th or 12th grade.

In conclusion, although participants in this study are from two very different locations, by choosing students from advanced classes in advanced schools in each of the two locations, the researchers managed to focus on mathematically advanced high school students in each of the two locations. Initially, 68 Chinese students and 77 U.S. students agreed to participate in this study. However, since some students had to miss one or two of the three tests, not all the participants' test papers were analyzed. In the end, 55 Chinese participants and 30 U.S. participants were present for all the tests. Among the 30 U.S. students, 17 were female and 13 were male; 17 were AP Calculus Course students and 13 were from Pre-Calculus Course students. Among the 55 Chinese students, 18 were female and 37 were male; all of the Chinese students were in the 12th grade. The Chinese students in this study were from one class; while the U.S. students were from four different classes. That is one of the reasons why more U.S. students than Chinese students missed some of the tests and ended up dropping out from this study.

MEASURES AND INSTRUMENTATION

The measures and instrumentation in this study include the mathematics content test, the Figural Torrance Test of Creative Thinking, the Verbal Torrance Test of Creative Thinking, and the mathematical problem-posing test. Since the researchers were based in the United States, all three tests were administered in Chinese by the mathematics teacher of the class in China. With the U.S. students, the first author conducted all of the tests in person, except the mathematics content test, which was given by the mathematics teacher of the class due to a time conflict.

The Mathematics Content Test

The purpose of the mathematics content test in this study is to measure the partici-pants' basic mathematical knowledge and skills. Instead of developing a test for this study, the researchers adapted the National Assessment of Educational Progress (NAEP) 12th grade Mathematics Assessment as the mathematics content test. The 2005 mathematics framework focuses on two dimensions: mathematical content and cognitive demand. By considering these two dimensions for each item in the assess-ment, the framework ensures that NAEP assesses an appropriate balance of content along with a variety of ways of knowing and doing mathematics. The 2005 framework describes five mathematics content areas: number properties and operations, measurement, geometry, data analysis and probability, and algebra. Although the NAEP assessment seems to fit the purpose of this study, the researchers conducted several pilot tests and made several changes to make sure that the items were cultural fair and that all the participants had learned the content.

The Torrance Tests of Creative Thinking

The Torrance Tests of Creative Thinking (TTCT) includes two tests, namely, the Figural TTCT, Thinking Creatively with Pictures, and the Verbal TTCT, Thinking Creatively with Words. According to the Scholastic Testing Service (2007), the Figural TTCT is appropriate at all levels, kindergarten through adult. It uses three picture-based exercises to assess five mental characteristics, fluency, resistance to premature closure, elaboration, abstractness of titles, and originality. Appropriate for first graders through adults, the Verbal TTCT uses six word-based exercises to assess three mental characteristics: fluency, flexibility, and originality. Both the Figural TTCT and the Verbal TTCT were used in this study, but only three mental characteristics, namely, fluency, flexibility, and originality, were analyzed.

The Mathematical Problem-Posing Test

Using Stoyanova and Ellerton's (1996) framework of mathematical problem posing, three situations were included in the mathematical problem-posing test, namely, free situation, semi-structured situation, and structured situation. Using Guilford's structure-of-intellect model, the problem-posing test was also analyzed using the three characteristics: fluency, flexibility, and originality.

The Translation of the Tests from English to Chinese

In the translation of the mathematics content test, two translation and back translation circles were done. The test was first translated into Chinese by the first author and then translated back into English by two mathematics education researchers in China. The two Chinese researchers held Ph.D degrees in mathematics education and had a high level of English proficiency. After a few changes were made, the test was then translated from Chinese into English by a science professor in the United States who is fluent in both Chinese and English. More details were discussed in the test development section. Instead of translating the TTCT, the Chinese versions of TTCT were purchased from the Taiwan Psychological Publishing Co., Lid. The Chinese versions of TTCT were not only translated by Li (2006a, 2006b) in Taiwan, but were also checked for validity and reliability in the context of Chinese students in Taiwan. Since the mathematical problem posing-test only included four tasks, the translating work was done be the first author and was then translated from Chinese into English by a mathematics education researcher in China. One translation and back translation circle was conducted.

DATA ANALYSIS

The Scoring of the Mathematics Content Test

Since the mathematics content test only includes multiple-choice problems and short answer problems, the scoring procedures are very straight forward. The first author scored all the mathematics content test and no inter-rater reliability was needed.

The Scoring of the TTCT Tests

The Figural TTCT was rated according to the *Streamlined Scoring Procedure* (Torrance, 1988). Similarly, the Verbal TTCT was rated according to the *Manual for Scoring and Interpreting Results* (Torrance 1988). As for the Chinese version of the TTCT, both the Figural TTCT and the Verbal TTCT were scored by the first author and an assistant researcher who speaks both English and Chinese.

The Scoring of the Mathematical Problem-posing Test

The problems posed by the participants in the mathematical problem-posing test were first judged as to their appropriateness. Responses that are non-appropriate were eliminated from further consideration. For example, for the first task, responses such as "How old are the children?" or "Do they know each other?" were eliminated. In addition, problems that lacked sufficient information for them to be solved were also eliminated from further analysis. For example, for the second task, responses such as "Find the area of the circle" and, for the third task, responses such as "How many girls and how many boys are there at the party?" were eliminated. The remaining responses that are appropriate and viable were scored according to the rubrics in terms of their fluency, flexibility, and originality. The rubrics were developed by the researchers following these steps:

1. Typed all the responses into a Microsoft Word document and recorded the frequency with which each of the responses occurred. The responses generated by the two groups of students were separated so that the researchers could see the differences among the groups.

2. Categorized the responses. The two groups of students' responses to the mathematical problem-posing test were categorized. It turned out that the categories are not the same for the two samples. For example, in the second problem posing task, the Chinese students have a category of "Dilation" but the U.S. students do not have this category. After the responses generated by each group of students were categorized, all the categories were combined to make a common rubric for both the two groups.

3. Determined the originality of each of the responses. The originality of the responses in this test was determined by their rareness. Since students in the two groups have different textbooks and instruction, one rare response in one group might not be rare in the other group. Therefore, the originality of the responses was relative to other students in the same group. For that reason, the originality was analyzed

separately among the two groups. For the U.S. group, 30 participants finished all the tests. The researchers decided that if one response was posed by three or more than three participants, which is more than but including 10 percent of the 30 participants, then it is considered as not original. For the Chinese group, in which there are totally 55 participants, the researchers decided that if one response was posed by six or more than six participants, which is about 10 percent of the 55 students, then it is considered as not original. In addition, there are problems that were posed by less than 10 percent of the total number of participants but were not considered as original, for example, the following problem is not considered as original because the mathematics involved in the problem is at a very low level to a high school student.

If there are four girls with brown hair and two more boys with brown hair than girls, how many people do not have brown hair?

RESULTS

Comparison of the Mathematics Content Test Scores

The purpose of the mathematics content test was to measure the participants' basic mathematical knowledge and skills. Table 1 shows the results for the two groups. Clearly, Chinese students achieved more highly on the mathematics content test than the U.S. group.

Table 1. Mathematics content test results

Groups	Average (out of 50)	Median (out of 50)
U.S. students	36.5 (73%)	36
Chinese students	45.8 (91.6%)	46

Comparison of TTCT Scores

The following two tables show the results of the Figural TTCT and Verbal TTCT. In the Figural TTCT: Norms-Technical Manual (Torrance, 2008b) and the Verbal TTCT: Norms-Technical Manual (Torrance, 2008c), Torrance and his colleagues listed the national percentiles for different grade levels of students based on surveys among the U.S. students. Li (2006 a, 2006b), who translated the TTCT, conducted surveys among Taiwan students and also listed the national percentiles for different grade levels students based on the data in Taiwan. In both manuals, the percentiles were given by grades. For example, in Table 2, in the U.S. manual, for both 11th graders and 12th graders, 24 is at the 81st percentile. In this study, however, in order to compare the two groups' performances, the U.S. manual was used for all two groups of students. Table 13 shows that, in the Figural TTCT test, Chinese students provided more responses than the U.S. students. In terms of originality of the responses, Chinese students and U.S. students had the same median.

Table 2. Figural TTCT results

Groups	Fluency median[a] (national percentile[b])	Originality median[a] (national percentile[b])
U.S. students (30 students)	24 (81%)	18 (75%)
Chinese students (55 students)	25 (84%)	18 (75%)

[a] The scores are medians in each group.
[b] The percentiles are obtained from the Figural TTCT Norms-Technical Manual (Torrance, 2008b).

Table 3 shows the results of the Verbal TTCT test. These are different from the results of the Figural TTCT test. In this test, U.S. students scored much more highly than the Chinese group. In addition, Chinese students' National percentile dropped to 55% on Fluency score and Flexibility score. It seems that U.S. students in this study achieved more highly in the Verbal TTCT than Chinese students.

Table 3. Verbal TTCT results

Groups	Fluency median[a] (national percentile[b])	Flexibility median[a] (national percentile[b])	Originality median[a] (national percentile[b])
U.S. students (30 students)	105 (78%)	54 (84%)	68 (84%)
Chinese students (55 students)	83 (55%)	43.5 (55%)	58 (75%)

[a] The scores are medians in each group.
[b] The percentiles are obtained from the Verbal TTCT Norms-Technical Manual (Torrance, 2008c).

Comparison of the Mathematical Problem-posing Test Scores

It is important to point out that, in counting the number of problems generated by the students in each group, the same problems generated by the same group of students were counted once. For example, the following two problems were counted as one problem and were categorized as "Given the three sides of the triangle, find the area of the inscribed circle".

Problem 1: Given that the three sides of the triangle are 3, 4, and 5, find the area of its inscribed circle.

Problem 2: Given that the three sides of the triangle are 5, 6, and 7, find the area of the circle.

Task 1. Table 4 and Figure 2 show the number of problems that each group of students posed for the different categories for task 1 in the mathematical problem-posing test. Notice that there is no zero in the numbers. In other words, each of the two groups' responses covered all the 8 categories.

Table 4. Summary of results on the mathematical problem-posing test–task 1

Group	1[a]	2	3	4	5	6	7	8	Total
U.S.	27	13	42	8	3	10	3	6	112
(%)	(24.1[b])	(11.6)	(37.5)	(7.1)	(2.7)	(8.9)	(2.7)	(5.4)	
Chinese	143	74	30	5	5	14	4	11	286
(%)	(50)	(25.9)	(10.5)	(1.7)	(1.7)	(4.9)	(1.4)	(3.8)	

[a] Category 1 in Figure 2.
[b] The percentage of the number of responses in each category.

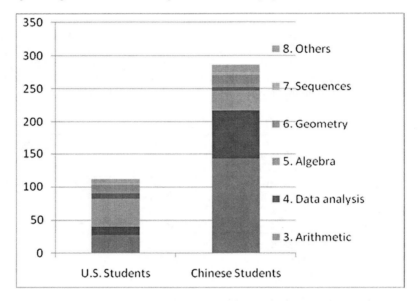

Figure 2. Summary of results on the mathematical problem-posing test, task 1.

Figure 2 shows the distribution of different categories in each of the two groups. Each of the bars represents the total number of problems students posed for Task 1 in the mathematical problem-posing test. A closer look at the percentages of the categories shows that 50% of Chinese students' responses for the first task are about Combination and Permutations; 29.5% are about Probability. The results for the U.S. students are very different from those for Chinese students. 37.5% of the responses are about Arithmetic problems and 24% are about Combination and Permutation. Among the 30 U.S. students, 11 were taking Pre-Calculus and 19 were taking AP Calculus. Students in the Pre-Calculus course had not learned the probability topic either.

Task 2. Table 5 and Figure 3 show the distribution of the different categories posed by different groups of students. Consistently, for the two groups, the biggest

Table 5. Summary of results on the mathematical problem-posing test–task 2.

Groups	1	2	3	4	5	6	7	8	9	10	Total
U.S.	1	39	44	3	0	3	6	3	0	7	106
(%)	(0.9)	(36.8)	(42)	(2.8)	(0)	(2.8)	(5.7)	(2.8)	(0)	(6.7)	
Chinese	11	48	61	8	1	24	14	8	10	15	200
(%)	(5.5)	(24)	(30.5)	(4)	(0.5)	(12)	(7)	(4)	(5)	(7.5)	

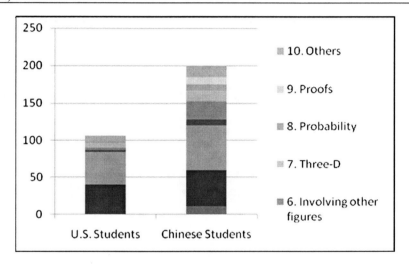

Figure 3. Summary of results on the mathematical problem-posing test, task 2.

two categories are Length and Area. For U.S. students and Chinese students, the Area category is the largest one and the Length category is the second one. Another observation is that Chinese students posed more problems that involve auxiliary figures (12%); while not many problems of that category were posed by the U.S. students (2.8%).

However, not both the two groups posed problems in all 10 categories. The 30 U.S. students whose tests were analyzed did not pose problem involving categories 5 and 9, which are Transformation and Proof. The 55 Chinese students whose tests were analyzed posed problems that covered all the ideas in the 10 categories. These results suggest that Chinese students are stronger in posing problems in geometry.

Task 3. Table 6 and Figure 4 show the distribution of the categories for Task 3. Consistently, for the two groups, Category 1, which is the Total number of people category, is one of the two top categories. For the U.S. group and the Chinese group, Category 8, which is the Number of things involved category, is the second largest category. Notice that 55 Chinese students' responses were analyzed, but only 30 U.S. students' responses were analyzed. Therefore, it may not be that surprising that Chinese students posed more number of different problems.

Table 6. Summary of results on the mathematical problem-posing test–task 3

Group	1	2	3	4	5	6	7	8	9	10	11	12	13	Total
U.S.	23	10	8	9	6	6	2	17	0	2	1	2	5	91
(%)	(25.3)	(11)	(8.8)	(9.9)	(6.6)	(6.6)	(2.2)	(18.7)	(0)	(2.2)	(1.1)	(2.2)	(5.5)	
Chinese	36	14	11	12	7	19	15	43	14	14	4	7	11	207
(%)	(17.4)	(6.8)	(5.3)	(5.8)	(3.4)	(9.2)	(7.2)	(20.8)	(6.8)	(6.8)	(1.9)	(3.4)	(5.3)	

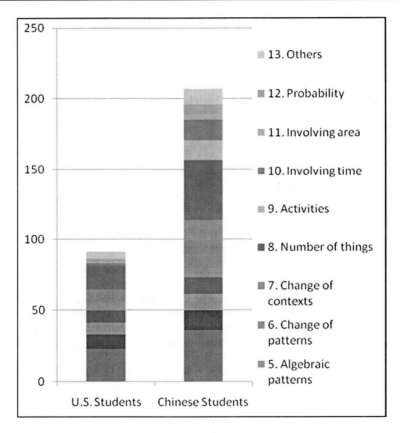

Figure 4. Summary of results on the mathematical problem-posing test, task 3.

Table 7 and Table 8 show the average number and medians of problems posed in each task by the two groups of students. As mentioned earlier, the originality of the problem posing test was determined relatively within each group. Therefore, originality should not be compared across groups. Comparison of the means indicates that, on average, Chinese students and U.S. students generated similar number of problems and the problems generated involved similar number of categories.

Table 7. Means of the fluency, flexibility, and originality of the mathematical problem-posing test

	Problem posing fluency mean	Problem posing flexibility mean
U.S. students	13.1	10.2
Chinese students	14.1	11.5

Table 8. Medians of the fluency and flexibility of the mathematical problem-posing test

	Problem posing fluency median	Problem posing flexibility median
U.S. students	13	10
Chinese students	15	12

Correlations between TTCT and the Mathematical Problem-posing Test

The scores in the TTCT and the mathematical problem-posing test were first converted to ordinal data before the correlations were calculated. Spearman's rho was calculated among the following variables:

a) fluency of the Figural TTCT and the fluency of the problem-posing test;
b) fluency of the Verbal TTCT and the fluency of the problem-posing test;
c) originality of the Figural TTCT and originality of the problem-posing test;
d) originality of the Verbal TTCT and originality of the problem-posing test;
e) flexibility of the Verbal TTCT and flexibility of the problem-posing test.

Table 9 suggests that among the fluency variables, there is no statistically significant correlation between problem-posing fluency and Figural TTCT fluency or Verbal Fluency. This result suggests that the numbers of responses produced for the two TTCT tests and the mathematical problem-posing test are weakly correlated according to Spearman's rho.

In the TTCT, only the Verbal TTCT has the variable flexibility. Table 10 shows that Verbal TTCT flexibility is weakly correlated to mathematical problem-posing test flexibility ($p < 0.05$). This result suggests that the numbers of categories U.S. students' responses in the Verbal TTCT are weakly correlated to those in the mathematical problem-posing test according to Spearman's rho.

Table 9. Correlation between mathematical problem-posing fluency and TTCT fluency–U.S. students

	Figural TTCT fluency	Verbal TTCT fluency	Problem posing test fluency
Figural TTCT Fluency	1.00		
Verbal TTCT Fluency	.55(**)	1.00	
Problem-Posing Test Fluency	0.29	0.34	1.00

** Significant with $p < 0.01$

Table 10. Correlation between mathematical problem-posing
flexibility and TTCT flexibility–U.S. students

	Verbal TTCT Flexibility	Problem posing test flexibility
Verbal TTCT Flexibility	1.00	
Problem Posing Test Flexibility	0.18	1.00

Table 11. Correlation between mathematical problem-posing originality
and TTCT originality–U.S.

	Figural TTCT Originality	Verbal TTCT Originality	Problem Posing Test Originality
Figural TTCT Originality	1.00		
Verbal TTCT Originality	0.53(**)	1.00	
Problem Posing Test Originality	0.32	0.22	1.00

** Significant with $p < 0.01$

Table 11 shows that for the U.S. group, among the originality variables, there is no statistically significant correlation among the problem posing originality and the Figural TTCT originality or the Verbal TTCT originality. This result suggests that the originality of students' responses produced in the two TTCT tests and those in the mathematical problem-posing test are again weakly correlated according to Spearman's rho.

Tables 12, 13, and 14 show the correlations for the Chinese students. In Table 12, the Spearman's rho shows that Chinese students' mathematical problem posing fluency is significantly correlated to Figural TTCT fluency ($p < 0.05$) and to Verbal TTCT fluency ($p < 0.01$). In other words, students who posed more problems in the mathematical problem-posing test also gave more responses in the Figural TTCT and the Verbal TTCT. As mentioned earlier, Figural TTCT does not have the flexibility variable. In Table 13, Spearman's rho shows that Chinese students'

Table 12. Correlation between mathematical problem posing fluency and
TTCT fluency—Chinese students

	Figural TTCT fluency	Verbal TTCT fluency	Problem posing test fluency
Figural TTCT Fluency	1.00		
Verbal TTCT Fluency	0.59**	1.00	
Problem-Posing Test Fluency	0.27*	0.53**	1.00

** Significant with $p < 0.01$
* Significant with $p < 0.05$

*Table 13. Correlation between mathematical problem posing flexibility
and TTCT flexibility—Chinese students*

	Verbal TTCT flexibility	Problem posing test flexibility
Verbal TTCT Flexibility	1.00	
Problem Posing Test Flexibility	0.48**	1.00

** Significant with $p < 0.01$

*Table 14. Correlation between mathematical problem-posing originality and TTCT
originality–Chinese students*

	Figural TTCT originality	Verbal TTCT originality	Problem-posing test originality
Figural TTCT Originality	1.00		
Verbal TTCT Originality	0.56**	1.00	
Problem-Posing Test Originality	0.18	.52**	1.00

** Significant with $p < 0.01$

Verbal TTCT flexibility and problem posing flexibility are significantly correlated ($p < 0.01$). In other words, students who posed more categories of problems in the mathematical problem-posing test also gave more categories of responses in the Verbal TTCT. In Table 14, Spearman's rho shows that Chinese students' problem posing originality is significantly correlated with their Verbal TTCT originality ($p<0.01$) but not Figural TTCT. In other words, students who posed more original problems in the mathematical problem-posing test also gave more original responses in the Verbal TTCT. But there is a weak correlation between problem posing and the Figural TTCT.

In summary, Spearman's rho in the tables above suggests that the correlations between TTCT and problem posing are not consistent among the two groups. For the Chinese students in this study, significant correlations occurred in fluency, flexibility, and originality between problem posing and Verbal TTCT; significant correlations occurred in fluency and flexibility, but not originality between problem posing and Figural TTCT. For U.S. students, no significant correlations were observed between problem posing and the two TTCT tests. However, although not all the correlations were statistically significant, notice the correlations between TTCT scores and problem posing scores were between 0.18 to 0.53 between the two groups. No negative correlation was observed. The correlations among the Chinese group were stronger than the U.S. group. Chinese students in this study also performed better than the U.S. group on the content test.

DISCUSSION

This study investigated the relationships between creativity and mathematical problem posing-abilities. Two groups of students from the United States and China were included. Three questions were addressed in this study. In this section, the findings in regard to the three questions are discussed.

Research Question 1: Are there Differences in the Mathematical Problem-posing Abilities in the Two Groups? If so, what are the Differences?

A comparison of the means and medians of the students' scores on the mathematical problem-posing test showed that Chinese students and U.S. students' fluency and flexibility are similar. Since the originality rubric was different for different groups, the originality was not compared.

In the task involving the free problem-posing situation, U.S. students tended to pose combinations and permutations problems and arithmetic problems. Chinese students' responses focused more on combinations and permutations, and probability. Consistently, both groups of students posed problems on combinations and permutations because the task scenario "ten boys and ten girls stand in a line" can very easily lead students to think of the different ways of arranging the 20 students. The fact that Chinese students posed many probability problems is because those students were in their senior year of high school and had learned the topic of probability by the time they took the problem-posing test. Among the 30 U.S. students, 11 were taking Pre-Calculus and 19 were taking AP Calculus. The AP Calculus students had learned probability in high school but probability was not a big category for the U.S. group. The differences in the free problem-posing situation among the two groups indicate that students' content knowledge does have a great influence on their problem posing.

In the task designed as a semi-structured problem-posing situation, consistently, the distribution of the problems in all two groups focused on the lengths category and the areas category. That may be because that lengths and areas are the two most familiar and basic topics in geometry. But the Chinese group also posed more problems involving auxiliary figures, while very few U.S. students did so. This difference might be due to the greater focus on geometry in the mathematics curriculum in China than that in the United States. In other words, students in Chinese might have seen or done more problems involving auxiliary figures in solving or proving geometry problems than the U.S. students.

In the task involving the structured problem-posing situation, for the U.S. group and the Chinese group, the largest category was the one involving total number of people (25.3% and 17.4% respectively) and the second largest category was the one involving numbers of things (18.7% and 20.8% respectively). It is not surprising that both groups posed more problems involving the number of people because in the part a of the task, it was asked "How many guests will enter on the 10th ring?" and most students posed similar problems to this one. Also, it is very easy to think of the amount of food, drinks, gifts, etc. because that is what happens in real life.

Research Question 2: Are there Differences in the Creativity of High School Students taking Advanced Courses in the Two Groups? If so, what are the Differences?

To answer the second research question, the Figural TTCT and Verbal TTCT were administered and the medians of the fluency, flexibility, and originality in the two different groups were compared. The comparison showed that the students in the two groups are not very different in the fluency and originality of the Figural TTCT. But U.S. students did much better than Chinese students on the fluency, flexibility, and originality on the Verbal TTCT. In the Figural TTCT, students were asked to express their ideas by drawing pictures. In the Verbal TTCT, students were asked to think with words. Therefore, the results of the TTCT suggested that although U.S. students and Chinese students are similar in their ability of drawing their ideas, U.S. students are more capable of expressing their ideas in words.

Research Question 3: Is there a Significant Relationship between Creativity and Mathematical Problem-posing Abilities of Students in the Two Groups?

To answer the third research question, Spearman correlation coefficients were calculated among the fluency, flexibility, and originality of the Figural TTCT and Verbal TTCT scores and the mathematical problem-posing test scores. In the Chinese group, mathematical problem-posing fluency is significantly correlated with Figural TTCT fluency ($p<0.01$) and with Verbal TTCT fluency ($p<0.05$); mathematical problem-posing flexibility is significantly correlated with Verbal TTCT flexibility ($p<0.01$); and mathematical problem-posing originality is significantly correlated with Verbal TTCT originality ($p<0.05$) but only weakly with Figural TTCT originality. However, in the U.S. group, no significant correlation was observed between the TTCT scores and mathematical problem posing test scores.

Although the TTCT scores and the mathematical problem-posing test scores were not all significantly correlated, all the Spearman's rho correlations were positive and were between 0.18 and 0.53. That suggests that there are trends in the correlations between creativity and mathematical problem-posing abilities.

To summarize, there is a significant relationship between creativity and mathematical problem-posing abilities of high school students taking advanced courses in the Chinese group but not in the U.S. group. Therefore, the relationship between creativity and mathematical problem-posing abilities is not consistent among the two groups. The consistent findings are that the correlations between the TTCT scores and the mathematical problem-posing test scores were all positive, which suggests in the practical sense, there are correlations between creativity and mathematical problem-posing abilities. Also, Chinese students greatly outperformed the U.S. students in this study and the correlations in the Chinese group were the strongest. That indicates that problem-posing abilities in mathematics might have something to do with students' mathematical knowledge and skills. But this is just a conjecture and needs further research to prove or disprove.

LIMITATIONS OF THIS STUDY

The Participants

In this study, participants were selected from two locations, a city in China and a town in the United States. The Chinese students were in the 12th grade. Some of the U.S. students were in the 11th grade and some were in the 12th grade. The students

23

in the two locations do not have the same mathematics curriculum. The Chinese students had not taken calculus in high school. Thus the differences in the mathematical background and contexts of the two groups constituted a limitation of this research. In addition, the students were not selected randomly within the two student populations. Therefore, the findings of this study cannot be generalized to other students in the two locations.

The Translation of the Instruments

Since this study involved participants who spoke different languages, namely, English and Chinese, the instruments were translated into two versions. Despite several pilot tests, there were still several problems affected by translation and those problems were excluded from analysis.

The Time and Distance Restrictions

Since four separate tests were to be administered, the researchers decided that in order to avoid interfering with students' regular learning, she had to work around the students' schedules. So far as the U.S. students were concerned, the four tests were given over two semesters. For the Chinese students, two tests were given at the beginning of the semester and two were given before the final examinations.

CONCLUSIONS AND IMPLICATIONS

In conclusion, the findings of this study suggested that there are differences in the mathematical problem posing abilities among the two groups. Although the number of Chinese students almost doubles the number of U.S. students in this study, the results of the problem posing test shows that as a group Chinese students posed almost twice as many or more different problems that the U.S. group. Given that the median of fluency and flexibility of students in the two groups are similar, that indicates that Chinese students were able to pose problems from their peers in the group. This result contradicts those found by Cai and Hwang (2002), who studied sixth-graders' mathematical problem posing and found out that although Chinese students did better in computation skills and solving routine problems, U.S. students performed as well as or better than those Chinese students in problem-posing tasks. This result may imply that, in this study, because students have spent 11 or 12 years learning mathematics, problem posing might involve more than posing but also recalling the problems learned in the past. Younger students, like sixth graders, have not been exposed to many problems in mathematics and, therefore, are more likely to create their own problems based on their prior knowledge.

Another implication is that students' problem posing abilities might be affected by their mathematical knowledge. Students from China in this study scored much more highly than the U.S. group in the mathematics content test and the Chinese students also did much better in the mathematical problem-posing test. The superior performances of Chinese students in the mathematics content test and the mathematical problem-posing test suggest that there might be some correlation between the two. In fact, in China, educators (e.g., Zhang, 2005) have reflected on mathematics education in the past and claimed that the basic knowledge and basic skills in mathematics could be highly related to creativity in mathematics, but there is definitely a kind of balance between them. Wong (2004, 2006), who summarized the characteristics of Confucian Heritage Culture (CHC) learners, pointed out that the Chinese students' focus on the basics might be related to the ancient Chinese tradition of learning from "entering" to "transcending the way." Wong's observation echoes that of Gardner (1989, as cited in Wang, 2008) that imitating the master is the starting point of the path to becoming the master one day. Ellerton (1986) and Leung (1993) both found a clear link between mathematical competence and problem posing, with the more able students being better able to generate problems. This study confirmed the link between the two. Also, this finding also verifies the framework of English (1997b) that, in generating new problems, students must recognize the critical items of information that are required for problem solution. Brown and Walter (2005) also claimed that knowledge is necessary for determining whether or how a posed problem structure constitutes a solvable problem, a basic element of problem posing.

As to creativity, U.S. students did much better in the Figural TTCT than the other two groups but on the Verbal TTCT there was not much difference between the two groups. Although statistically significant correlations between creativity and mathematical problem posing were found in the Chinese group, no such statistically significant correlation was found in the other two groups. This finding seems to suggest that there might not be consistent correlations between creativity and mathematical problem-posing abilities or at least that the correlations between creativity and mathematical problem-posing abilities are complex.

Nevertheless, the authors wanted to emphasize that Silver's (1997) statement suggests any relationships between creativity and problem posing might be the product of previous instructional patterns. Haylock (1987) and Leung (1993), who did not agree that there was correlation between creativity and problem posing in mathematics, did not take instruction into consideration. In other words, if the participants were students who had formal instruction on posing problems in mathematics before this study, the results might be very different, but this conjecture requires further research. In conclusion, this exploratory study revealed some of the characteristics of creativity, mathematical problem-posing abilities, and the correlations between the two among high school students who were taking advanced mathematics in United States and China. The different findings from the two different groups of students suggest that both creativity and mathematical problem-posing abilities and the correlations between them are complex entities to explore.

REFERENCES

Bai, G. (2004). Discussion of mathematical creativity in middle school through the example of mathematics education in the United States [以美国数学教学为例谈中学生创新能力的培养]. *Shu Xue Tong Bao [数学通报]*, *4*, 17–18.

Brown, S. I., & Walter, M. I. (2005). *The art of problem posing*. Hillsdale, NJ: Lawrence Erlbaum Associates.

Cai, J. (2000). Mathematical thinking involved in U.S. and Chinese students' solving process-constrained and process-open problems. *Mathematical Thinking and Learning: An International Journal, 2,* 309–340.

Cai, J., & Hwang, S. (2002). Generalized and generative thinking in U.S. and Chinese students' mathematical problem solving and problem posing. *Journal of Mathematical Behavior, 21*(4), 401–421.

Csikszentmihalyi, M., & Getzels, J. W. (1971). Discovery-oriented behavior and the originality of creative products: A study with artists. *Journal of Personality and Social Psychology, 19,* 47–52.

Dillon, J. T. (1982). Problem finding and solving. *Journal of Creative Behavior, 16,* 97–111.

Dunn, J., Zhang, X., & Ripple R. (1988). Comparative study of Chinese and American performance on divergent thinking tasks. *New Horizons, 29,* 7–20.

Ellerton, N. F. (1986). Children's made-up mathematics problems: A new perspective on talented mathematicians. *Educational Studies in Mathematics, 17,* 261–271.

English, L. D. (1997a). Development of fifth grade children's problem posing abilities. *Educational Studies in Mathematics, 34,* 183–217.

English, L. D. (1997b). Development of seventh grade students' problem posing. In E. Pehkonen (Ed.), *Proceedings of the 21st annual conference for the International Group for the Psychology of Mathematics Education* (Vol. 2, pp. 241–248). Lahti, Finland: University of Helsinki and Lahti Research and Training Center.

English, L. D. (1997c). Promoting a problem-posing classroom. *Teaching Children Mathematics, 4,* 172–181.

Guilford, J. P. (1959). Traits of creativity. In H. H. Anderson (Ed.), *Creativity and its cultivation* (pp. 142–161). New York: Harper & Brothers Publishers.

Haylock, D. W. (1987). A framework for assessing mathematical creativity in school children. *Educational Studies in Mathematics, 18,* 59–74.

Jay, E. S., & Perkins, D. N. (1997). Problem finding: The search for mechanism. In M. A. Runco (Ed.), *The creativity research handbook* (Vol. 1, pp. 257–293). Cresskill, NJ: Hampton Press.

Jia, T., & Jiang, Q. (2001). Cultivating students' creativity in mathematics education in the United States [美国数学教育培养学生创新能力窥见]. *Mathematics Education Abroad [外国中小学教育], 4,* 34–37.

Jensen, L. R. (1973). *The relationships among mathematical creativity, numerical aptitude, and mathematical achievement.* Unpublished Dissertation. The University of Texas at Austin, Austin, TX.

Leung, S. S. (1993). Mathematical problem posing: The influence of task formats, mathematics knowledge, and creative thinking. In J. Hirabayashi, N. Nohda, K. Shigematsu, & F. Lin (Eds.), *Proceedings of the 17th International Conference of the International Group for the Psychology of Mathematics Education* (Vol. III, pp. 33–40). Tsukuba, Japan.

Li, Y. (2006a). *Torrance tests of creative thinking: Manual for scoring and interpreting results for verbal forms A and B[陶伦斯创造思考测验语文版指导手册].* Taiwan: Psychological Publishing Co., Ltd.

Li, Y. (2006b). *Torrance tests of creative thinking: Streamlined scoring guide for figural forms A and B[陶伦斯创造思考测验图形版指导手册].* Taiwan: Psychological Publishing Co., Ltd.

Lubart, T. I. (1990). *International Journal of Psychology, 25*(1), 39–59.

Mann, E. L. (2006). Creativity: The essence of mathematics. *Journal for the Education of the Gifted, 30*(2), 236–260.

Markus, H., & Kitayama, S. (1991). Culture and the self: Implications for cognition, emotion, and motivation. *Psychological Review, 98,* 224–253.

Mathematics Curriculum Development Group of Basic Education of Education Department [教育部基础教育司数学课程标准研制组]. (2002). *The interpretation of mathematics curriculum* (Trial Version). [数学课程标准（实验稿）解读]. Beijing: Beijing Normal University Press.

National Center for Educational Statistics. (2009). *The national assessment of educational progress overview.* Retrieved August 28, 2009, from http://nces.ed.gov/nationsreportcard/mathematics/

National Council of Teachers of Mathematics. (1989). *Curriculum and evaluation standards for school mathematics.* Reston, VA: National Council of Teachers of Mathematics.

Plucker, J. A., & Beghetto, R. A. (2004). Why creativity is domain general, why it looks domain specific, and why the distinction does not matter. In R. J., Sternberg, E. L. Grigorenko, & J. L. Singer (Eds.), *Creativity: From potential to realization* (pp. 153–168). Washington, DC: American Psychological Association.

Polya, G. (1954). *Mathematics and plausible reasoning*. Putnam: Princeton University Press.

Presmeg, N. C. (1981). *Parallel threads in the development of Albert Einstein's thought and current ideas on creativity: What are the implications for the teaching of school mathematics*. Unpublished M.Ed. dissertation in Educational Psychology, University of Natal.

Rudowicz, E., & Hui, A. (1998). *Gifted Education International, 36*(2), 88–104.

Scholastic Testing Service. (2007). *Gifted Education*. Retrieved March 29, 2008, from http://ststesting.com/2005giftttct.html

Shriki, A. (2010). Working like real mathematicians: Developing prospective teachers' awareness of mathematical creativity through generating new concepts. *Educational Studies in Mathematics*.

Silver, E. A. (1994). On mathematical problem posing. *For the Learning of Mathematics, 14*(1), 19–28.

Silver, E. A. (1997). *Fostering creativity through instruction rich in mathematical problem solving and problem posing*. Retrieved July 29, 2007, from http://www.emis.de/journals/ZDM/zdm973a3.pdf

Sriraman, B. (2005). Are giftedness and creativity synonyms in mathematics? *Journal of Secondary Gifted Education, 17*(1), 20–36.

Sriraman, B. (2009). The characteristics of mathematical creativity. *The International Journal on Mathematics Education [ZDM], 41*, 13–27.

Stevenson, H. W., & Stigler, J. W. (1992). *The learning gap: Why our schools are failing and what we can learn from Japanese and Chinese education*. New York: Summit Books.

Stigler, J., & Hilbert, J. (1999). The teaching gap: Best ideas from the world's teachers for improving education in the classroom. New York: Free Press.

Stoyanova, E. (1997). *Extending and exploring students' problem solving via problem posing: A study of years 8 and 9 students involved in mathematics challenge and enrichment stages of Euler enrichment program for young Australians*. Unpublished doctoral dissertation submitted to Edith Cowan University, Perth, Australia.

Stoyanova, E., & Ellerton, N. F. (1996). A framework for research into students' problem posng in school mathematics. In P. C. Clarkson (Ed.), *Technology in mathematics education* (pp. 518–525). Mathematics Education Research Group of Australasia. The University of Melbourne.

Sun, C. (2004). Severe critique from mathematician Shing-Tung Yau: Mathematics Olympiad in China kills children's curiosity [数学家丘成桐棒喝奥数热：奥数扼杀好奇心]. *Yangcheng Evening*. Retrieved May 7, 2006, from http://news.xinhuanet.com/edu/2004-12/25/content_2379632.htm

Torrance, E. P. (1966). *Torrance tests of creative thinking: Norms-technical manual*. Princeton, NJ: Personnel Press, Inc.

Torrance, E. P. (1988). The nature of creativity as manifest in its testing. In R. J. Sternberg (Ed.), *The nature of creativity: Contemporary psychological perspectives* (pp. 43–75). New York: Cambridge University Press.

Torrance. E. P. (2008a). *Torrance tests of creative thinking: Streamlined scoring guide for figural forms A and B*. Bensenville, IL: Scholastic Testing Service, Inc.

Torrance. E. P. (2008b). *Torrance tests of creative thinking Norms-Technical manual: Figural (streamlined) forms A and B*. Bensenville, IL: Scholastic Testing Service, Inc.

Torrance. E. P. (2008c). *Torrance tests of creative thinking norms-technical manual: Verbal forms A and B*. Bensenville, IL: Scholastic Testing Service, Inc.

Vogt, W. P., (2007). *Quantitative research methods for professionals in education and other fields*. New Jersey: Allyn & Bacon, Inc.

Wong, N. Y. (2004). The CHC learner's phenomenon: Its implications on mathematics education. In L. Fan, N. Y. Wong, J. Cai, & S. Li (Eds.), *How Chinese learn mathematics: Perspectives from insiders* (pp. 503–534). Singapore: World Scientific.

Wong, N. Y. (2006). From "Entering the Way" to "Exiting the Way": In search of a bridge to span "basic skills" and "process abilities". In F. K. S. Leung, G.-D. Graf, & F. J. Lopez-Real (Eds.), *Mathematics education in different cultural traditions: The 13th ICMI study* (pp. 111–128). New York: Springer.

Wong, N. Y. (2008). Confucian heritage culture learner's phenomenon: From "exploring the middle zone" to "constructing a bridge". *The International Journal on Mathematics Education [ZDM]*, *40*, 973–981.

Ye, Z. (2003). *Investigation and practice of the mathematics teaching mode of creative education [创新教育下的数学教学模式的探索与实践]*. Unpublished M. Ed. thesis, Fujian North Normal University.

Yang, G. (2007). *A comparison and reflection on the school education of China and the U.S. [中美基础教育的比较与思考]*. Retrieved March 25, 2007, from http://www.sm.gov.cn/bmzd/jcck/200111/Findex.htm

Yue, X., & Rudowicz, E. (2002). Perception of the most creative Chinese by undergraduates in Beijing, Guangzhou, Hong Kong, and Taipei. *Journal of Creative Behavior*, *36*(2), 88–104.

Zha, P. J., Walczyk, J. J., Griffith-Ross, D. A., Tobacyk, J, J., & Walczyk, D. F. (2006). The impact of culture and individualism-collectivism on the creative potential and achievement of American and Chinese adults. *Creativity Research Journal*, *18*(3), 355–366.

Zhang, D. (2005). *The "two basics": Mathematics teaching in Mainland China*. Shanghai, China: Shanghai Educational Publishing House.

Zhao, X. (2007).

Zhao, Y. (2008). *What knowledge has the most worth?* American Association of School Administrators. Retrieved April 10, 2008, from http://www.aasa.org/publications/saaricaledetail.cfm?ItemNumber=9737

Zhu, H., Bai, G., & Qu, X. (2003). Mathematics education in the United States [谈美国数学教学]. *Mathematics Education Abroad [外国中小学教育]*, *8*, 41–42.

Xianwei Yuan
Dept of Mathematics
Illinois State University
USA

Bharath Sriraman
Dept of Mathematical Sciences
The University of Montana
USA

EUN-SUNG KO AND KYEONG HWA LEE

3. ARE MATHEMATICALLY TALENTED ELEMENTARY STUDENTS ALSO TALENTED IN STATISTICS?

INTRODUCTION

There is little doubt in the education field that mathematically talented students should develop statistical literacy because they are expected to contribute to advances in non-mathematical areas, including physics, biology, medical science, and genetic engineering as well as mathematics. Research needs to examine whether mathematically talented students are indeed more gifted in statistics than non-talented students. Research also needs to look at the types of approaches and techniques that can lead to improved ability in statistics for mathematically talented students. This study focuses on mathematically talented students' understanding of the concept of average, whether they have a greater understanding of average than non-talented students, and how mathematically talented students' ability in statistics, especially as it relates to average, can be improved.

The need for differentiated instruction for mathematically talented students has long been established (Greenes, 1981; Heinze, 2005; Krutetskii, 1976; Schneider, 2000; Sriraman, 2003; Wieczerkowski, Cropley & Prado, 2000). Assouline and Lupkowski-Shoplik (2005, p. 223), for example, recommend key curricula and materials requirement for mathematically talented students, which place priority on differentiating the curricula. The following summarize their major suggestions: (1) it is important to develop differentiated curricula and materials for talented students in mathematics; (2) mathematically talented students should be taught a variety of topics including problem solving, geometry, algebra, arithmetic, number system, probability, statistics, and spatial visualization; and (3) the essence of the curriculum offered to mathematically talented students needs to be enhanced systemically. To succeed with the first recommendation, in particular, to develop differentiated curricula and materials for mathematically talented students, information is needed on: (1) the cognitive and affective characteristics of mathematically talented students, (2) their approach to the learning of major concepts or ideas in different areas, and (3) their needs in statistics learning.

According to prior studies, mathematically talented students show different characteristics from their non-talented peers. They show good cognitive ability in the pace and depth of learning and high level thinking such as generalizing, abstracting, and intuiting (Assouline & Doellinger, 2001; Benbow & Minor, 1990; Dreyfus & Tsamir, 2004; Greenes, 1981; Heinze, 2005; Krutetskii, 1976; Na, Han, Lee, & Song, 2007; Schneider, 2000; Sriraman, 2003, 2004; Wieczerkowski et al., 2000). And, they

B. Sriraman and K.H. Lee (eds.), The Elements of Creativity and Giftedness in Mathematics, 29–43.

also possess high quality affective aspects such as curiosity, patience, and spontaneity (Krutetskii, 1976; Limm, 1984; Schneider, 2000; Sriraman, 2003). For mathematically talented students, their potential can be maximized at the height of their curiosity. Moreover, when properly instructed, patience seems to best suit their pace and depth of learning and high level thinking. Thus, it is crucial to provide curricula and materials that are appropriate for their cognitive and affective distinctiveness.

Previous research into the characteristics of mathematically talented students in learning geometry, algebra, and probability have had several ramifications in the teaching of and material development for mathematically talented students (Greenes, 1981; Heinze, 2005; Krutetskii, 1976; Lee, 2005; Lee, Kim, Na, Han, & Song, 2007; Lee, Ko, & Song, 2007; Na et al., 2007; Sriraman, 2003, 2004). However, there are few studies that investigate how mathematically talented students learn major concepts or ideas in statistics. It is not disconnected with deemphasizing statistics in school mathematics. At this point, different views concerning the relation between mathematics ability and statistics ability have been proposed. Hawkins (1996), for example, claims that a mathematically educated person can be statistically illiterate, and Moore (1998) claims that statistical thinking is different from mathematical thinking since the former mainly depends on reasoning about data, variation, and chance. Ullman (1995) suggests that statistical thinking requires something inherent since one should deal with uncertain empirical data.

Although research on the relationship between statistical and mathematical thinking is inconclusive (e.g., delMas, 2004), there have been several arguments about the early introduction of statistics into school mathematics (Cobb & McClain, 2004; Cobb & Moore, 1997; Shaughnessy, Garfield, & Greer, 1996). Nevertheless, there is little doubt in the education field that mathematically talented students should develop statistical literacy because they are expected to contribute to advances in non-mathematical areas, including physics, biology, medical science, and genetic engineering as well as mathematics. Many aspects of diverse scientific disciplines such as physics and chemistry have been reconceptualized due to statistics; and, statistical thinking has played important roles in the formulation of ideas in the fields of economics and archaeology (Wheatley, 1983, p. 141). Therefore, research needs to examine whether mathematically talented students are indeed more gifted in statistics than non-talented students. Research also needs to look at the types of approaches and techniques that can lead to improved ability in statistics for mathematically talented students. This study focuses on mathematically talented students' understanding of the concept of average, whether they have a greater understanding of average than non-talented students, and how mathematically talented students' ability in statistics, especially as it relates to average, can be improved.

CONCEPTUAL ANALYSIS OF AVERAGE

A crucial aspect of statistical data analysis is the description and prediction of aggregate features of data sets (Bakker & Gravemeijer, 2004). Cobb (1999) and Bakker and Gravemeijer (2004) also consider distribution a core idea behind statistical reasoning. However, students tend to think of a data set not as an aggregate having certain properties, but as a collection of individual values (Ben-Zvi, 2004). According to

Bakker and Gravemeijer (2004), average is an important concept that enables inter-action between data as individual values and distribution as conceptual entities. Average serves as the means of describing how specific data sets are distributed within a space of values. Wild and Pfannkuch (1999) and Reading and Shaughnessy (2004) argue that students should learn the concept of average as 'central tendency' to attain proper understanding of variation. Additionally, Konold and Pollatsek (2002) suggest that core ideas taught to students should include conscious-raising activities through which students realize the investigation of noisy processes is statistics. Students should be able to see that these processes contain signals, which can be detected through careful examination of sufficient data. According to Konold and Pollatsek (2002), the main purpose for finding average is to represent one such signal attained from the noise of individual values. The concepts of average are very powerful in statistical reasoning since average includes mean, mode, and median to summarize information about a set of data.

Reports have suggested that students develop diverse ideas about average from the various standard meanings of average just as they do for many other concepts in mathematics. Mokros and Russell (1995, p. 26), for example, have identified five tactics used by fourth, sixth, and eighth graders to depict average: (1) a mode, (2) a product attained from an algorithm, (3) a value deemed reasonable, (4) a midpoint, and (5) a mathematical point of balance. Students depicting average as a mode view mode as "the most"; they fail to represent the data set as a whole and lack flexibility in solving average-based problems whereas students who view average as an algorithm believe average is a value computed from an arithmetic mean algorithm. These students often employ a variety of useless circular strategies that confuse total, average, and data. Students who consider average via reasonability see average as a tool for making sense of a set of data, and they choose average values that are representative of entire data sets. Next, students following a median approach look for a "middle" value among a data set and use symmetry to construct data distribution around the average. Lastly, students who view average as a mathematical point of balance seek a point of balance for a set of data by taking into account the values of all data points. In other words, the first two approaches do not recognize average as being representative whereas the last three approaches embody the idea of representativeness.

Research has shown that comprehension of the true meaning of average, even in a variety of social contexts, is not easy. Mokros and Russell (1995), for example, report that children and adults alike, puzzle over the statistical claim that a house-hold has a mean of 3.2 persons. The idea of mean as "fair share" is of no use in this situation. Even if the value had not been expressed as a decimal number, it would still be difficult for many to accept that a mean value can be a number not actually present in the data set. Understanding of the value and power of this strange abstraction requires movement toward more abstract mathematics. Watson (2006, p. 101) reports that students tend to confuse "on average" with "every". In general, students interpret the statement "people watch 3 hours of TV per day on average" as "people watch 3 hours of TV every day."

To summarize the aforesaid discussion, students need to recognize that (1) average represents a data set, (2) average is a mathematical construction that expresses a relationship among particular numbers, and (3) average interacts with variation. This research examines these issues in relation to mathematically talented students' under-standing of average. More specifically, the paper looks at differences between mathematically talented and non-talented primary school students with regard to i) recognition of the notion of representativeness, ii) construction of an abstract mathematical to express the relationship among particular numbers, and iii) coping with variation.

METHOD

Participants

This study investigates differences between mathematically talented and non-talented elementary students' statistical thinking, especially their understanding of average. 70 mathematically talented and 62 non-talented students in grade 5 participated in this study, and each of the participants and their parents gave informed consent prior to inclusion in the study. The mathematically talented students in this study are all receiving instruction at a university-attached institute for a scientifically talented student education that focuses on mathematics and science. The students are also categorized as being in the upper 5 percentile group nation-wide. The non-talented students were randomly sampled from two grade 5 classes at one school. Both the mathematically talented and non-talented students have learned about arithmetic mean in their regular mathematics curricula.

Tasks

Figure 1 displays questions presented to participants. For this study, the questions, taken from prior research studies (Konold & Pollatsek, 2002; Watson, 2006), were translated into Korean.

Q1. Explain the word 'average'. What do you think the word 'average' means?
Q2. A research study found that "Korean primary school students watch an average of 3 hours of TV per day." What does the word 'average' mean in this sentence?
Q3. Let's say you are watching TV, and you hear: "On average, Korean families have 1.7 children." How can the average be 1.7, and not a counting number like 1, 2, or 3?
Q4. Numbers of comments made by 8 students during a class period were 0, 5, 2, 22, 3, 2, 1, and 2. What was the number of comments made by one student on average that day?
Q5. A small object was weighted on the same scale separately by nine students in a science class. The weights (in grams) recorded by each student were 6.2, 6.0, 6.0, 15.3, 6.1, 6.3, 6.2, 6.15, 6.2. What would you give as the best estimate of the actual weight of this object?

Figure 1. Questionnaire items.

Watson (1997, 2006) proposed a three-tiered hierarchy of statistical literacy that involves various skills related to statistical reasoning: (a) basic understanding of statistical terminology, (b) understanding of statistical terms and concepts included in the context of a social discussion, and (c) questioning of inappropriate claims made without proper statistical underpinning. According to Watson, the understanding of average begins with an understanding of the definition of the word 'average'. However, students at this basic level understand only terminology. Students at the second level are able to interpret and understand the meaning of average in a variety of social contexts, and students at the highest level are able to criticize statistical statements related to average. Q1 and Q2 (Figure 1) investigate the level—basic or second—of students' understanding of average. Both questions look at the concept of average as it relates to representativeness to address research question (i). That is, Q1 asks students to describe the term 'average' irrespective of a specified context, and Q2 requests students to explain 'average' in a specific context.

Q3 and Q4 (Figure 1) provide insight on the answer to the second research question (ii); i.e., differences between mathematically talented and non-talented primary school students' ability to generate an abstract mathematical construction for average. Q3 asks students to rationalize a decimal number value as the average for a set of real entities, an average value that has no specific referent in the real world. Q4 explores whether students accept a decimal number average for a set of physical object data knowing the value cannot physically be expressed with a decimal number. Lastly, Q5 (Figure 1) provides answers to the last research question (iii) regarding differences between mathematically talented and non-talented primary school students' handling of variation during the calculation of average. In other words, Q5 requires students to consider an extreme value in a set of data during the calculation of average.

Administration and Analysis

Students are asked to complete questionnaires within a 30-minute time frame, then mini-interviews are conducted with certain students on the basis of their responses. Students' written responses are entered on a spreadsheet and categorized using an iterative technique (Miles & Huberman, 1994). The technique involves refining categories and subcategories by comparing and contrasting features of responses.

Mokros and Russell (1995) proposed five distinct average categories based on student images of average after close examination of how students develop the meaning of average while solving problems related to average. The categories were then organized into two classes: one in which students recognize average as being representative and a second in which students do not recognize average as being representative. Mokros and Russell's two classes set the groundwork for Q1 and Q2 in this study. Researcher judged students' mention of a midpoint, a standard value, a middle value, and a value that minimizing errors among data in their answer as recognizing representativeness, and hence, placed the students in the group 'representative'. Students who give answers that make mention of a mode or algorithm, are placed in the group 'not representative'.

For Q3 responses, students that propose examples of 1.7 persons or mention a non-real person are seen to 'offer proper interpretation'. Examples of this grouping are

KO AND LEE

responses like, "If ten families have 1, 2, 3, 2, 1, 1, 2, 3, 1, 1 child respectively, the average would be 1.7 persons" and "An average of 1.7 does not really mean 1.7 persons; it is an approximation." The group 'reliance on an algorithm' consists of students who depend solely on an algorithm to describe average. Q4 separates students into two additional groupings. The first, 'acceptance of a decimal number average', consists of students that provide decimal number averages as answers. The second group, 'non-acceptance of a decimal number average', is made up of students that offer answers of whole numbers instead of decimal number averages because of rounding results up or down (see student 5).

For Q5 responses, students with answers that exclude the extreme value and calculate average via an algorithm, or employ a mode, are categorized as 'proper treatment' because each of these approaches are not affected by variation while all other student answers—calculating average by using all nine data values or concluding that average cannot be determined (give up)—place students in the group 'improper treatment'.

RESPONSES AND FINDINGS

Average as Being Representative

Participant answers to Q1 and Q2 were separated into two class types: one for students that recognize the notion of representativeness, i.e., students who consider average to be reasonable as in midpoint or mathematical point of balance, and another for students that do not accept the notion of representativeness, students who view average as a mode or algorithm. According to Table 1, when they are asked to define average out of context, 51.4% of the mathematically talented students in this study can be placed in the first class while 48.6% fall into the second class. The table also shows that after evaluation of their explanations of average in a social context, 47.1% of the mathematically talented students are class type one students while 52.9% are class type two students. For Q1, the percentage of mathematically talented students who recognize average as being representative is slightly higher than that of students who do not recognize the representativeness of average. Interestingly, the percentage of mathematically talented students that recognize average as being representative decreases with Q2.

Table 2 also highlights the finding that 50.0% of the non-talented students fall into class type one and 50.0% fall into class type two when these students are asked to define average out of context. Additionally, student definitions for average in a social context resulted in 30.7% of the non-talented students being catalogued class type one students and 69.3% catalogued class type two students. While the percentage of non-talented students, who consider average as being representative, and the percentage of non-talented students, who do not recognize the representativeness of average, are equal for Q1, the percentage of non-talented students who do not recognize average as being representative more than doubles the percentage of their peers for Q2. In terms of Q1 and Q2, a chi-square test indicated no significant difference between the mathematically talented and non-talented students of this study: Q1, X^2 (1, N = 132) = 0.027, p > 0.05, and Q2, X^2 (1, N = 132) = 3.748, p > 0.05.

34

Table 1. Mathematically talented student responses to Q1 and Q2

Q2 ＼ Q1	Representative	Not representative	Total
Representative	37.1%	10.0%	47.1%
Not representative	14.3%	38.6%	52.9%
Total	51.4%	48.6%	100.0%

Table 2. Non-talented student responses to Q1 and Q2

Q2 ＼ Q1	Representative	Not representative	Total
Representative	21.0%	9.7%	30.7%
Not representative	29.0%	40.3%	69.3%
Total	50.0%	50.0%	100.0%

Taken together, both conditions, in context and out of context, indicate that 37.1% of the mathematically talented students accepted the notion of representativeness for average (Table 1) whereas only 21.0% of the non-talented students recognized the notion (Table 2). Student 1 below best summarizes students' understanding of average as being representative.

Student 1: *[Q1]* People use average to remove errors among data and to express the set of data with one number. *[Q2]* It's the middle value among a set of data.

Although 14.3% of the mathematically talented students and 29.0% of the non-talented students recognized average as being representative in Q1, the percentages falter in Q2. According to Konold and Pollatsek (2002), this phenomenon occurs because students perceive average as something that must be calculated. Student 2 provides a good précis of students' idea of average as an algorithm.

Student 2: *[Q1]* It is a data set standard. *[Q2]* It is calculated by adding all the hours elementary students in our country watch TV per day and then dividing the total by the number of students.

Interestingly, percentages clearly show how students' notion of representativeness changes according to context. While only 10.0% of the mathematically talented students and 9.7% of the non-talented students excluded the notion of representativeness in their answers to Q1, a greater percentage excluded the notion in their answers to Q2. Student 3 illustrates how context enabled students to employ ideas related to the notion of representativeness such as midpoint: a large number of data prevent them using an algorithm to find the mean.

Student 3: *[Q1]* A value gained by summing all data in a set and then dividing the sum by the total number of data. *[Q2]* The middle value for how much time elementary students in our country watch TV per day.

38.6% of the mathematically talented students and 40.3% of the non-talented students failed to recognize the notion of representativeness for average in their responses to both Q1 (out of context) and Q2 (in a social context). Hence, it can be said that even mathematically talented students are unable to grasp the notion of representativeness for average. Also, like their non-talented peers, they too perceived average to be a mere algorithm or a procedure through which mean is calculated.

Mathematical Abstract Construction

To investigate whether the students constructed a mathematical abstract for average, students were asked to answer questions Q3 and Q4. Q3 evaluated students' interpretation of a decimal number average attained from real entities, a value that cannot be duplicated in the real world. Q4 explored students' acceptance of a decimal number average for a set of physical object data, a number that can, also, not be physically expressed. Table 3 and 4 are summaries of responses to Q3 and Q4. The tables indicate that 55.7% of the mathematically talented students properly interpreted a decimal number average whereas only 14.5% of the non-talented students were able to properly interpret the value (Q3). Also, 54.2% of the mathematically talented students accepted a decimal number average for a set of physical object data. On the other hand, only 30.7% of the non-talented students accepted the decimal number as being the value for average.

For Q3 and Q4, a chi-square test indicated that the difference between the mathematically talented and non-talented students in this study was statistically significant: Q3, X^2 (1, $N = 132$) = 24.116, p < 0.01, and Q4, X^2 (1, $N = 132$) = 7.489, p < 0.01.

Table 3. Mathematically talented student responses to Q3 and Q4

Q3 / Q4	Offer of proper interpretation	Reliance on an algorithm	Total
Acceptance of a decimal number average	32.8%	21.4%	54.2%
Non-acceptance of a decimal number average	22.9%	22.9%	45.8%
Total	55.7%	44.3%	100.0%

Table 4. Non-talented student responses to Q3 and Q4

Q3 / Q4	Offer of proper interpretation	Reliance on an algorithm	Total
Acceptance of a decimal number average	8.1%	22.6%	30.7%
Non-acceptance of a decimal number average	6.4%	62.9%	69.3%
Total	14.5%	85.5%	100.0%

32.8% of the mathematically talented students and 8.1% of the non-talented students properly interpreted a decimal number average for Q3 and accepted a decimal number as the value for average (Q4). It could be said that since these students have good understanding of a decimal number average, they can make a mathematical abstract construction for average. Student 4 exemplifies this proposed thought.

Student 4: *[Q3]* An average of 1.7 does not really mean 1.7 persons, it is an approximation, an estimate. *[Q4]* I got an average value of 4.625 from the eight data, so I can say around 4.5 times. *How can the number of comments be 4.5?* It's an average; it's not real. It doesn't mean that a student made four and half comments.

Answers to Q3 suggested 22.9% of the mathematically talented students and 6.4% of the non-talented students are able to correctly explain a decimal number average. Oddly, students avoided a decimal number average in Q4. Although students appeared to have a good understanding of average versus algorithm, they could not construct a mathematical abstract for average. Student 5 best summarizes students' behaviour and thinking.

Student 5: *[Q3]* For example, if there were one hundred pairs of parents and one hundred seventy children at my school, it would also average 1.7 persons. *[Q4]* The average is 4.625, so I can say the number of comments made is about 5. *Why not say 4.625 times?* Well, you asked for the number of comments, so I think I should say 5.

Answer summaries show that 21.4% of the mathematically talented students and 22.6% of the non-talented students explain a decimal number average through an algorithm (Q3) and accept a decimal number average (Q4). Even though there is clear indication students accept a decimal number average, Student 6 showed unmistakably that they in fact, do not fully accept that the value for average could be a decimal number (4.625). It may be that students naïvely employed an arithmetic mean algorithm instead of constructing a mathematical abstract for average.

Student 6: *[Q3]* A decimal number average is possible because the value is what you get when the total number of children in families is divided by the number of families. *[Q4]* It's 4.625. Sometimes you have to keep dividing the dividend by the divisor to a few decimal places to compute computing average, if the dividend is not divisible by the quotient.

22.9% of the mathematically talented students and 62.9% of the non-talented students relied on an algorithm to explain a decimal number average (Q3). Moreover, they showed a tendency to avoid a decimal number average (Q4). Hence, despite being able to calculate average through an arithmetic mean algorithm (Q4), students are still regarded as having a scanty understanding of average.

Treatment of Variation

Students were asked to answer Q5 in order to examine how students deal with variation within a set of data when calculating average. Table 5 summarizes student

Table 5. Mathematically talented and non-talented student Q5 answers

Answer type		Talented students	Non-talented students
Proper Treatment	Omission of the extreme value	20.0%	1.5%
	Use of the concept of mode	2.9%	17.7%
	Subtotal	22.9%	19.2%
Improper Treatment	Use of the concept of mean	67.1%	38.7%
	Desist average calculation	10.0%	8.2%
	Other	0.0%	33.9%
	Subtotal	77.1%	80.8%
Total		100.0%	100.0%

responses to Q5. Only 22.9% of the mathematically talented students and 19.2% of the non-talented students could properly manage variation within a data set to calculate average. To determine if the 3.7% difference between the two groups was significant a chi-square test was done. The test indicated no significant difference between the mathematically talented and non-talented students: X^2 (1, $N = 132$) = 0.241, p > 0.05. Although there was no statistically significant difference between groups, the two groups utilized different approaches to deal with the variation. Generally, students either excluded the extreme value or employed the idea of mode. For a majority of the mathematically talented students (20.0%) the extreme value was discarded from their calculations while most non-talented students saw average as the mode.

Student 7 estimated object weight by calculating average from the eight "normal" data values. He felt the weight value 15.3 was inappropriate. He claimed that because the data measurement was much heavier than the other eight values, it must have been a measuring mistake. This student properly dealt with variation in the process of calculating average by considering the origin of the variation, in this case, an incorrect measurement. Student 8 employed the idea of mode to control the variation within the data set. This student concluded the mode had to be the average for the set of 9 data after arranging the data set into a weight scale with a range of 6.0 to 15.3.

Student 7: Average is achieved by using only eight of the data values; it does not include 15.3. I think the weight value 15.3 was estimated improperly because it is too large compared to the others.

Student 8: I think the answer is 6.2 because the weight measurements are so different and the range is so wide. The value 6.2 occurs most frequently.

77.1% of the mathematically talented students and 80.8% of the non-talented students failed to properly address variation. Moreover, 67.1% of the mathematically talented students and 38.7% of the non-talented students simply ignored variation within the data set and proceeded to calculate average using all nine data values; i.e., they included the extreme value. Interestingly, Student 9 correctly became conscious of the need to employ the idea of mean to obtain an approximation of weight since the weight values differed; unfortunately, he failed to control variation because he did not consider the extreme value.

Student 9: It is 7.16, an average of all nine data values. Because they [data] are different, we need to calculate average to gain an approximate degree of accuracy.

Regrettably, 10.0% of the mathematically talented students and 8.2% of the non-talented students discontinued with the calculation of average. For instance, although Student 10 anticipated object weight to be between 6 and 7 since most measurements were recorded at between 6 and 7, he felt an average for the data set was unattainable. He did not know how to deal with an extreme value, in this case a weight of 15.3. In other words, he failed to approximate the object's weight because of an incompetency at managing extreme values due to variation. In addition, Student 11 shows that although 33.9% of the non-talented students managed to estimate the weight of the object, their values were incorrect, and the bases of their average determination were also improper.

Student 10: It's impossible to calculate. If all the weight data values had been between 6 and 7, it would have been possible. But one [15.3] of the values is greater than the others by about 9.

Student 11: It's 15.3 because it is the heaviest recorded weight.

SUMMARY AND DISCUSSION

An out-of-context investigation of students' understanding of the term 'average'— the first step in statistical literacy (Watson, 2006)—revealed little difference between mathematically talented students (51.4%) and non-talented students (50.0%) in the ability to recognize average as being representative. However, examination of students' understanding of the term 'average' in a specific social context, the second step in statistical literacy (Watson, 2006), found that a larger percentage of mathematically talented students (47.1%) considered average to be representative than non-talented students (30.7%). These findings suggest difference exists between mathematically talented and non-talented students' recognition of average as being representative.

Further analysis, however, shows this difference to be small. Only 38.6% (Table 1) of the mathematically talented students failed to include the notion of representativeness in their definitions or explanations of average for both Q1 and Q2. Hence, 61.4% of the mathematically talented students do indeed consider the representativeness of average. The 14.3% of mathematically talented students who considered average as being representative in Q1 but not in Q2 centred their attention on the actual calculation of an average for Q2. Given a specific social context, these students believed average involves consideration of how and why average is calculated. Also, the 10.0% of mathematically talented students who viewed average as being representative in Q2 but not in Q1 seemed to associate the term 'average' with an averaging algorithm or formula learnt in school textbooks for Q1. They also realized the notion of representativeness for average by reflecting on average with reference to a given context for Q2. These results confirm that the 24.3% of mathematically talented students indeed recognize average as being representative. In comparison,

40.3% (Table 2) of the non-talented students did not include the notion of representativeness in their definitions or explanations of average for both Q1 and Q2. Also noteworthy is the finding that 59.7% of the non-talented students also viewed average as being representative.

The idea of average is very powerful in statistical reasoning since average includes mean, mode, and median, concepts that are used to summarize information about a set of data. Additionally, average viewed as being representative enables data as individual values to interact with distribution as a conceptual entity. Thus, statistics education for the talented should pay special attention to the notion of average as being representative.

While 55.7% of the mathematically talented students properly interpreted a decimal number average for Q3, only 14.5% of the non-talented students showed a proper understanding. Also, 54.2% (Q4) of the mathematically talented students accepted a decimal number average for a set of physical object data, a value that cannot be physically expressed in the real world. On the other hand, only 30.7% of the non-talented students accepted the value as the average. Although results show that mathematically talented students are good at interpreting the meaning of a decimal number average and constructing a mathematical abstract for average in comparison to non-talented students, 44.3% of the mathematically talented students provided proper interpretation of a decimal number average in Q3. Moreover, 45.8% of the mathematically talented students were reluctant to accept a decimal number average for Q4. Poor understanding of a decimal number average and difficulty in constructing a mathematical abstract for average could be the reasons for these findings. Hence, average and its related concepts need to be factored into statistics education for mathematically talented students.

The 32.8% of mathematically talented students who showed proper understanding of a decimal number average in Q3 and accepted a decimal number average in Q4 are believed to have generated an abstract mathematical construction for average. For the 22.9% of mathematically talented students that provided appropriate explanations for a decimal number average in Q3 but were reluctant to accept a decimal number average in Q4, it may be that students psychologically could not accept a decimal number average despite having clear proper understanding of it due to the inability to physically construct the average result. Students relied on examples (e.g. Student 5 spoke of one hundred families and one hundred and seventy children) to interpret a decimal number average in Q3, but they could not postulate any real examples for Q4.

According to results, 22.9% of mathematically talented students and 19.2% of non-talented students properly controlled variation within a set of data to find average; that is, there is little difference in terms of percentages between the two groups. For 67.1% of the mathematically talented students and 38.7% of the non-talented students variation was disregarded and an arithmetic mean was calculated by including all nine data values. Percentages indicate this tendency was carried out more frequently by mathematically talented students than by non-talented students. Averages that are attained without consideration of variation within a data set cannot be true representatives of data sets. In other words, these averages cannot be considered true summarizing data tools. Thus, researchers and educators should focus on assisting mathematically talented students to recognize and deal with variation within a set of data.

The abilities of mathematically talented students in terms of generalizing, abstracting, and intuiting in geometry, algebra, probability, and problem solving have been long demonstrated (Assouline & Doellinger, 2001; Benbow & Minor, 1990; Greenes, 1981; Heinze, 2005; Krutetskii, 1976; Na et al., 2007; Schneider, 2000; Sriraman, 2003, 2004; Wieczerkowski et al., 2000). However, according to the findings of this study on statistical thinking, there is little actual difference between mathematically talented and non-talented students' appreciation of the notion of representativeness for average and treatment of variation for average. The only clear difference is in construction of a mathematical abstract for average. Since a mathematically educated person can be statistically illiterate (Hawkins, 1996), mathematically talented students need to develop statistical thinking. Mathematically talented students should be equipped with greater competence in statistical thinking because they will be responsible for decisions and judgments as researchers, leaders, and pioneers in various areas requiring statistics such as physics, chemistry, biology, medical science, genetic engineering, economics, archaeology, and so on. Statistics involves a unique mode of thinking in addition to being a field of mathematics (Moore, 1992), and statistical thinking needs communication between statistics' user and context. Therefore, mathematically talented students should be provided with more experiences and opportunities to learn and explore statistical ideas and concepts in real contexts.

REFERENCES

Assouline, S., & Lupkowski-Shoplik, A. (2005). *Developing math talent: A guide for education gifted and advanced learners in math.* Waco, TX: Prufrock Press.

Assouline, S. G., & Doellinger, H. L. (2001). Elementary students who can do junior high math: Policy or pedagogy. In N. Colangelo & S. G. Assouline (Eds.), *Talent development IV: Proceedings from the 1998 Henry B. and Jocelyn Wallace National Research Symposium on Talent Development* (pp. 123–134). Scottsdale, AZ: Great Potential Press.

Bakker, A., & Gravemeijer, K. P. E. (2004). Learning to reasoning about distribution. In D. Ben-Zvi & J. Garfield (Eds.), *The challenge of developing statistical literacy, reasoning and thinking* (pp. 147–168). Dordrecht, The Netherlands: Kluwer.

Benbow, C. P., & Minor, L. L. (1990). Cognitive profiles of verbally and mathematically precocious students: Implications for identification of the gifted. *Gifted Child Quarterly, 34*(1), 21–26.

Ben-Zvi, D. (2004). Reasoning about data analysis. In D. Ben-Zvi & J. Garfield (Eds.), *The challenge of developing statistical literacy, reasoning and thinking* (pp. 121–145). Dordrecht, The Netherlands: Kluwer.

Cobb, G. W. (1999). Individual and collective mathematical development: The case of statistical data analysis. *Mathematical Thinking and Learning, 1*(1), 5–43.

Cobb, G. W., & McClain, K. (2004). Principles of instructional design for supporting the development of students' statistical reasoning. In D. Ben-Zvi & J. Garfield (Eds.), *The challenge of developing statistical literacy, reasoning and thinking* (pp. 375–395). Dordrecht, The Netherlands: Kluwer.

Cobb, G. W., & Moore, D. S. (1997). Mathematics, statistics, and teaching. *American Mathematical Monthly, 104*, 801–823.

delMas, R. C. (2004). A comparison of mathematical and statistical reasoning. In D. Ben-Zvi & J. Garfield (Eds.), *The challenge of developing statistical literacy, reasoning and thinking* (pp. 79–95). Dordrecht, The Netherlands: Kluwer.

Dreyfus, T., & Tsamir, P. (2004). Ben's consolidation of knowledge structures about infinite sets. *Journal of Mathematical Behavior, 23*(3), 271–300.

Greenes, C. (1981). Identifying the gifted student in mathematics. *Arithmetic Teacher, 28*(6), 14–17.

Hawkins, A. (1996). Can a mathematically-educated person be statistically illiterate? *Mathematics for the Millennium-What needs to be changed and why?* (pp. 107–117). Nuffield Foundation: Pre-conference paper.

Heinze, A. (2005). Differences in problem solving strategies of mathematically gifted and non-gifted elementary students. *International Education Journal, 6*(2), 175–183.

Konold, C., & Pollatsek, A. (2002). Data analysis as the search for signals in noisy processes. *Journal for Research in Mathematics Education, 33*, 259–289.

Krutetskii, V. A. (1976). *The psychology of mathematical abilities in school children* (J. Teller, Transl. from the Russian, J. Kilpatrick & I. Wirszup, Editors). Chicago: University of Chicago Press. (Original work published 1968)

Lee, K. (2005). Three types of reasoning and creative informal proofs by mathematically gifted students. In *Proceedings of the 29th conference of the International Group for the Psychology of Mathematics Education* (Vol. 3, pp. 241–248). Melbourne, Australia.

Lee, K., Kim, M., Na, G., Han, D., & Song, S. (2007). Induction, analogy, and imagery in geometric reasoning. In *Proceedings of the 31th conference of the International Group for the Psychology of Mathematics Education* (Vol. 3, 145–152). Seoul, Korea.

Lee, K., Ko, E., & Song, S. (2007). The analysis of activity that gifted students construct definition of regular polyhedra. In *Proceedings of the 31th conference of the International Group for the Psychology of Mathematics Education* (Vol. 3, pp. 153–160). Seoul, Korea.

Limm, S. (1984). The characteristics approach: Identification and beyond. *Gifted Child Quarterly, 28*(4), 181–187.

Miles, M. B., & Huberman, A. M. (1994). *Qualitative data analysis: An expanded sourcebook* (2nd ed.). Thousand Oaks, CA: Sage.

Mokros, J., & Russell, S. J. (1995). Children's concepts of average and representativeness. *Journal for Research in Mathematics Education, 26*(1), 20–39.

Moore, D. S. (1992). Teaching statistics as a respectable subject. In F. & S. Gordon (Eds.), *Statistics for the twenty-first century*. MAA Notes, no. 26 (pp. 14–25). Washington, DC: Mathematical Association of America.

Moore, D. S. (1998). Statistics among the liberal arts. *Journal of the American Statistical Association, 93*(444), 1253–1259.

Na, G., Han, D., Lee, K., & Song, S. (2007). Mathematically gifted students' problem solving approaches on conditional probability. In *Proceedings of the 31th conference of the International Group for the Psychology of Mathematics Education* (Vol. 4, pp. 1–8). Seoul, Korea.

Pollatsek, A., Lima, S., & Well, A. D. (1981). Concept or computation: Students' understanding of the mean. *Educational Studies in Mathematics, 12*, 191–204.

Reading, C., & Shaughnessy, J. M. (2004). Reasoning about variation. In D. Ben-Zvi & J. Garfield (Eds.), *The challenge of developing statistical literacy, reasoning and thinking* (pp. 201–226). Dordrecht, The Netherlands: Kluwer.

Schneider, W. (2000). Giftedness, expertise, and exceptional performance: A developmental perspective. In K. A. Heller, F. J. Mönks, R. J. Sternberg, & R. F. Subotnik (Eds.), *International handbook of giftedness and talent* (pp. 165–178). New York: Elsevier.

Shaughnessey, J. M., Garfield, J., & Greer, B. (1996). Data handling. In A. J. Bishop, K. Clements, C. Keitel, J. Kilpatrick, & C. Laborde (Eds.), *International handbook of mathematics education* (Pt. 1, pp. 205–237). Dordrecht, The Netherlands: Kluwer.

Sriraman, B. (2003). Mathematical giftedness, problem solving, and the ability to formulate generalizations: The problem-solving experiences of four gifted students. *Journal of Secondary Gifted Education, 14*, 151–165.

Sriraman, B. (2004). Gifted ninth graders' notions of proof: Investigating parallels in approaches of mathematically gifted students and professional mathematicians. *Journal for the Education of the Gifted, 27*(4), 267–292.

Ullman, N. (1995). *Statistical or quantitative thinking as a fundamental intelligence.* Unpublished paper, County College of Morris, Randolph, NJ.

Watson, J. M. (1997). Assessing statistical thinking using the media. In I. Gal & J. B. Garfield (Eds.), *The assessment challenge in statistics education* (pp. 107–121). Amsterdam: ISO Press.

Watson, J. M. (2006). *Statistical literacy at school: Growth and goals.* Mahwah, NJ: Lawrence Erlbaum Associates.

Wheatley, G. H. (1983). Mathematics curriculum for the gifted and talented. In J. VanTassel-Vaska & S. M. Reis (Eds.), *Curriculum for gifted and talented students* (pp. 137–146). Thousand Oaks, CA: Corwin Press.

Wieczerkowski, W., Cropley, A. J., & Prado, T. M. (2000). Nurturing talents/gifts in mathematics. In K. A. Heller, F. J. Mönks, R. J. Sternberg, & R. F. Subotnik(Eds.), *International handbook of giftedness and talent* (pp. 413–426). New York: Elsevier.

Wild, C. J. & Pfannkuch, M. (1999). Statistical thinking in empirical enquiry. *International Statistical Review, 67*(3), 223–265.

Eun-Sung Ko and Kyeong-Hwa Lee
Seoul National University
Korea
kes-7402@hanmail.net
khmath@snu.ac.kr

KRISTINA JUTER AND BHARATH SRIRAMAN

4. DOES HIGH ACHIEVING IN MATHEMATICS = GIFTED AND/OR CREATIVE IN MATHEMATICS

INTRODUCTION

A student at a university, let us call him John, was always the first to answer questions posed by the teacher. Problems that took 15 minutes for his peers to solve took him a split second. John attended all compulsory lectures, but he did not do all compulsory tasks and hence did not pass the course. He was always late and not very focused on the course, other than on occasional problems posed by his teacher. He saw mathematical relations but was not particularly interested in the university setting and he did not adjust to it which led him to fail the course. He was clearly mathematically gifted, and a creative thinker in his ability to see solutions to problems quickly, but in the course statistics, he would be regarded a low achieving student. This conflicting scenario leads to several questions.

What characterizes high achieving in mathematics? Does it require certain extraordinary skills, skills you are born with or skills you can acquire by hard work, i.e., can anyone become a high achiever? On the other hand, what does it mean to be gifted in mathematics? What does it mean to be creative in mathematics? What does it mean to be intelligent in mathematics? Is it enough to work hard from an average level of understanding to become gifted? What are the relations between gifted, high achieving, creative, intelligent? Are these terms synonyms? antonyms? Or is there more complexity to these terms and the need to understand the subtleties in their usage? In this chapter we unpack the various definitions of these terms as well as construct seven hypothetical case studies based on the theories in the literature.

CREATIVITY AND MATHEMATICAL CREATIVITY

Humanity's innovative spirit and creativity lies beneath the comforts and security of today's technologically evolved society. Creativity is a paradoxical construct to study because in many ways it is self defining. In other words, we are able to engage or judge acts of everyday creativity such as improvising on a recipe, use a tool in a way it wasn't intended, or intuit emotions and intended meanings from gestures and body language in day-to-day communication. Children are particularly adept at engaging in creative acts such as imaginary role playing or using toys and other objects in imaginative ways. "Aha!" experiences occur not only in individuals working on scientific problems but also in day-to-day problems such as realizing a person's name or relational identity after having forgotten it. However it is important to distinguish between everyday creativity and domain specific or paradigm

B. Sriraman and K.H. Lee (eds.), The Elements of Creativity and Giftedness in Mathematics, 45–65.
© 2011 Sense Publishers. All rights reserved.

shifting creativity. Domain specific creativity or "extraordinary creativity" causes paradigm shifts in a specific body of knowledge and it is generally accepted that works of "extraordinary creativity" can be judged only by experts within a specific domain of knowledge. Some researchers have described creativity as a natural "survival" or "adaptive" response of humans in an ever-changing environment.

The Handbook of Creativity edited by Robert Sternberg which contains a comprehensive review of all research available in the field of creativity suggests that most of the approaches used in the study of creativity can be subsumed under six categories: mystical, pragmatic, psychodynamic, psychometric, social-personality and cognitive. The mystical approach to studying creativity suggests that creativity is the result of divine inspiration, or is a spiritual process. In the history of mathematics, Blaise Pascal claimed that many of his mathematical insights came directly from God. This is somewhat analogous to the ancient Greeks' belief in muses as a source of inspiration for artistic works. The pragmatic approach is focused on developing creativity. For instance, George Polya's emphasis on the use of a variety of heuristics for solving mathematical problems of varying complexity is an example of a pragmatic approach. The psychodynamic approach to studying creativity is based on the Gestaltist idea that creativity arises from the tension between conscious reality and unconscious drives as popularized by Jacques Hadamard who constructed case studies of eminent creators such as Albert Einstein. This approach is discussed in the chapter by Sriraman, Yaftian and Lee (this volume). The psychometric approach to studying creativity entails quantifying the notion of creativity with the aid of paper and pencil tasks such as the Torrance Tests of Creative Thinking developed by Paul Torrance. These tests are used by many gifted programs in middle and high schools, to identify students that are gifted/creative and show traits of divergent thinking. The test is scored for fluency, flexibility, and the statistical rarity of a response. Some researchers also call for use of more significant productions such as writing samples, drawings, etc to be subjectively evaluated by a panel of experts instead of simply relying on a numerical measure. The psychometric approach is discussed in the context of problem posing activities given to U.S and Chinese student in the chapter by Yuan and Sriraman (this volume). The social-personality approach to studying creativity focuses on personality and motivational variables as well as the socio-cultural environment as sources of creativity. Finally the cognitive approach to the study of creativity focuses on understanding the mental processes that generate new and novel ideas. Most of the contemporary literature on creativity suggests that creativity is the result of confluence of factors from the six aforementioned categories. Two of the most commonly cited confluence approaches to the study of creativity are the "systems approach" of Mihaly Csikszentmihalyi; and "the case study as evolving systems approach" of Doris Wallace and Howard Gruber.

The systems approach takes into account the social and cultural dimensions of creativity, instead of simply viewing creativity as an individualistic psychological process and studies the interaction between the individual, domain and field. The field consists of people who have influence over a domain. For example, editors of research journals would have influence on any given domain. The domain is defined a cultural organism that preserves and transmits creative products to other individuals in the field.

Thus creativity occurs when an individual makes a change in a given domain, and this change is transmitted through time. The personal background of individuals and their position in a domain naturally influence the likelihood of their contribution. It is no coincidence that in the history of science, there are significant contributions from clergymen such as Pascal, Copernicus and Mendel, to name a few, because they had the means and the leisure to "think". Csikszentmihalyi argues that novel ideas that result in significant changes are unlikely to be adopted unless they are sanctioned by a group of experts that decide what gets included in the domain. In contrast to Csikszentmihalyi's argument that calls for focus on communities in which creativity manifests, "the case study as evolving systems approach" treats each individual as a unique, evolving system of creativity and ideas, where each individual's creative work is studied on its own. The case study as an evolving system of Gruber & Wallace has the following components to it. First, it views creative work as multi-faceted. So, in constructing a case study of a creative work, one has to distil out the facets that are relevant and construct the case study based on the chosen facets. These facets are: uniqueness of the work, epitome (a narrative of what the creator achieved), systems of belief (an account of the creator's belief s system), modality (whether the work is a result of visual, auditory or kinesthetic processes), multiple time-scales (construct the time-scales involved in the production of the creative work), dynamic features of the work (documenting other problems that were worked on simultaneously by the creator), problem-solving, contextual frame (family, schooling, teachers influences), and values (the creator's value system) (Sriraman, 2005).

Cultural and social aspects play a significant role in what the community, in general, and the school system, in particular, considers as "creativity" and how they deal with it. Numerous studies indicate that the behavioural traits of creative individuals very often go against the grain of acceptable behaviour in the institutionalized school setting. For instance, negative behavioural traits such as indifference to class rules, display of boredom, cynicism or hyperactivity usually result in disciplinary measures as opposed to appropriate affective interventions (Sriraman, 2005). In the case of gifted students who 'conform' to the norm, these students are often prone to hide their intellectual capacity for social reasons, and identify their academic talent as being a source of envy. History is peppered with numerous examples of creative individuals described as "deviants" by the status quo. Even at the secondary and tertiary levels there have been criticisms about the excessive amount of structure imposed on disciplines by academics as well as Euro-centric attitudes and male episte-mology centred attitudes towards knowledge generation. Such a criticism particularly resonates in the world of science and mathematics, especially during elementary and secondary schooling experiences level, where minority, ethnic minorities, first nation and female gifted/creative students are marginalized by practices that are alien to their own cultures.

Based on extensive classroom based research and informed by findings from the field of psychology, creativity and the history of science, five pedagogical principles to maximize general creativity in the classroom have been posited by Sriraman (2005). The five principles are: (a) the Gestalt principle, (b) the Aesthetic principle, (c) the free market principle, (d) the scholarly principle, and (e) the uncertainty principle.

The Gestalt principle: Although psychologists have criticized the Gestalt model of creativity because it attributes a large "unknown" part of creativity to unconscious drives during incubation, numerous studies with scientists and mathematicians have consistently validated this model. In all these studies after one has worked on a problem for a considerable time (preparation) without making a breakthrough, one puts the problem aside and other interests occupy the mind. Jacques Hadamard put forth two hypotheses regarding the incubation phase: (1) The 'rest-hypothesis' holds that a fresh brain in a new state of mind makes illumination possible. (2) The 'forgetting-hypothesis' states that the incubation phase gets rid of false leads and makes it possible to approach the problem with an open mind. The Soviet psychologist Krutetskii explained that the experience of sudden inspiration is the result of previous protracted thinking, of previously acquired experience, skills, and knowledge the person amassed earlier. This period of incubation eventually leads to an insight on the problem, to the "Eureka" or the "Aha!" moment of illumination. Most of us have experienced this magical moment. Yet the value of this archaic Gestalt construct is ignored in the classroom. This implies that it is important that teachers encourage the gifted to engage in suitably challenging problems over a protracted time period thereby creating the opportunities for the discovery of an insight and to experience the euphoria of the "Aha!" moment.

The Aesthetic principle: Many eminent creators have often reported the aesthetic appeal of creating a "beautiful" idea that ties together seemingly disparate ideas, combines ideas from different areas of knowledge or utilizes an atypical artistic technique. In mathematics, Georg Cantor's argument about the uncountability of the set of real numbers is an often quoted example of a brilliant and atypical counting technique.

The Free market principle: Scientists in an academic setting take a huge risk when they announce a new theory or medical breakthrough or proof to a long standing unsolved problem. The implication for the classroom is that teachers should encourage students to take risks. In particular they should encourage the gifted/creative students to pursue and present their solutions to contest or open problems at appropriate regional and state math student meetings, allowing them to gain experience at defending their ideas upon scrutiny from their peers.

The Scholarly principle: Teachers should embrace the idea of "creative deviance" as contributing to the body of knowledge, and they should be flexible and open to alternative student approaches to problems. In addition, they should nurture a class-room environment in which students are encouraged to debate and question the validity of both the teachers' as well as other students' approaches to problems. Gifted students should also be encouraged to generalize the problem and/or the solution as well as pose a class of analogous problems in other contexts. Allowing students problem posing opportunities and understanding of problem design helps them to differentiate good problems from poor, and solvable from non-solvable problems. In addition, independent thinking can be cultivated by offering students the opportunity to explore problem situations without any explicit instruction.

The Uncertainty principle: Real world problems are full of uncertainty and ambiguity. Creating, as opposed to learning, requires that students be exposed to the uncertainty as well as the difficulty of creating original ideas in science, mathematics, and other disciplines. This ability requires the teacher to provide affective support to students who experience frustration over being unable to solve a difficult problem. Students should periodically be exposed to ideas from the history of mathematics and science that evolved over centuries and took the efforts of generations of artists, scientists and mathematicians to finally solve. At the elementary and secondary schooling levels, one normally does not expect works of extraordinary creativity, however the literature indicates that it is certainly feasible for students to offer new insights into existing/current scientific problems or a new interpretation or commentary to a literary, artistic or historical work.

INTELLIGENCE AND MATHEMATICAL INTELLIGENCE

Mathematical intelligence is considered a strong indicator of general intelligence and items requiring numerical and spatial reasoning have historically been a component of what constitutes an IQ score or "g" score. The traditional view of mathematical intelligence as a construct measurable by a standardized battery leaves little room for the role of imaginative thinking and does not take into consideration the extra-cognitive and socio-cultural factors that influence a person's mathematical creativity. Since mathematical intelligence is often associated with mathematical giftedness and mathematical creativity, a differentiation of the various terms is necessary and explained in this entry. Mathematical intelligence is described from the point of view of extant research findings in the domains of mathematical cognition, psychology, socio-cultural research, and gifted education.

The construct of intelligence in general and mathematical intelligence in particular have been topics of great controversy since the advent of psychometric testing. For example most modern day intelligence tests which have evolved out of the original Binet-Simon test and the Stanford-Binet test developed by Lewis Terman consist of subtests which measure numerical reasoning, digit memory, letter-number sequencing, digit symbol-coding, picture completion, block design, matrix reasoning, symbol and object assembly. In other words logical, quantitative and visual-spatial reasoning play a significant role in IQ tests. However this view of intelligence has been criticized as being problematic as the items do not take into consideration socio-cultural and environmental variables that can influence performance particular among minorities and non-native English speakers. High scores on the Stanford-Binet have been traditionally used as an indicator of giftedness and a predictor of academic success in school and beyond. Similarly psychometric batteries such as the SAT, ACT and GRE consist of a mathematics portion which claim to predict academic success in college.

In the studies conducted in the domain of cognition, mathematical intelligence in an individual can be defined in terms of: (1) the ability to abstract, generalize and discern mathematical structures; (2) data management; (3) ability to master principles of logical thinking and inference; (4) analogical, heuristic thinking and posing related problems; (5) flexibility and reversibility of mathematical operations; (6) an intuitive awareness of mathematical proof; (7) ability to independently discover mathematical principles; (8) decision making abilities in problem solving situations; (9) the ability to visualize problems and/or relations and (10) distinguish between empirical and theoretical principles.

Mathematical intelligence in the general population has been classified by numerous theorists using a hierarchical model. For instance, Zalman Usiskin, a mathematics educator at the University of Chicago proposed an eight-tiered hierarchy to classify mathematical talent, which ranges from Level 0 to Level 7. In this hierarchy Level 0 (No Talent) represents adults who know very little mathematics, Level 1 (Culture level) represents adults who have rudimentary number sense as a function of cultural usage and their mathematical knowledge is comparable to those of students in grades 6–9. It is obvious that a very large proportion of the general population would fall into the first two levels. The remaining population is thinly spread out into levels 2 through 7 on the basis of mathematical talent. Level 2 represents the honors high school student who is capable of majoring in mathematics as well as those that eventually become secondary math teachers. Level 3 (the "terrific" student) represents students that score in the 750–800 on the SAT's or 4 or 5 in the Calculus AP exams. These students have the potential to do beginning graduate level work in mathematics. Level 4 (the "exceptional" student) represents students that excel in math competitions and receive admission into math/science summer camps and/or academies because of their talent. This student is capable of constructing mathematical proofs and able to "converse" with mathematicians about mathematics. Level 5 represents the productive mathematician. It represents a student that has successfully completed a Ph.D in the mathematics or related mathematical sciences and is capable of publishing in the field. Level 6 is the rarified territory of the exceptional mathematician, which represents mathematicians that have made significant contributions to their particular domains and conferred recognition for their work. Finally Level 7 are the all-time greats, including the Fields medal winners in mathematics. The Fields Medals was established by John Charles Fields (1863–1932) and is the equivalent of the Nobel Prize for the field of mathematics. This level is the exclusive territory of giants or exemplary geniuses like Leonard Euler, Karl Friedrich Gauss, Bernhard Riemmann, Srinivasa Ramanujan, David Hilbert, Henri Poincaré among others. The hierarchical model of Usiskin has been extended further by Sriraman (2005) by taking into consideration the need to differentiate between the constructs of mathematical giftedness and mathematical creativity implicitly assumed in the model.

In the former Soviet Union in the time period 1950–1970 numerous experiments were conducted with mathematically capable students in order to discern their specific mathematical abilities. This research characterized the mathematical abilities of gifted children holistically as comprising of analytic, geometric and harmonic components and argued that gifted children usually have a preference for one component over the others. The analytic 'type' has a mathematically abstract cast of mind, the geometric 'type' has a mathematically pictorial cast of mind, whereas a harmonic 'type' is a combination of analytic and geometric types. For instance, given the same problem, one gifted child might pursue an analytic approach, whereas another would pursue a geometric approach. Another classification of 'styles' of mathematical giftedness suggests the 'empirical type' and the 'conceptual type'. In this classification the empirical type would have a preference for applied situations, immediately observable relations and induction, whereas the conceptual type would have a preference for theoretical situations and deduction. The Soviet psychologist, V.A. Krutetskii observed that one of the attributes of mathematically gifted students was the ability to switch from a direct to a reverse train of thought (reversibility), which gifted students performed with relative ease. The mathematical context in which this reversibility was observed was in transitions from usual proof to proof via contradiction (reductio ad absurdum), or when moving from a theorem to its converse. The researchers cited in this paragraph acknowledged the use of 'intuitive' ability for mathematics in gifted children.

Another aspect of mathematical intelligence is that of mathematical creativity. Most extant definitions of mathematical creativity found in the mathematics and mathematics education literature is vague or elusive. This may be because of the difficulty of describing this complex construct. For instance mathematical creativity has been defined by mathematicians like Henri Poincaré via the use of various metaphors such as the ability to discern, choose; to distinguish between acceptable and unacceptable patterns; and non-algorithmic decision-making. The literature on students that are mathematically creative at the pre-university level is also vague. Exceptional mathematical ability has been associated with the Einstein syndrome and the Asperger syndrome. The Einstein syndrome is characterized by exceptional mathematical ability but delayed speech development, whereas the Asperger syndrome is a mild form of autism. At the pre-university level, one normally does not expect works of extraordinary creativity, however it is certainly feasible for students to offer new insights into a math problem or a new interpretation or commentary to a literary or historical work. The psychologist Robert Sternberg defines creativity as the ability to produce unexpected original work, which is useful and adaptive. Other definitions such as those formulated by Paul Torrance usually impose the requirement of novelty, innovation or unusualness of a response to a given problem. As reviewed earlier, confluence theories of creativity define creativity as a convergence of knowledge, ability, thinking style, motivational and environmental variables. A synthesis of the numerous definitions of creativity leads to a generally accepted definition of mathematical creativity as the ability to produce original work that significantly extends the body of knowledge, and/or opens up avenues of new questions for others. The existing research also indicates that mathematically creative individuals are prone to reformulating the problem or finding analogous problems. They are also different from their peers in that they are fiercely independent thinkers, tend to persevere and to reflect a great deal. Although some of the cognitive and affective aspects of mathematical creativity are now known, some theorists claim that numerous extra-cognitive factors play an important role in the manifestation of mathematical intelligence in creative acts. These factors include beliefs, aesthetics, intuitions, intellectual values, self imposed subjective norms and standards, and chance as contributing towards astonishing acts and products of creative endeavours.

Some theorists contend that although the field of psychology has an established body of research which has examined factors such as the influence of personality and socio-cultural influences contributing to creative behaviour, the study of beliefs, aesthetics, intuitions, values and chance are necessary to complement and convey a complete picture of creativity. In socio-cultural frameworks for mathematics such as that proposed by Alan Bishop doing mathematics is viewed as being engaged in and aware of the six pan-cultural human activities which are (1) playing, (2) designing, (3) locating, (4) explaining, (5) counting, and (6) measuring.

One important implication for teachers of mathematics is that many of the traits of highly able individuals are in fact cultivatable in the classroom. For instance the role of analogical reasoning is highlighted as a trait of exceptional creativity, yet the use of analogies and metaphors vanishes in the school curricula as imagination is replaced by conformity as students progress through elementary and secondary grades particularly in science and mathematics. Problem solving research in the 1980's partly focused on analogical behaviours engaged in by expert and novice problem solvers. This research revealed that expert problem solvers in mathematics and science engaged in metaphorical processes as they constructed problem representations and they looked for analogies between the problem at hand and other familiar situations. A recent longitudinal cross-cultural study conducted with young children in Australia and the United States, reported that spontaneous analogies employed by children in everyday language in natural settings were by and large absent when children employed the language of mathematics, that is engaged in mathematical reasoning, which suggests that practitioners need to encourage this natural facility in mathematics classrooms.

Real world problems are full of uncertainty and ambiguity. Creating, as opposed to learning, requires that students be exposed to the uncertainty as well as the difficulty of creating original ideas in mathematics, science and other disciplines. This ability requires the teacher to provide affective support to students who experience frustration over being unable to solve a difficult problem. Students should periodically be exposed to ideas from the history of mathematics and science that evolved over centuries and took the efforts of generations of mathematicians to finally solve. Cultivating this trait will ultimately serve the mathematically gifted student to make the transition into the professional realm. The Hamburg Model in Germany, which is focused on allowing gifted students to engage in problem posing activities, followed by time for exploring viable and non-viable strategies to solve the posed problems, captures an essence of the nature of professional mathematics, where the most difficult task is often to correctly formulate the problem (theorem).

GIFTEDNESS AND MATHEMATICAL PRECOCIOUSNESS

Exceptional Abilities from a Young Age

Precocity in mathematical ability is a well documented phenomenon in the history of science and mathematics. Mathematical precocity is typically found in anecdotes of child prodigies such as Blaise Pascal (1623–1666), Carl Friedrich Gauss

(1777–1855), Rowan Hamilton (1805–1865), Srinivasa Ramanujan (1887–1920), Shakuntala Devi (1939–) and Terrence Tao (1975–), among others. Many of these prodigies were known for their phenomenal computing abilities which involved complex arithmetic and number theoretic operations on large numbers.

Some well documented and historically accurate anecdotes will indicate the profound nature of such individual's precocity. At the age of eleven, Pascal had composed a treatise on the sounds of vibrating bodies in spite of his father Étienne forbidding him from studying mathematics lest it interfere with Pascal's schooling in the classical languages. At the age of 12, Pascal constructed an independent proof that the sums of the angles of a Euclidean triangle are invariant and equal two right angles, with a piece of coal on a wall. Pascal was then allowed the luxury of sitting in on meetings held in the monastery housing Mersenne, where mathematical geniuses like Descartes, Desargues and Gassendi often gathered.

Rowan Hamilton displayed unusual precocity in the realm of languages and by the age of 13, under the tutelage of his uncle learned most classical and modern European languages, in addition to Hindustani, Persian, Sanskrit and Arabic. His genius in mathematics only manifested after his entry into Trinity College in Dublin, culminating in his discovery of the mathematical structure of quaternions in 1843. Srinivasa Ramanujan, labeled as one of the greatest mathematical geniuses of the 20th century was self-taught and found his love and astonishing ability for mathematics at the age of 13 by mastering an advanced trigonometry book by S.L. Loney and the nearly 5000 theorems found in A synopsis of elementary results in pure and applied mathematics by George S. Carr. Later with the help of G.H. Hardy at Cambridge, who recognized his brilliance, Ramanujan made profound contributions to analytic number theory, analysis, series and continued fractions. During his lifetime Ramanujan is said to have discovered nearly 4000 mathematical theorems in the forms of identities and equations. Shakuntala Devi, the daughter of a trapeze artist was a calculating prodigy who demonstrated her unusual counting talents in card games at the age of 3. She had the ability to perform mathematical computations faster than computers, an ability that did not wane in adulthood. She mentally extracted the 23rd root of a 201 digit number in 1977 and in 1980 demonstrated her abilities to the Computer Science department at Imperial College in London by correctly multiplying two randomly selected 13-digit numbers in 28 seconds. Finally Terence Tao, whose early mathematical precocity is well documented in the current gifted education literature, was attending already high school level courses at the age of 8, and scored a 760 on the SAT math. He was recently awarded the Fields Medal in Mathematics, the highest honor given to mathematicians under the age of 40, who have made seminal contributions to the development of the field.

Late Development of Mathematical Giftedness

Even though mathematical precocity is most frequently found among child prodigies, the literature contains eminent samples of precocious individuals who were relatively late bloomers in their seminal contributions to mathematics, such as

Abraham DeMoivre (1667–1754), Karl Weierstrass (1815–1857), Emmy Noether (1882–1935) and Abraham Robinson (1918–1974).

Identifying Precociuosness

Julian Stanley's landmark Study of Mathematically Precocious Youth (SMPY) started at Johns Hopkins in 1971 introduced the idea of above-level testing for the identification of highly gifted youth. From 1980–1983, in SMPY, 292 mathematically precocious youth were identified on the basis of the Scholastic Aptitude Test (SAT). These students scored at least 700 on SAT-Mathematics before the age of 13. Other tests that have good validity and reliability are The Stanford-Binet Intelligence Scale (Form L-M) and the Raven's Advanced Progressive Matrices which is useful with students from culturally diverse and English as a second language backgrounds. SMPY also generated a vast amount of empirical data gathered over the last 30 years, and resulted in many findings about the types of curricular and affective interventions that foster the pursuit of advanced coursework in mathematics.

Recently David Lubinski and Camilla Benbow compiled a comprehensive account of 35 years of longitudinal data obtained from the Study of Mathematically Precocious Youth (SMPY). They reported the findings from 20-year follow ups on various cohort groups that participated in SMPY. These researchers found that the success of SMPY in uncovering antecedents such as spatial ability, tendency to independently investigate and research oriented values were indicative as potential for pursuing lifelong careers related to mathematics and science. The special programming opportunities provided to the cohort groups played a major role in shaping their interest and potential in mathematics, and ultimately resulted in "happy" choices and satisfaction with the career paths chosen. Another finding was that significantly more mathematically precocious males entered into math oriented careers as opposed to females, which Lubinski and Benbow argue is not a loss of talent per se, since the females did obtain advanced degrees and chose careers more oriented to their multidimensional interests such as administration, law, medicine, and the social sciences. Programs such as SMPY serve as a beacon for other gifted and talented programs around the world, and provide ample evidence on the benefits of early identification and nurturing the interests of mathematically precocious individuals.

Mattsson (in press) studied 34 Swedish upper secondary teachers' characterization of mathematically gifted students. The teachers' descriptions were divided in cognitive and non-cognitive attributes. Creative ability, logical ability and management of school mathematics with great ease were the top three cognitive attributes with 11, 8 and 7 teachers using respective description. Only two teachers mentioned easy learning and five mentioned ability to see formal structure, which has similarities with logical ability. Motivation was the dominating non-cognitive attribute mentioned by 15 teachers followed by independence (4 teachers), systematic work (3) and reluctance to standardized teaching (3). The teachers were also asked how they identified mathematically gifted students and the most common way was through the students' own initiative in for example desire to finish courses faster or learning new things. Oral reasoning and test results were the second and third indicators the teachers described to detect gifted students.

Programmes for the Highly Gifted Youth

Given the profound abilities of mathematically precocious students programming can be delivered for these students via acceleration, curriculum compacting, differentiation. There exists compelling evidence from longitudinal studies conducted in the former Soviet Union by Krutetskii that highly mathematically gifted students are able to abstract and generalize mathematical concepts at higher levels of complexity and more easily than their peers in the context of arithmetic and algebra. These results were recently extended for the domains of problem solving, combinatorics and number theory by Sriraman (2002). The literature indicates that acceleration is perhaps the most effective way of meeting precociously gifted student programming needs. Mathematics unlike any other discipline lends itself to acceleration because of the sequential developmental nature of many elementary concepts. The very nature of acceleration suggests that the principles of curriculum compacting are applied to trim out the excessive amount of repetitive tasks. In addition, the effectiveness of radical acceleration and exclusive ability grouping, as extensively reported by Miraca Gross (see citations) in her longitudinal study of exceptionally and profoundly gifted students in Australia indicates that the benefits far out-weigh the risks of such an approach. Most of the students in Gross's studies reported high levels of academic success in addition to normal social lives. Simply put the purpose of curricular modifications such as acceleration, compacting and differentiation for mathematically precocious students is to tailor materials that introduce new topics at a faster pace which allow for high level thinking and independence reminiscent of research in the field of mathematics. Besides the use of curriculum compacting, differentiating and acceleration techniques, many school programs offer all students opportunities to participate in math clubs, in local, regional and statewide math contests. Typically the exceptionally talented students benefit the most from such opportunities. In many countries (such as Hungary, Romania, Russia and also the U.S), the objective of such contests is to typically select the best students to eventually move on to the national and international rounds of such competitions. The pinnacle of math contests are the prestigious International Math Olympiads (IMO) where teams of students from different countries work together to solve challenging math problems. At the local and regional levels, problems typically require mastery of concepts covered by a traditional high school curriculum with the ability to employ/connect methods and concepts flexibly. However at the Olympiad levels students in many countries are trained in the use of undergraduate level algebraic, analytic, combinatorial, graph theoretic, number theoretic and geometric principles.

Whereas most extant models within the U.S such as those used in the Center for Talented Youth (CTY) at Johns Hopkins tend to focus on accelerating the learning of concepts and processes from the regular curriculum, thus preparing students for advanced coursework within mathematics, other models such as Hamburg Model in Germany, are more focused on allowing gifted students to engage in problem posing activities, followed by time for exploring viable and non-viable strategies to solve the posed problems. This approach in a sense captures an essence of the nature of professional mathematics, where the most difficult task often is to correctly formulate the problem and pose related problems. Another successful model of identifying and developing mathematical precocity is found in historical case studies of mathematics gifted education in the former USSR. The Russian mathematician and pedagogue Gnedenko claimed that personal traits of creativity can appear in different ways in different people. One person could be interested in generalizing and a more profound examination of already obtained results. Others show the ability to find new objects for study and to look for new methods in order to discover their unknown properties. The third type of person can focus on logical development of theories demonstrating extraordinary sense of awareness of logical fallacies and flaws. A fourth group of gifted individuals would be attracted to hidden links between seemingly unrelated branches of mathematics. The fifth would study historical processes of the growth of mathematical knowledge. The sixth would focus on the study of philosophical aspects of mathematics. The seventh would search for ingenious solutions of practical problems and look for new applications of mathematics. Finally, someone could be extremely creative in the popularisation of science and in teaching.

The history of Soviet mathematics provides with a striking example of a co-existence of two different approaches to mathematics education, one embedded into the general lay public educational system implementing the blueprint based on the European concepts of the late 19th century, and the other one focusing mainly on gifted children and having flourished starting from 1950s onwards. The latter took the form of a complex network of activities including "mathematics clubs for advanced children" (Russian "кружки" (kruzhki), literally "circles" or "rings", usually affiliated with schools and universities but some were also home-based), Olympiads, team mathematics competitions, (mat-boi, literally "mathematical fight"), extracurricular winter or summer schools for gifted children, publication of magazines on physics and mathematics for children (the most famous being the Kvant, literally "Quantum"), among others (Freiman & Volkov, 2004). All these activities were free for all partici-pating children and were based solely on the enthusiasm of mathematics teachers or university professors. This process led to the creation of a system of formation of a "mathematical elite" in the former USSR focused first and foremost on "extremely gifted children", which was in a sharp contrast with the "egalitarian" regular state-run schools targeting "average students". The young Andrey Kolmogorov (1903–1987), a highly precocious child, who went on to become one of the most eminent mathe-maticians of the 20th century, was able to benefit from the unique extra-curriculum pedagogical environment provided by this system.

In conclusion, the history of mathematics and the literature in gifted education indicates that mathematical precocity is a relatively rare trait in the general population and one that typically manifests at a young age. Fortunately, it can be identified via above-level testing. Such individual's abilities develop and thrive when they are mentored early in their lives and provided affective support in addition to curricular programming appropriate for their abilities.

SEVEN CASES OF VARIOUS LEVELS OF GIFTEDNESS AND ACHIEVEMENT

In what follows, we have gathered a set of caricature cases portraying possible mathematical development. The cases are partly authentic based on the existing literature summarized in the previous sections but fictitious in the sense that they have not been identified explicitly by the authors in a particular classroom.

John, Gifted but not High Achieving in Mathematics

John, the student from the introduction, went through school as a distracted boy. He thought school was boring and he did not see any benefits of school mathematics which he regarded to be trivial games and tasks. He could instantly solve the problems the teachers gave him and he was cognitively creative (Sternberg, 2000) as he saw mathematical relations and structures enabling him to understand whole sets of mathematical constructs. At age 15 he had started to cut class frequently, particularly in the mornings as he tended to stay up in the evenings reading or designing computer programs. He was intrigued by alternative worldviews and was quite a philosopher. John barely managed to pass his upper secondary school exams and started at a teacher education program at the university. He chose mathematics and computer science as his subjects but he was often cutting classes and he missed compulsory seminars and tasks causing him to fail courses and become somewhat of an outsider in his class. He tried to fit in at the university, but he kept forgetting when and where he was supposed to be and what was expected from him. Eventually he was unable to continue at the university due to financial issues. He started to work wher-ever he could find employment, at a computer company as a programmer and later at a greenhouse taking care of plants, with the intention to continue his teacher education once he got enough money. When he was 34 he concluded that teaching was not for him and started his own computer company which he ran with moderate success due to his deficient social abilities and his tendency to spend his workdays creating intricate program codes. He could sit by his computers, forgetting time and the assignments his clients expected him to work with, and be overwhelmed by the flow of his creations. He had an aesthetic sense of his work in line with Sriraman's (2005) aesthetic pedagogical principle, which by itself was insufficient for his creativity to flourish in an institutional or societal sense.

Lisa, High Achieving Merely through Hard Work

All through her first years in school Lisa worked hard to please her parents and teachers in all school subjects. After school she took piano lessons and sang in a choir. She had top grades at age 14, except in sports and handicrafts, when she started to feel overwhelmed by the workload to keep her grades. She had to cut back on her after school activities until she spent most of her waking time studying. Her abilities to understand mathematical deduction was at an intermediate level, but she had a well developed study technique and a good memory so she was able to learn huge parts even though she sometimes was unable to understand the core features of the concepts at hand. She remained a high achiever in mathematics but had to work harder and harder to compensate for her difficulties to see relations between concepts.

Lisa went to university to become an engineer. She realized that she was no longer the highest achieving student in her mathematics class and her self esteem sunk even though she was above average, and she became depressed. She persisted but after a year she decided to switch to economics instead where the mathematics courses were easier. The mathematics she had learned at the engineering program made her a top student again. She never became very good at deduction and problem solving in advanced mathematics, but what she lacked in depth she compensated in her broader skills which made her a flexible and appreciated economist.

Steve, Late Discovery of Mathematical Precociousness

Steve was an average schoolboy, both in terms of achievement and socially. He had a lot of friends and was a member of the local soccer team. He thought mathematics was great fun and he did what he was supposed to do, but not more, throughout school for which he was awarded medium marks after his last year at upper secondary school. He did not see himself as a person able to get high marks and was pleased with his results. After school Steve was employed at a local harbour where his father had been working for many years. None of Steve's parents were academically trained. Steve was content and productive at his workplace and soon became head of his department due to his distributional and organizational skills. At age 29 he was no longer challenged by his work and he started studying mathematics as a leisure activity in the evenings. He realized that he was able to see structures and cope with logical deduction and he kept on taking courses at the university. This late discovery of his mathematical precociousness, like DeMoivre or Weierstrass aforementioned in this chapter, made him re-evaluate the purpose of his life. He soon became a top student in whatever mathematics topic he studied and was encouraged by his professors to consider a professional career within mathematics. After some years of study he had a PhD in mathematics and a position at the university teaching and doing research performing at level 5 in Usiskin's hierarchy. Steve was successful and his creativity helped him in his teaching and research. He got several international publications about his new findings and kept working at the university for many years.

Annie, Initially a High Achiever by Strategic Social and Mathematical Behaviour

Annie was a good judge of character from an early age. She was outgoing and enjoyed predicting people's actions. She did not particularly enjoy school work, but she liked school so she used her social skills to avoid as much work as possible. Mathematics was a subject she wanted to have high grades in, mainly because both her parents and her brother were science academics, but she did not think she was mathematically talented enough. Whenever there was group work at school she selected the peers with the highest abilities and since she was popular and socially able, she was welcome to join them. She gave the impression that she was interested and the group did not see her as a burden. She would take notes of what the others said so she seemed to contribute and she had the answers that way. Individual tests were harder to manage, but the teacher was rather conventional and his tests were mostly of routine character, similar to the tasks in the textbooks, since problem solving was done in the groups. Annie soon decoded the teacher's compositions of tests and learned what to look for in the textbook. Her creativity, even though it was at a low level, could be categorized as pragmatic and social-personality rather than cognitive or any of the other categories listed by Sternberg (2000). She made sure that she did not miss the group work and if she was uncertain to get a good grade on an individual test, she stayed at home that day. This shallow, yet when it comes to her grades successful, way of learning continued and Annie made it through upper secondary school after which she continued to university. She had a strong self confidence from her experiences of school so far but was choked by the demands at university. She was no longer able to get good grades and she failed her courses forcing her to drop out of the university. Annie had her social abilities and creative nature, even if not mathematically so, to fall back on and she ended up working at a museum as a tourist guide. She was humbled by her shortcomings at the university and initially embarrassed, but she soon replaced that feeling with pride of what she could do when she realized that her family and friends did not think less of her.

Chris, from Above Average to Low Achieving

At age seven, Chris was able to determine if a number was a divisor to another number or not. He could do this for rather large numbers but he could not explain how he did it. The factors of a number came to him intuitively in what could be labelled a mystical approach (Sternberg, 2000). He was also able to see some other number theoretical relations, an ability which puzzled his teachers and parents since he did not show any other signs of extraordinary giftedness. He was a content schoolboy, well above average achieving, but not a high achiever. His ability to handle numbers gave him a good self esteem, but he had to work with problem solving and analytical tasks. His father used to work with him in the evenings both with his homework and his particular talent. Chris' gift in number theory did not evolve and as Chris grew older, the abilities diminished and at age 13 his mathematical abilities were at the level of any other well achieving child his age. He was good at solving routine problems and was able to follow a sequence of mathematical reasoning, but he had never been able to understand how to perform mathematical deduction himself. Every time he tried, his mind went blank and he did not know where to begin. He felt that he had failed his father who used to help him with his mathematics and he did not want to discuss mathematics with him anymore. That way he thought that his father would not notice his lost gift. Chris went from feeling special to worthless and at upper secondary school he had lost all inspiration for mathematics and everything that was school related with it. All his life, school had been about mathematics and science and with that part lost, he decided to do something utterly different. His marks from upper secondary school were not sufficient for him to be able to go to university and he was not interested in further schooling so he did not mind. Chris started to work at a local sandwich store, but his parents were worried that he would settle with that and they tried to make him go back to school and improve his marks. Chris was happy working at the store and would not listen to his parents. After a year he started feeling that he was not doing anything with his life and he felt insignificant. He was aware of his parents' standpoint regarding his career choice and wanted them to be proud of him like they were when he was a child. He went back to school, but had lost so much that he barely was able to pass and graduate from upper secondary school. He did not continue to university but he got a better job at a shoe factory and started to work himself up through the hierarchies at the factory. He felt that he had found something he was good at and a place where he could blossom and show his value.

Mary, High Achieving, Gifted and Creative

As long as Mary could remember she had loved to arrange numbers in different sequences and sets, and to play and experiment with them. She could see patterns and solutions to equations at an early age. At school she would always get the highest marks in mathematics and she did well in the other subjects as well. Once she had seen or heard something she remembered it. Her remarkable results made her some-what of an outcaste at school and she often kept to herself, feeling different. She did not know how to act around other children her own age. Mary's teachers gave her books and exercises for higher grades in an accelerated individualisation to meet her needs and challenge her intellect. Her love for the subject endured through upper secondary school and at her graduation she had already finished the first year of university mathematics. She was at Level 4 in Usiskin's hierarchical model of mathematical intelligence. At the university she was more comfortable and found friends to discuss mathematics with. All her friends were older than her but she was accepted, and sometimes admired, for whom she was and what she was able to do mathematically. She was still always awarded the highest marks and her mathema-tical abilities were developing in all 10 areas of mathematical intelligence listed in the Intelligence and mathematical intelligence section of this chapter. Mary lived a quiet life and stayed devoted to her research in mathematics and she stayed at the university where she got a position as a researcher in mathematics. She was productive, at an intelligence level 6 in Usiskin's hierarchy, and her results were published internationally. She did not want to give up her research to raise a family, although she did not see that as a sacrifice. She regarded her ability a gift, as precious as a family.

Nelly, Gifted but not Creative

Nelly was born in a large city where she lived with her sister and mother after her parents' divorce when she was five. She managed school well and was particularly fascinated by mathematical relations. At first she was intrigued by relations such as the relation between division and multiplication and her proficiency developed to proofs of the Pythagorean theorem and other geometrical properties, then further to algebra and calculus. Nelly understood mathematical reasoning and deduction presented in her textbooks or by her teachers, but she was unable to create a proof new to her. Her mental representations were not flexible enough for her to see possibilities, new combinations and relations in new mathematical contexts. Her gift was more as a mathematics observer than as a mathematics performer. If she read or heard new mathematical pieces, she could integrate them to her existing knowledge and understand the relations. She could repeat what she had learned but not create further from it. Her talent made the schoolwork quite easy as the tasks and assessment methods were designed for repeating rather than creating. She was pleased with the fact that she never had to study, but also discontented from the frustration of not being able to go further and experience progress in her own mathematical creativity. The combination of the two conflicting feelings resulted in a medium achievement level at school. She continued to university and studied to become an upper secondary school teacher in mathematics. She never developed any higher abilities to create mathematically on her own, a shortage she was well aware of, and compensated for it by broadening her knowledge reading as much as she could to be able to meet her students at whichever level. She became a skilled teacher and in time she had a large knowledge base to work from. Her positive experience from teaching mathematics gradually replaced her frustration over not being able to become a productive mathematician.

DISCUSSION

The seven cases are discussed from the various questions of interplay between mathematically gifted, creative and degrees of achievement posed in the introduction, and framed by the theories presented. Figure 1 shows a model of the cases in relation to achievement, giftedness and creativity. The axes in the squared plane are levels of achievement (A), giftedness (G), and the heights of the piles indicate the level of creativity (C) respectively. The letters by the poles are the first letters in each of the characters' names. Steve, Chris and Annie each have two poles with a line suggesting a direction between them. This is to indicate their development as described above.

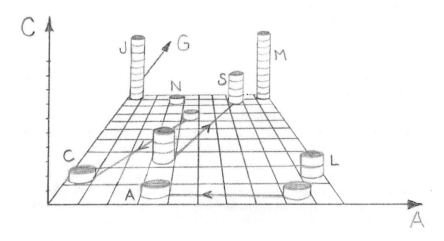

Figure 1. A model of the seven cases in a coordinate system illustrating the relations of achievement, giftedness and creativity.

The Labels High Achiever, Gifted and Creative in Mathematics

All seven cases portray special mathematical features. Mary's high levels in all three variables in Figure 1 stand in contrast to Chris and Annie who both had a promising start, Chris in his gift at a young age and Annie in her ability to adjust to the social conditions she was in, but were unable to maintain their advantages. Chris and Annie both lack mathematical creativity and the ability to see possible alternatives to conventional methods, such as Cantor's method to show the uncountability of the set of real numbers, is out of their reach. With the component of creativity added, like in Mary's case, a new dimension opens up enabling bold and unexpected combinations and paths leading to new insights.

John and Lisa are both exceptional in their mathematical endeavours if compared to the average student. John's ability and Lisa's hard work single them out from their peers. Yet they are profoundly different from each other regarding input and results in their mathematical work. John could effortlessly have been a high achiever if he had adjusted to the social requirements of the university, but he was not willing to do so. Lisa, on the other hand, could not change her situation as easily since giftedness and creativity are traits partly defining boundaries, or lack of boundaries, of the mind, which is essentially different from the ability to work hard. Mathematical precociousness is rather clearly setting the boundaries, whereas confinements from personal levels of creativity are of various characters if creativity is defined through Sternberg's (2000) six categories. Mystical and psychodynamic creativity are influenced by forces beyond one's own control, you either have divine inspiration or unconscious drives or you do not have it! Cognitive creativity is closely related to the level of giftedness as it depends on the mental processes generating new ideas. The strength and flexibility of the mental representations confine the potential of cognitive creativity. Pragmatic, psychometric and social-personal aspects of creativity are more dependent on the self for practice and social settings, and personal boundaries become less obvious in those perspectives.

Social Impact and Changed Development

Social influences can affect both positively and negatively, as the cases illustrate. A sense of belonging in a social context takes the aspect of being different out of the situation, as it did in Mary's case when she came to the university, allowing her mathematical creativity to flourish. Krutetskii's (1976) and Sriraman's (2005, 2009 various, 2010) research on programmes for gifted children and Gross' (1986, 1993) ability grouping all indicate positive results on the students' learning abilities. Steve, who started in a socially secure context, did not feel the pressure from being different, as John and Mary did, or to please his parents, as Lisa and Annie, and it was not until he had been in the same situation for a while that he felt under stimulated and hence motivated to explore his mathematical possibilities, not to prove anything to anyone but as a challenge to himself. He had nothing to defend and was free to go as far as he could. Steve's case is an example of hidden abilities which surface under certain conditions. The motivation to work with mathematics and reach for, and expand, their own boundaries can come from various situations. Chris, who had discovered his gift early, was unable to develop the way his parents and teacher expected. He followed the other children's pace and, in his case, the father's efforts to help Chris gave an opposite result to the intended and Chris' motivation was replaced by shame, which prompted Chris' deterioration to become a low achiever.

Both Steve's and Chris' changed trajectories in Figure 1 were prompted from outer social situations as well as inner responses to those prompts. Steve was in an un-challenging situation and in his need for a challenge, he started his mathematics exploration, whereas Chris' reason to change was his counter reaction to what he thought his father expected. Annie, who was a high achiever at first but could not maintain the achievement level through her strategy of using the social settings she was in, did not change her strategy or intention like Steve and Chris did. Her strategy was just not working any longer as the demands were continuously increasing and her changed trajectory was the result.

Assessment and School Practice

The label 'High achiever' in a school context could say something about gifted or creative if the assessment measured some, or all, of the 10 categories of mathematical intelligence (Sriraman, 2009 various, 2010), and not just what has been learned in routine tasks. Students such as Annie who used the systems, both teaching and assess-ment, to appear gifted through social creativity would then be mathematically assessed instead.

Mattsson's (in press) study of teachers' characterization of mathematically gifted students showed that creative and logical abilities and management of school mathe-matics were the most common features to define a gifted student. A student like Nelly, who could reproduce whatever she had heard or read but was unable to see new compositions in mathematical problem solving or proving, would be characterized differently depending on what emphasis the assessing teacher had in his or her evaluation. Test results, which are one way to identify giftedness in Mattsson's (in press) results, often show how well students can perform routine operations and repeat already seen patterns. Annie, Lisa and Nelly would benefit from such tests, whereas students with higher creativity like Mary and John could be inspired from a more open assessment of mathematical originality and inventiveness.

REFERENCES

Benbow, C. P., Lubinski, D., & Sushy, B. (1996). The impact of SMPY's educational programs from the perspective of the participant. In C. P. Benbow & D. Lubinski (Eds.), *Intellectual talent* (pp. 266–300). Baltimore: Johns Hopkins University Press.

Bishop, A. J. (1988). *Mathematical enculturation: A cultural perspective on mathematics education.* Dodrecht: Kluwer Academic Publishers.

Bredo, R. (2006). Conceptual confusion and educational psychology. In P. Alexander & P. Winne (Eds.), *Handbook of educational psychology* (2nd ed., pp. 43–58). Mahwah, NJ: Lawrence Erlbaum & Associates.

Craft, A. (2002). *Creativity in the early years: A life wide foundation.* London: Continuum.

Csikszentmihalyi, M. (1996). *Creativity.* New York: Harper.

Davidson, H. M. (1983). *Blaise Pascal.* Boston: Twayne Publishers.

English, L. (Ed.). (2004). *Mathematical and analogical reasoning of young learners*. Mahwah, NJ: Lawrence Erlbaum & Associates.

Feldman, D. H. (1993). Child prodigies: A distinctive form of giftedness. *Gifted Child Quarterly, 37*(4), 188–193.

Freiman, V., & Volkov, A. (2004). Early mathematical giftedness and its social context: The cases of imperial China and Soviet Russia. *Journal of Korea Society of Mathematical Education Series D: Research in Mathematical Education, 8*(3), 157–173.

Fomin, D., Genkin, S., & Itenberg, I. (1996). *Mathematical circles: Russian experience*. American Mathematical Society.

Gross, M. U. M. (1986). Radical acceleration in Australia: Terence Tao. *Gifted Child Today*.

Gross, M. U. M. (1993). Nurturing the talents of exceptionally gifted children. In K. A. Heller, F. J. Monks, & A. H. Passow (Eds.), *International handbook of research and development of giftedness and talent* (pp. 473–490). Oxford: Pergamon Press.

Gnedenko B. V. (1991) Introduction in specialization: Mathematics (Введение в специальность: математика), Nauka, p. 235 (In Russian).

Kiesswetter, K. (1992). Mathematische Begabung. Über die Komplexität der Phänomene und die Unzulänglichkeiten von Punktbewertungen. *Mathematik-Unterricht, 38*, 5–18. (In German).

Krutetskii, V. A. (1976). *The psychology of mathematical abilities in school children* (J. Teller, Trans., J. Kilpatrick & I. Wirszup, Eds.). Chicago: University of Chicago Press.

Lubinski, D., & Benbow, C. P. (2006). Study of mathematically precocious youth after 35 years: Uncovering antecedents for the development of math-science expertise. *Perspectives on Psychological Science, 1*, 316–345.

Mattsson, L. (in press). Head teachers' conceptions of gifted students in mathematics in Swedish Upper Secondary School. *Nordic Studies in Mathematics Education*.

Persson, R. (2005). Voices in the wilderness: Counselling gifted students in a Swedish Egalitarian Setting. *International Journal for the Advancement of Counselling, 27*(2), 263–276.

Persson, R. (2009). The unwanted gifted and talented: A sociobiological perspective of the societal functions of giftedness. In L. V. Shavinina (Ed.), *International handbook on giftedness* (pp. 913–924). Dordrecht: Springer Science+Business Media B.V.

Shavinina, L. V., & Ferrari, M. (Eds.), (2004). *Beyond knowledge: Extra cognitive aspects of developing high ability*. Mahwah, NJ: Lawrence Erlbaum & Associates.

Sriraman, B. (2002). How do mathematically gifted students abstract and generalize mathematical concepts. *NAGC 2002 Research Briefs, 16*, 83–87.

Sriraman, B. (2003a). Mathematical giftedness, problem solving, and the ability to formulate generalizations. *The Journal of Secondary Gifted Education, 14*(3), 151–165.

Sriraman, B. (2003b). Can mathematical discovery fill the existential void? The use of conjecture, proof and refutation in a high school classroom (feature article). *Mathematics in School, 32*(2), 2–6.

Sriraman, B. (2004). Gifted ninth graders' notions of proof: Investigating parallels in approaches of mathematically gifted students and professional mathematicians. *Journal for the Education of the Gifted, 27*(4), 267–292.

Sriraman, B. (2005). Are mathematical giftedness and mathematical creativity synonyms? A theoretical analysis of constructs. *Journal of Secondary Gifted Education, 17*(1), 20–36.

Sriraman, B., & Freiman, V. (2007). Does mathematics gifted education need a philosophy of creativity. *Mediterranean Journal for Research in Mathematics Education, 6*(1 & 2), 23–46.

Sriraman, B., & Steinthorsdottir, O. (2008). Secondary mathematics- research into practice: Implications of research on mathematics gifted education for the secondary curriculum. In J. Plucker & C. Callahan (Eds.), *What the research says: Encyclopedia on research in gifted education* (pp. 355–367). Waco, TX: Prufrock Press.

Sriraman, B. (2009a). General creativity. In B. Kerr (Ed.), *Encyclopedia of giftedness, creativity and talent* (Vol. 1, pp. 369–372). Thousand Oaks, CA: Sage Publications.

Sriraman, B. (2009b). Aha! Experiences. In B. Kerr (Ed.), *Encyclopedia of giftedness, creativity and talent* (Vol. 1, pp. 37–39). Thousand Oaks, CA: Sage Publications.

Sriraman, B. (2009c). Mathematical intelligence. In B. Kerr (Ed.), *Encyclopedia of giftedness, creativity and talent* (Vol. 2, pp. 544–547). . Thousand Oaks, CA: Sage Publications.

Sriraman, B. (2009d). Mathematics curriculum. In B. Kerr (Ed.), *Encyclopedia of giftedness, creativity and talent* (Vol. 2, pp. 553–556). Thousand Oaks, CA: Sage Publications.

Sriraman, B. (2009e). Mathematical precociousness. In B. Kerr (Ed.), *Encyclopedia of giftedness, creativity and talent* (Vol. 2, pp. 547–550). Thousand Oaks, CA: Sage Publications.

Sriraman, B. (2009f). Collaborative learning. In B. Kerr (Ed.), *Encyclopedia of giftedness, creativity and talent* (Vol. 1, pp. 158–159). Thousand Oaks, CA: Sage Publications.

Sriraman, B., & Kÿymaz, Y. (2009). Relationship of creativity to intelligence. In B. Kerr (Ed.), *Encyclopedia of giftedness, creativity and talent* (Vol. 2, pp. 726–728). Thousand Oaks, CA: Sage Publications.

Sriraman, B., & Dahl, B. (2009). On bringing interdisciplinary ideas to gifted education. In L. V. Shavinina (Ed.), *The international handbook of giftedness* (Vol. 2, pp. 1235–1256). Springer Science & Business.

Sriraman, B. (2010). Expertise report on the state of mathematics gifted education. In press-*Deutsche Telekom/Humboldt-Universität Expert Reports in Education.*

Sternberg, R. J. (Ed.). (2000). *Handbook of creativity.* Cambridge University Press.

Sternberg, R. & Ben-Zeev, T. (Eds.). (1996). *The nature of mathematical thinking.* Mahwah, NJ: Lawrence Erlbaum & Associates.

Torrance, E. P. (1974). *Torrance tests of creative thinking: Norms-technical manual.* Lexington, MA: Ginn.

Usiskin, Z. (2000). The development into the mathematically talented. *Journal of Secondary Gifted Education, 11*(3), 152–162.

Wallace, D. B., & Gruber, H. E. (1992). *Creative people at work: Twelve cognitive case studies.* Oxford University Press.

Kristina Juter
Linnaeus University and Kristianstad University College
Sweden

Bharath Sriraman
Dept of Mathematical Sciences
The University of Montana
USA

JENNIFER M. SUH AND KERRI FULGINITI

5. DEVELOPING MATHEMATICAL POTENTIAL IN UNDERREPRESENTED POPULATIONS THROUGH PROBLEM SOLVING, MATHEMATICAL DISCOURSE AND ALGEBRAIC REASONING

INTRODUCTION

The following study explored strategies for developing mathematical potential and enhancing mathematics instruction for diverse learners from a low socio-economic population identified as "young scholars". The intentional focus on designing and creating opportunities to foster mathematical potential and build collective knowledge influenced many of the pedagogical decisions made by the teacher and researcher in their jointly planned research lessons. The most salient features in developing mathematics potential in these young scholars were giving opportunities to 1) engage in rich mathematical tasks and sequence of related problems, b) use multiple representations to develop representational fluency, and c) develop mathematical communication where reasoning and proof and sense-making became a habit of mind and the focus of classroom discourse. Through encouragement and participation in problem solving, mathematical discourse and algebraic reasoning, students exhibited confidence, competence and more of the behavioural characteristics of mathematically proficient students.

The following research project aimed at developing mathematical potential in under-represented groups by giving access to authentic and rigorous mathematics problem based learning focused on developing mathematical communication and algebraic reasoning. Research indicates that children of color are underrepresented in gifted programs and are less likely to be nominated by teachers as potential candidates for gifted programs when using such traditional measures as IQ and achievement tests for identification (Ford, Harris, Tyson, & Trotman, 2002). The issue of underrepresentation of economically disadvantaged and culturally diverse students in advanced academic programs is multifaceted and complex (see Figure 1). Some major themes in research concerning underrepresentation of minorities and students living in poverty are: a) the biased assessment measures; b) the low self esteem and expectation set by the individual or others; and c) the lack of strong advocacy or referral from parents and guardians (Van Tassel-Baska, Johnson, & Avery, 2002). Some of the recommendations for the biased assessment is to have multidimensional assessments such as portfolios, case studies and anecdotal records which would give more diverse learners opportunity to entry to advanced programs with an advanced curriculum. Some efforts are underway in broadening the identification procedures

B. Sriraman and K.H. Lee (eds.), The Elements of Creativity and Giftedness in Mathematics, 67–79.

The Underrepresentation of Economically Disadvantaged and Culturally Diverse Students in Advanced Academic Programs		
Issues	*Recommendations*	*Outcomes*
Biased assessment measures	Multidimensional assessments (portfolios, case studies, anecdotal records)	Access Entry into advanced programs with advanced curriculum
Low expectations (self and others)	Raise expectations through more rigorous and challenging curriculum	Affirmation Increase expectations and student efficacy
Few parent/guardian referrals	Increase communication/administrator and teacher referrals/parent advocacy training	Advocacy Support students in reaching their fullest potential

Figure 1. Issues related to underrepresentation of diverse students in advanced academics.

to increase the number of minority children in gifted education programs (Van Tassel-Baska, Johnson, & Avery, 2002). Many researchers and practitioners suggest using multiple tests and alternative methods for finding gifted minority students, including performance-based assessment measures based on Gardner's theory of multiple intelligences or other models (Van Tassel-Baska et al., 2002) and nonverbal ability assessments, such as the Naglieri Nonverbal Abilities Tests or Raven's Matrix Analogies Tests (Ford et al., 2002). Raising expectation in academics can begin with raising the bar for teaching the standards of learning and providing more rigorous and challenging curriculum before these students. Finally, parents, guardians and family members from disadvantaged and culturally diverse population need to have frequent and meaningful advocacy training so that collectively they can support, affirm and advocate for their youngsters in reaching their fullest potential.

THEORETICAL FRAMEWORK

Participation Gap among Diverse Learners in Accessing Rigorous Mathematics

Sociocultural approaches emphasize the interdependence of social and individual processes in the co-construction of knowledge (Vygotsky, 1986). "Through participation in activities that require cognitive and communicative functions, children are drawn into the use of these functions in ways that nurture and 'scaffold' them" (pp. 6–7). Vygotsky (1986) described learning as being embedded within social events and occurring as a child interacts with people, objects, and events in the environment. Through socially shared activities learners also internalized processes. Following this approach, researchers have explored sociomathematical norms and how teachers actively guide the development of classroom mathematical practices and individual learning through capitalizing on opportunities that emerge through students' activities and explanations (Ball, 1993; Cobb, Wood & Yackel, 1993; Lampert, 1990; McClain & Cobb, 2001). However, recent research offers some important insight on participation gaps which exist among students from diverse social, cultural, and racial backgrounds in mathematics classrooms and how classrooms can be structured to better afford opportunities to participate in mathematics by a wider range of students (DIME, 2007).

Typically, school systems that serve economically disadvantaged or minority student struggle to meet academic achievement and traditionally reform movements have aimed at remedial models to improve students' achievement. According to this model, students from diverse population get more of the basic skill learning without the opportunity to participate in learning opportunities that develop unique talents, creative thinking and problem solving strategies. According to a report issued by the Partnership for 21st Century Skills, today's graduates need to be critical thinkers, problem solvers, and effective communicators who are proficient in both core subjects and new, twenty-first-century content and skills. These include learning and thinking skills, information- and communications-technology literacy skills, and life skills.

In reform oriented approaches like problem based learning, students work in teams to explore real-world problems and create presentations to share what they have learned. Compared to learning primarily from textbooks, this approach has many benefits for students, including deeper knowledge of subject matter, increased self-direction and motivation, improved research and problem-solving skills, and under-standing how academics connect to real-life and careers. The study by Boaler (1999) found that students at the problem-based school did better than those at the more traditional school both on math problems requiring analytical or conceptual thought and on those considered rote, that is, those requiring memory of a rule or formula. The focus of the mathematics communication was to place more emphasis in the mathematical reasoning and communication which is reflected through cognitive actions such as justifying, proving, investigating, analyzing and explaining. This increased emphasis on proving and justifying results in the algebraic reasoning and the habits of mind that will prepare students for more advanced studies in mathematics.

This design research focused on developing mathematical potential of diverse learners by building collective mathematical knowledge in the classroom through mathematical discourse, students' reasoning and proof and algebraic reasoning. In addition, the research team was intentional in the use of pedagogical content tools defined as "devices such as graphs, diagrams, equations, or verbal statements that teachers use to connect students' thinking while moving the mathematical agenda forward" (Rasmussen & Marrongelle, 2006, p. 388).

The research questions that guided this design research were:

1) What designed learning opportunities afforded access, affirmation and develop-ment of mathematics potential for under-represented students?
2) How do pedagogical content tools promote development of mathematical commu-nication, algebraic connections and generalizations methods among elementary students?

METHODOLOGY

Participants

The participants in this study were sixteen "young scholars" in fourth through sixth grade students who participated in the summer program focused on problem based learning. Many of these students' former classroom teachers recommended them based on their exhibition of mathematically promising traits during the academic year. These students attended a Title I (low socio economic) elementary school in a major metropolitan area with a diverse population of 600 students at the school: 51% Hispanics, 24% Asians, 16% Caucasians, 3% African Americans and 6% others, with over 50% receiving free and reduced lunch. Using multiple instruments, students were selected for the "Young Scholar: MATH 4-1-1" Project which provided supplementary educational experiences for a select group of bright African American, Hispanic, and economically disadvantaged students. The project focused on exposing students to a variety of high-achieving peer groups that would enhance and develop the "scholar identity" of these students. These classes and support sessions began in the summer and continued into the school year through after school meetings. The classes and sessions were designed to enrich and support the mathematics learning. The research and design team for this project consisted of a university mathematics educator and researcher and a gifted and talented specialist at an elementary School. This team co-designed and co-taught the lessons and analyzed student learning to make adjustment each day to the follow up lessons.

Design Features of the Project

The focus of the summer program was to immerse students in authentic mathematics problem solving while utilizing local community resources such as invited community speakers and culturally relevant and contextualized tasks. The idea was to expose students from diverse backgrounds to new, engaging and rigorous mathematics while fostering their algebraic thinking and positive attitude towards mathematics. The project was called MATH 4-1-1: Young Mathematicians On Call where students solved rich engaging, meaningful and mathematically authentic problems presented by the community. The structure of the enrichment fell into three main categories based on Renzulli's Schoolwide Enrichment Model (SEM). This enrichment cluster design defines authentic learning as *applying* relevant knowledge, thinking skills, and interpersonal skills to the solution of real problems (Renzulli, Gentry & Reis, 2003).The idea was to expose students to new engaging and rigorous mathematics content which was classified as Type I activities. Type II activities were skill training that connected to what practitioners do within their field. Finally during Type III activities, students utilized the developed interest areas (Type I) and newly acquired skills (Type II) to create an authentic project or service for an authentic audience. However, central to enrichment clusters was the idea that students would direct their learning and invest in their interest areas. Some of the enrichment projects included the following:

– *Math 411: Helping the community solve problems with mathematics.* Meet some people in your community with real life problems in their work places or their lives. Together with your teammates, help people in your community solve problems using your math skills.

– *Be a statistician: Survey your community to know what they want.* Do you want to find out what people think about things? Survey your friends, family and community about something you've always wanted to know. Organize your responses in a creative way. Decide how to share this information. Develop and conduct a survey and communicate your results in this exciting enrichment cluster.

– *MATH 4 US: Starting a business.* Research a need in your community and plan a business. Present your idea to investors and determine the resources needed to run your business. Keep a budget of expenses and profit.

The fundamental nature of such authentic high-end learning activities created an environment in which students applied the relevant knowledge and skills to solving real problems (Renzulli et al., 2004). Emphasis was placed on creating authentic learning situations where students were thinking, feeling, and doing what practicing professionals did in solving daily problems (Renzulli, Leppien & Hays, 2000).

Focusing on the Core Traits of Mathematically Proficient Students

The research team used the Rating scale (see table 1) developed by Gavin (2003) to identify scholarly identities and the National Research Council's (2001) Five Strands of mathematical proficiency (NRC, 2001) to focus on the learning goals. The researcher team mapped out the behaviour characteristics from the rating scale and the Five Strands of Mathematics Proficiency (see Figure 2) and found a direct correlation among the behaviour traits and the strands of mathematical proficiency. The mapping exercise allowed both the teacher and the research to agree on a set of core behaviour characteristics that would be the focus of the student outcome for the diverse learners in the *"MATH 4-1-1: Young Mathematicians on Call"* project. For example, conceptual understanding, which is the comprehension of mathematical concepts, operations, and relations matched up with Gavin's (2003) Rating Scale 2, 4: organizes data and information to discover mathematical pattern and understands new math concepts and processes more easily than other students and displays a strong number sense (e.g., makes sense of large and small numbers, estimates easily and appropriately). In addition, strategic competence which is the ability to formulate, represent, and solve mathematical problems, matched up with Rating Scale 5, 7, 9 and 10: has creative (unusual and divergent) ways of solving math problems; frequently solves math problems abstractly, without the need for manipulatives or concrete materials; when solving a math problem; can switch strategies easily, if appropriate or necessary; regularly uses a variety of representations to explain math

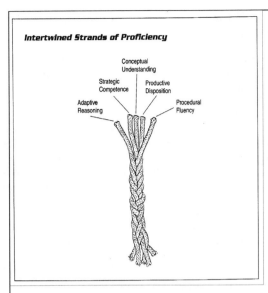

Intertwined Strands of Proficiency

Conceptual Understanding

Strategic Competence

Productive Disposition

Adaptive Reasoning

Procedural Fluency

Five Strands of Mathematical Proficiency
National Research Council's (2001)

- conceptual understanding - comprehension of mathematical concepts, operations, and relations
- procedural fluency - skill in carrying out procedures flexibly, accurately, efficiently, and appropriately
- strategic competence - ability to formulate, represent, and solve mathematical problems
- adaptive reasoning - capacity for logical thought, reflection, explanation, and justification
- productive disposition - habitual inclination to see mathematics as sensible, useful, and worthwhile, coupled with a belief in diligence and one's own efficacy.

Figure 2. Five strands of mathematical proficiency, NRC (2001).

Table 1. Rating the behavioral & mathematical characteristics (Gavin, 2003)

Rating the Behavioral & Mathematical Characteristics (Gavin, 2003)

1. is eager to solve challenging math problems (A problem is defined as a task for which the solution is not known in advance).
2. organizes data and information to discover mathematical patterns.
3. enjoys challenging math puzzles, games, and logic problems.
4. understands new math concepts and processes more easily than other students.
5. has creative (unusual and divergent) ways of solving math problems.
6. displays a strong number sense (e.g., makes sense of large and small numbers, estimates easily and appropriately).
7. frequently solves math problems abstractly, without the need for manipulatives or concrete materials.
8. has an interest in analyzing the mathematical structure of a problem.
9. when solving a math problem, can switch strategies easily, if appropriate or necessary.
10. regularly uses a variety of representations to explain math concepts (written explanations, pictorial, graphic, equations).

concepts (written explanations, pictorial, graphic, equations). Adaptive reasoning, which is capacity for logical thought, reflection, explanation, and justification (matched up with Rating Scale #8, 10: has an interest in analyzing the mathematical structure of a problem; regularly uses a variety of representations to explain math concepts (written explanations, pictorial, graphic, equations). Most importantly, having productive disposition which is the habitual inclination to see mathematics as sensible, useful, and worthwhile, coupled with a belief in diligence and one's own efficacy aligned with the behavioural characteristic of 1 & 3: is eager to solve challenging math problems and enjoys challenging math puzzles, games, and logic problems.

Procedures

The study used qualitative methods of collaborative action research using the design research approach and research memos. Design-based research method is a research methodology aimed to improve educational practices through systematic, flexible, and iterative review, based upon collaboration among researchers and practitioners in real-world settings, and leading to design principles or theories (Brown, 1992; The Design-Based Research Collective, 2003). Using design research which emphasizes the processes of iteration, feedback loops and narrative reports, we refined the key components of our design. As teacher researchers, we took active notes and memos as we proceeded with the research exploring the interplay between the individual and collective knowledge in the mathematics classroom through discourse and the development of new ideas through records of students' thinking. We collected video recordings of each class sessions, retained copies of students work and work displayed in the "collective workspace" and recorded observations and reflections throughout the planning, teaching, and debriefing phases of the study. Daily debriefing meetings allowed for formative analysis of the design process by focusing on what was revealed during each class session and to plan for subsequent classes while modifying the task, tools and teaching methods based on feedback. In addition, these memos and artifacts (i.e. students' written work contained drawings, solution procedures, numeric notations and explanations) were analyzed for emerging themes at the end of the project for a summative analysis. Student responses, memos, and classroom videotapes were used to triangulate students' understanding.

RESULTS

Qualitative analysis from the teacher-researchers' memos indicated that the process of collaborative planning, teaching and debriefing focused on fostering mathematical potential and building collective knowledge impacted many pedagogical decisions. The most salient features in developing mathematics potential in these young scholars were giving opportunities by a) selecting tasks and sequences of related problems, b) integrating pedagogical content tools to develop representational fluency, and c) orchestrating classroom discourse through questioning that focused on reasoning, proof and sens.

Selecting Tasks and Sequences of Related Problems

In selecting the problems, the teacher researchers were deliberate in developing and posing problems that were related yet increasingly more complex. This allowed for students to naturally make connections to previous problems solved in class and to build upon the knowledge they had acquired. By having the previous problems displayed on the generalization posters and readily accessible, students had entry to problems and to solution strategies and built new knowledge based on previous knowledge. Through a real life service project for the school to raise money for a natural habitat for the school courtyard, we used a business theme to work on many classes of real life math problems such as budgeting, analysing cost and revenue, maximizing profits, figuring out combination problems, using discounts and comparing prices using unit pricing. Another design feature that allowed for students to extend their thinking by exploring related problems with increasing complexity was through Thinking Connection cards. Due to the nature of the multi-age and grades of the students, Thinking Connection cards allowed for differentiation and extension for students who were ready to go beyond.

Integrating Pedagogical Content Tools to Extend Students' Reasoning

Pedagogical content tools such as "devices such as graphs, diagrams, equations, or verbal statements" were used "intentionally to connect students thinking while moving the mathematical agenda forward" (Rasmussen & Marrongelle, 2006, p. 388). Representational fluency, the ability to use multiple representations and translate among these models, has shown to be critical in building students' mathematical understanding (Goldin & Shteingold, 2001; Lamon, 2001). Therefore, the research team agreed that it was important to develop students' abilities to represent mathematical ideas in multiple ways including manipulatives, real life situations, pictures, verbal symbols and written symbols. Translations among the different representations assess whether a student conceptually understands a problem. Some of the ways to demonstrate translation among representations in mathematics is to ask students to restate a problem in their own words, draw a diagram to illustrate the problem, or act it out.

In order to promote representational fluency, the research team focused on developing students' mathematical reasoning in the classroom by implementing a design feature called Collective Workspace, Poster Proofs, and Generalization Posters. Collective Workspace (see Figure 3) was a method for students to bring their individual work to their group and discuss different solution strategies and compare each others' strategies specifically looking for connections, efficiency, multiple representations and generality. This collective space and time allowed for students to connect their way of knowing to others strategies, in addition, it allowed students a chance to debate on which strategy was most efficient and effective to broader classes of problems.

Generalization Posters (see Figure 4) were created as a class to summarize the essential mathematical learning. Pictures of individual strategies were attached to these posters so that students use them as a reference for future problems. It also allowed for students to build on each other's ideas as a class so that every student can have ownership of the collective thinking. Just as mathematicians over centuries built on conjectures and theorems, these young mathematicians were given the same opportunity to engage in this mathematical activity.

Figure 3. "Collective workspace" to build collective mathematical knowledge.

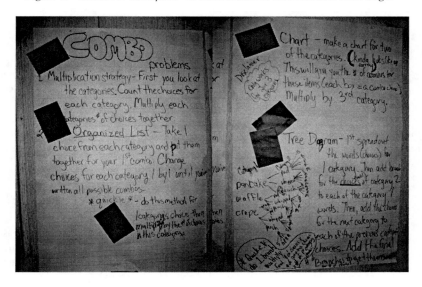

Figure 4. Generalization posters with strategy photos.

Orchestrating Classroom Discourse through Pedagogical Moves and Questioning

The teacher's role in extending students' thinking during this task was in engaging students to determine share strategies and to look for an efficient way to solve

Orchestrating Math Communication
PEDAGOGICAL MOVES and QUESTIONING

 Zooming in and zooming out: making generalization

 Connecting: making connections among representations or algebraic concepts

 Marking: marking critical features which the students should pay attention to

 Directing: keeps the students on task and encouraged to persist

 Extending: Pressing on for justification

 Scaffolding: simplifying or clarifying

*Figure 5. Orchestrating mathematics communication through
pedagogical moves and questioning.*

combination problem and to generate a rule. To analyse the mathematical discourse, teacher researchers used these codes and instructional strategies to make sense of pedagogical moves and questioning strategies.

In one of the combination problem, students were asked to determine the number of flavors that an ice cream shop owner could offer her customers. Some of the students began by drawing the ice cream cones with different flavors but quickly found that drawing a picture was not an efficient strategy. Below is an excerpt from the discussion that took place during the collective workspace.

Teacher: Let's look closely how your classmates solved this problem. *(PMQ: Zooming In)*

Lana: I drew a picture of the icecream with its topping and syrup but it was not easy so I decided to list all the different combinations. Then I noticed my partner was using the first letter of the flavor, topping and syrup and it seemed like a short cut then writing out the whole word, like strawberry.

Teacher: So you decided to use S to stand for strawberry and C for chocolate and V for vanilla. I see that you have listed the possible icecream. How did you know you had all the possible combinations? *(PMQ: Connecting and Marking)*

Jose: I decided to create a chart with the flavors going down and the topping going across and had a 3 by 4 table. But then I realized for each I also had to decide it I wanted caramel or chocolate syrup. So I had to take the 12 types of ice creams and double them for the syrup and got 24 different combinations.

Mariam: I used a tree. I started with the 3 flavors and each flavor had 4 topping choices and then from there I had 2 syrup choices, so I knew that it would be 3 x 4 x 2 = 24 different kinds.

Teacher: I see that Mariam used multiplication to help her see how many combinations she had. Do others see how this equation may appear in your solution? *(PMQ: Connecting)* So how are your different strategies similar or different from each other? Take a few minute to look at your own and turn to a partner and share. *(PMQ: Zooming in and zooming out)*

Frances: I noticed that Lana's list was done in a similar fashion as Mariam's tree. She seemed to start with one flavour and go to the next topping and then to the syrup. She wrote it each time making sure she did not double it up.

Teacher: Frances said categories for the flavor, topping, and syrup. What were in each category? *(PMQ: revoicing and extending)*

Brandon: There were many choices, for example, there were four topping Choco chip(CC), oreo cookies(OC), rainbow sprinkles(RS) and fresh berries(FB).

Teacher: So what can we write on our Generalization Poster about combination problems? *(PMQ: Zooming out)*

At the end of class, the Generalization Poster read,

IN GENERAL, when solving a combination problem with categories and choices, you can find the number of possible combination by multiplying the choices in each category, for example: Number of flavors x number of toppings x number of syrups = Number of possible combinations. F x T x S = total.

But multiplying will only tell you the total number, not the different types of combinations. For a list of combinations, the tree method works quite well and keeps the list organized. A table is easy if you have two categories but when you have more, you might have to make another table. A smart way to save time is to use a shorten form or just the first letter of the choice so that you are not wasting time writing it all out.

It was during the conversation that took place in the collective workspace that students negotiated the meaning of solving combination problems and concretized the learning for individuals and for the collective group. As evidenced by the excerpt, the advancement of ideas that resulted from students' reasoning became a collective record through the Generalization Poster. In addition, student generated representations, such as, the table, tree diagram, equation and verbal explanation became an important pedagogical content tool for scaffolding questions for algebraic connections, explanations and generalizations and for students to compare, connect and extend their thinking.

CONCLUSIONS

Through this study, the research team developed a guiding framework called *Building Collective Knowledge to Develop Mathematical Proficiency*. Principles to this framework included: a) *adhering to the authenticity of problems*, which proved to be motivating for students. The research team ensured that the task required students to use higher ordered thinking skills, to consider alternate solutions, and to think like a mathematician; b) *making connections and generalizations* to important mathematical ideas that goes beyond application of algorithms by elaborating on definitions and making connections to other mathematical concepts, which led to; c) *navigating through guided reinvention*, (Gravemeijer & Galen, 2003) where students go through similar processes as mathematicians so that they see the mathematical knowledge as a product of their own mathematical activity (p. 117); d) *elaborating and communication through justification*, where students demonstrate a concise, logical, and well-articulated explanation or argument that justifies mathematical work; e) *participating in shared learning* and the interdependence of social and individual processes in the co-construction of knowledge.

In this study, the research team made up of the university mathematics educator and gifted and talented specialist benefited from the opportunity to plan and debrief together which allowed them to determine when, what kind and how to use tools such as graphs, diagrams, equations, spreadsheets, or verbal statement to connect students thinking and to build collective mathematical knowledge in the classroom. This process required the combination of pedagogical and mathematical knowledge. This study suggests that well-intentional and purposeful integration of mathematical tools such as representations, notations and explanations and the use of critical pedagogical moves and questioning can help build collective mathematical knowledge in the classroom and build mathematical potential in diverse learners. In addition, having a shared understanding of the core traits of mathematically proficient students allowed for the research team to provide frequent opportunities for "young scholars" to exhibit those traits and encouraged those behaviour characteristics when students demonstrated them in class. Developing mathematical potential and enhancing mathematics instruction for diverse learners from a low socio-economic population is a critical need in education. Through encouragement and participation in problem solving, mathematical discourse and algebraic reasoning, these students began to exhibit more confidence and competence in exhibiting the traits of mathematically proficient students and developed these as habits of young mathematicians.

REFERENCES

Ball, D. L. (1993). With an eye on the mathematical horizon: Dilemmas of teaching elementary school mathematics. *The Elementary School Journal, 90*, 449–466.

Boaler, J. (1999). Mathematics for the moment, or the millennium? *Education Week*. Downloaded from www.edweek.org/ew/ewstory.cfm?slug=29boaler.h18&keywords=boaler*

Brown, A. L. (1992). Design experiments: Theoretical and methodological challenges in creating complex interventions in classroom settings. *Journal of the Learning Sciences, 2*(2), 141–178.

Cobb, P., Wood, T., & Yackel, E. (1993). Discourse, mathematical thinking and classroom practice. In N. Minick, E. Forman, & A. Stone (Eds.), *Education and mind* (pp. 91–119). New York: Oxford University Press.

Design-based Research Collective. (2003). Design-based research: An emerging paradigm for educational inquiry. *Educational Researcher, 32*(1), 5–8.

Diversity in Mathematics Education Center for Learning and Teaching. (2007). Culture, race, power and mathematics education. In F. Lester (Ed.), *The second handbook of research on mathematics teaching and learning* (pp. 405–434). Reston, VA: NCTM.

Ford, D. Y., Harris, J. J., III, Tyson, C. A., & Frazier Trotman, M. (2002). Beyond deficit thinking: Providing access for gifted African American students. Beyond self-concept and self-esteem for African American students: Improving racial identity improves achievement. *The High School Journal, 87*(1), 18–29.

Gavin, S. (2003). *Scales for rating the behavioral characteristics of superior students.* Mansfield Center, CT: Creative Learning Press.

Goldin, G., & Shteingold, N. (2001). Systems of representations and the development of mathematical concepts. In A. A. Cuoco & F. R. Curcio (Eds.), *The roles of representations in school mathematics* (pp. 1–23). Reston, VA: National Council of Teachers of Mathematics.

Gravemeijer, K. (1999). How emergent models may foster the constitution of formal mathematics. *Mathematical Thinking and Learning, I*(2), 155–177.

Gravemeijer, K., & van Galen, F. (2003). Facts and algorithms as products of students' own mathematical activity. In J. Kilpatrick, W. G. Martin, & D. Schifter (Eds.), *A research companion to principles and standards for school mathematics* (pp. 114–122). Reston, VA: NCTM.

Lamon, S. (2001). Presenting and representating from fractions to rational numbers. In A. A. Cuoco & F. R. Curcio (Eds.), *The roles of representation in school mathematics, 2001 yearbook* (pp. 146–165). Reston, VA: National Council of Teachers of Mathematics.

Lampert, M. (1990). When the problem is not the question and the solution is not the answer: Mathematical knowing and teaching. *American Educational Research Journal, 27*(1), 29–63.

Lesh, R., Cramer, K., Doerr, H., Post, T., & Zawojewski, J. (2003). Using a translation model for curriculum development and classroom instruction. In Lesh, R. & Doerr, H. (Eds.), *Beyond constructivism. Models and modeling perspectives on mathematics problem solving, learning, and teaching.* Mahwah, NJ: Lawrence Erlbaum Associates.

McClain, K., & Cobb, P. (2001). An analysis of development of sociomathematical norms in one first grade classroom. *Journal for Research in Mathematics Education, 32*(3), 238–266.

National Research Council. (2001). Adding it up: Helping children learn mathematics. In J. Kilpatrick, J. Swafford, & B. Findell (Eds.), *Mathematics learning study committee, center for education, division of behavioral and social sciences and education.* Washington, DC: National Academy Press.

Rasmussen, C., & Marrongelle, K. (2006). Pedagogical content tools: Integrating student reasoning and mathematics in instruction. *Journal for Research in Mathematics Education, 37*(5), 388–420.

Renzulli, J., Leppien, J., & Hays, T. (2000). *The multiple menu model: A critical guide for developing differentiated curriculum.* Manfield Center, CT: Creative Learning Press.

Renzulli, J. S., Gentry, M., & Reis, S. M. (2003). *Enrichment clusters: A practical plan for real-world, student-driven learning.* Mansfield Center, CT: Creative Learning Press.

VanTassel-Baska, J., Johnson, D., & Avery, L. D. (2002). Using performance tasks in the identification of economically disadvantaged and minority gifted learners: Findings from Project STAR. *Gifted Child Quarterly, 46*(2), 110–123.

Vygotsky, L. (1986). *Thought and language.* Cambridge, MA: The MIT Press.

Jennifer Suh
George Mason University
USA

Kerri Fulginiti
Fairfax County Public School
USA

LINDA MATTSSON AND SAMUEL BENGMARK

6. ON TRACK TO GIFTED EDUCATION IN MATHEMATICS IN SWEDEN

INTRODUCTION

No-one must believe they are special. It is improper to feel pride in oneself. These words catch the basic ethos by which individual excellence has commonly been viewed in Sweden (Persson, Joswig & Balogh, 2000). This deeply rooted cultural heritage has been strengthened by an exceptional egalitarian display and enact, that has implied a deplorable situation for gifted students (Persson, 1998b, 2010). Special provision for gifted students has been conspicuous by its absence since it has been viewed as means of elitism (Edfeldt & Wistedt, 2009).

However the winds are changing and in this article we provide a description of the status of gifted education in mathematics in Sweden by highlighting the development of four components - a) national policies, b) advocacy groups, c) research, teacher education and curriculum development, and d) implementation in schools. All four of these components are important in the development of gifted education (Phillipson, Kaur & Phillipson, 2003). Sweden has recently taken important steps regarding some of these components. By considering the progress in gifted education in other countries (see e.g. Alencar, Fleith, & Arancibia, 2009; Brody, 2009; European Commission, 2006; Eyre, 2009; Peyser, 2005; Phillipson, Shi, Zhang, Tsai, Quek, Matsumura & Cho, 2009) we then discuss steps to be taken in order to stay on track towards successful gifted education in Sweden.

A HISTORICAL REVIEW – DEVELOPMENT OF THE SCHOOL SYSTEM AND THE CURRICULUM

Since 1842 it has been the duty of every Swedish citizen to acquire certain know-ledge and skills, including some mathematics (Wallby, Carlsson & Nyström, 2001). Throughout the 19th century there were parallel school systems for different social groups, and home-schooling was still common. Higher education was a privilege for the wealthy, particularly for boys (*ibid.*). During the 1880s influential groups started to argue that there was a need to integrate the various school systems to bridge tension between social groups, and facilitate the transition for talented pupils from disadvantaged home to higher education (Axelsson, 2007).

In the beginning of the 20th century discussions about talent and intelligence was an essential part of the Swedish debate about school and society. Of central interest was if the principle task of the Swedish school should be to educate an elite group or if it was to nurture the masses. On one hand it was considered important to take

B. Sriraman and K.H. Lee (eds.), The Elements of Creativity and Giftedness in Mathematics, 81–101.

advantage of the talented in order to ensure the prosperity in the country, particularly in view of the, at that time, recent and extensive emigration to America. On the other hand there was a worry for the less talented since they were thought to be associated with immorality and social problems. Critics expressed great concern that a unified school system would lead to that the talented students would become under-stimulated and bored, and would developed inertia and laziness (*ibid.*).

It was however broadly accepted that there were differences in intelligence between individuals and necessary to separate students accordingly. The issues were *when* this differentiation should take place and *how* the selection should be done (*ibid.*). A combination of scores and knowledge tests was primarily used for the selection to higher education. Intelligence tests were sparsely used, and if so, as an instrument to exclude weaker individuals from citizenship or from normal teaching. In contrast to many other countries intelligence tests were not commonly used to detect talented students (*ibid.*). While it became increasingly common with support activities for weak students, special measures for talented students were rare in practice.

The question at what age differentiation should start was dealt with in various reforms and came over time to be postponed to older and older ages. By 1950 Sweden had nine years of compulsory school for all. In 1962 this became six years of joint elementary school and which followed by three years with alternative courses, including one in mathematics. The students themselves chose between these alternative courses and hence the question of how to differentiate students lost its actuality. Over time alternative courses were gradually taken away. Mathematics was one of two subjects that had alternative courses in the national curriculum from 1969 and 1980. From the 1994 curriculum the alternative courses disappeared. Since then Sweden has a nine year compulsory school with the same curriculum for all students.

At the first non-compulsory educational level, the upper secondary school, there are still different curricula to choose between. Different programs, appealing to different interest and academic ambitions are offered. High enough average marks may be needed to be admitted at certain programs. Each individual program follows a national curriculum and national syllabi. There are seven national courses in mathematics; Mathematics A to Mathematics E, Mathematics - Breadth and Mathematics - Discrete. Independently of which program the student is studying the mathematics course is regulated by one and the same syllabus. Mathematics A is included in every program. Hence, even after leaving the non-differentiating compulsory school the students study exactly the same mathematics course regardless whether the students had chosen vocational education or an academic program.

Grades are given to the students per course, i.e. the student normally has several grades in mathematics, which all are included in the average mark used when applying to university. Even interested students hesitate to take on an elective mathematics course since it is more likely to have a negative effect on their average mark compared with other, elective, basic level courses.

During the development of the educational structure that emerged during the 20th century there was special focus in a group that came to be known as the *talent pool*, that is, individuals who are suitable for further studies but who chose not continue for example because of low motivation or social status (Husén & Härnqvist, 2000).

The research about the *talent pool* influenced the decisions concerning the educational structure, but did not imply any special efforts for students with great talent. From the 1940s until 1994 the school debate, with the very influential Alva Myrdal as a portal figure, was less and less about cognitive development while social development replaced it as the main educational task (Axelsson, 2007; Edfeldt, 2003). In addition, the Swedish research in mathematics education mostly focused on students' difficulties with mathematics (Engström, 2003; Magne 2001, 2006).

Altogether this has led to a difficult situation for gifted mathematics students in Sweden. The alternative courses were removed and the debate focused more and more on the social development and on the weaker students. The Swedish mathematics education has not been a success in an international comparison. According to TIMMS Advanced, Swedish upper secondary school student's mathematical knowledge has dropped dramatically between 1995 and 2008, more than any other country in the study (Mullis, Martin, Robitaille & Foy, 2009). Also the student in the top five percentile has a lower score 2008 compared with 1995. Further, universities from all over Sweden have reported on the descending level of knowledge in mathematics among first year university students (e.g. Swedish National Agency for Higher Education, 2005).

NATIONAL POLICIES

The Swedish education is controlled by national laws, regulations and international agreements. The Education Act (Swedish statute-book, 1985) sets out the overarching objectives such as for example every citizen's right to education including the number of hours of instruction every pupil is entitled to. The national curricula from 1994 (National Agency for Education, 2006a, 2006b) contains learning objectives but also norms and values that the school should stimulate students to embrace, among other things. In these documents there are no formulations that explicitly mention the students that internationally are labeled gifted or talented. However, in both the Education Act and in the curricula there are formulations, implying that the education should be specifically adapted to each student's circumstances and needs, not least for "students in need of special support". Hence the 1994 curricula seemed to open a door for provision for gifted students (Edfeldt & Wistedt, 2009). There is no explicit definition of the group of "students in need of special support" in the documents. There are however some concretizations of the notion in both the Education Act and in the national curricula, but since these concretizations only mentions students with disabilities and students on the lower part of the ability-scale the gifted students have not generally been included in Special Pedagogy.

The objectives in the national curricula, and in the national course syllabi, are divided into *goals to attain* and *goals to aim for*. All students are expected to reach the goals to attain and most students are expected to go further, towards the goals to aim for. According to the 1994 curriculum these goals are meant to be met through individualized teaching.

In May 2008 the Swedish government published a memorandum announcing a five year trail period for cutting-edge program (spetsutbildning) (Ministry of

Education and Research, 2008). Twenty upper secondary schools where selected to arrange special classes for gifted students in mathematics or some other academic subjects. The schools are allowed to use admission test and to have national admission. According to Swedish legislations nothing but the average mark may otherwise be used in the selection process. Hence these schools are able to admit students with a specific talent for mathematics even if the student has not succeeded well in other subjects.

It is worth noticing that the labels "students with talent" (talangfulla elever) and "students with specific abilities" (elever med särskilda förmågor) are used in the memorandum (Ministry of Education and Research, 2008). However, in the final legislation this group of students is not mentioned, and only the activities where described (Swedish statue-book, 2008).

ADVOCACY

There has been hardly any public debate in the Swedish press about gifted students in mathematics or gifted education in general. The little debate there has been has mainly been triggered by actions by politicians or by reports like TIMMS. Right before the elections in 2006 the two political blocks began to argue publically for and against the idea of having special classes for talented students. The critics argued that such classes would not give equal opportunities to all students and would disunify classes (Axelsson, 2008, October 16). Two years later, when the Minister of Education announced the coming pilot with the cutting-edge programs, there was mainly positive responses in the press. Support came from both the teacher union and individual teachers (Olsson, 2008, May 24). A common argument was that all students should have the same right to develop in their own pace, including the gifted. In the memorandum these special classes were labeled cutting-edge programs but many journalists chose to use words like "elite educations" (elitutbildning) which can be perceived to be in disharmony with the egalitarian tradition in Swedish education.

The government in power in August 2010 promised to start cutting-edge programs at 10 secondary schools in Sweden, if reelected (Ministry of Education and Research, 2010). Fully developed the programs would involve about 150 mathematics and natural science students, about 0,15% of the student group each year. No extra financial support would be given to the schools to educate teachers, develop or implement the programs. At the press conference where cutting-edge programs for secondary schools where announced the Minister of Education made clear that special financial support is only given to support students that have problems reaching the goals (Björklund, 2010). Once again the word "elite education" was used in the press and this time critics argued that that the students should not be forced to make a choice like that already at the age of 12 or 13 (Ström, 2010).

Some support for gifted education has been given by the National Center for Mathematics Education (NCM, Nationellt centrum för matematikutbildning) which is an organization that is very active in promoting the development of mathematics education at all levels of, and for all students in, the educational system. Through a mathematics magazine, which a large part of the Swedish schools subscribe to, information about developmental projects, research projects, conferences and mathematical problems are spread to schools, including topics on gifted education.

In 2003 the Delegacy of Mathematics (Matematikdelegationen), appointed by the ministry of education at the request of the Swedish government and organized by NCM, was given the task to propose measures for changing the attitudes towards mathematics, for making mathematics more interesting as well as for developing mathematics education. The final report included the standpoint: "Students that exhibit mathematical talent should be given specific challenges to broaden and deepen their knowledge" (Swedish Government Official Report, 2004, p. 27). This rapport of the Delegacy of Mathematics rendered in 2006 into a Government decision to improve mathematics teaching in Sweden (Government Offices of Sweden, 2006). None of these improvements addresses gifted education directly. One of the actions was to introduce Mathematics Developers (Matematikutvecklare) who are committed to promoting the development of mathematics and give guidance into recent research and other inspirational material. In 2010 there are Mathematics Developers at 276 of the 290 Swedish municipalities. The hub for the Mathematics Developers at the national level is NCM which organizes conferences on a variety of themes twice a year. At a conference 2009 half a day was devoted to lectures and discussions on gifted students in mathematics. The evaluations showed that mathematics developers welcomed the opportunity to discuss gifted education. Several of the teachers subsequently offered the corresponding information and discussion theme for mathematics teachers in their home communities.

A concrete supportive activity for gifted students are the different mathematical competitions arranged by Swedish organizations like the Swedish Mathematical Society and NCM, individual schools and universities, commercial companies and devoted individuals. Among the most well known one finds the *Kangaroo Competition* for primary and secondary school students, *Pythagoras Quest* for secondary school, *Högstadiets matematiktävling* for secondary school, and *Skolornas matematiktävling* for upper secondary school. These competitions are very diverse in nature. There are team competitions, individual competitions, multiple choice questions and free text problems, and practical everyday problems as well as abstract problems. The Kangaroo Competition, which is held nationwide within the classrooms once per year is not aimed at the gifted students particularly, but feed-back from teachers indicate that a number of gifted students are discovered every year by the students unexpected results. In the other end there is Skolornas matematiktävling, through which students qualify for the *International Mathematics Olympiad*. The students who qualify for the national final are offered to participate in a distance course in mathematics given by university staff.

Other advocacy groups are for example Mensa Sweden that has a gifted child-program with the aim of raising the understanding of the gifted children's specific circumstances. Also several universities and university colleges offer various kinds of math circles, clubs or courses intended for students with special interest for mathematics. These activities, however, are all too often very dependent on the commitment of individuals, driving spirits, and are hence not always sustainable.

GIFTED EDUCATION RESEARCH RELEVANT FOR MATHEMATICS EDUCATION

During the 20th century there was a focus on social development and equal opportunities for all in Sweden, there was no room for research within gifted education.
Only at the end of the last century, after the 1994 school reform, research in this
field was started in the country and in the forefront we have Roland S. Persson with
his studies about gifted (särbegåvade) individuals (see e.g. Persson, 1998a, 1999,
2005, 2009a, 2010). With gifted Persson means a person who is clearly different from
others in his or her field of competence and interest area, a person who surprises
you at repeated occasions with his or her exceptional ability in one or more areas, both
in school and in everyday life. It is clear that Persson do not rank gifted individuals
in the same category as high achievers. In addition to his studies of giftedness in
music (see e.g. Persson, 2009b) Persson has focused on the social situation and the
gifted student's roll within education and society. Special attention has been directed
towards the ideal of egalitarianism and how this affects perception and management
of highly gifted individuals. The results of his studies show that Swedish primary
school teachers view of gifted individuals in large coincide with international studies
of cognitive attributes such as level of knowledge and ability to apply knowledge
in different contexts and to effectively process information and that these students
generally are creative (Persson, 1998b). But the results also show that teachers value
social attributes highly when identifying gifted students, attributes such as helpful-
ness, leadership abilities and being a good role-model. The gifted students are also
seen as being secure individual and able to keep the spirit up in the classroom,
which according to Persson are expectations that can be harmful for the situation of
the gifted. Moreover, Persson's studies show that gifted students perceive the Swedish
school as hostile and although it improves somewhat in higher grades it is not
considered satisfactory by the gifted students themselves (Persson, 2010). Persson also
suggest that, within an equalitarian school system, mentoring is a way of providing
the legitimate support to gifted students (Persson, 2005). Although Persson's research
gets international recognition, it has so far received little attention within the Swedish
education system.

Simultaneously Åke Edfeldt has studied high achieving students' reading comprehension while at a national level advocating the establishment of gifted education
in Sweden (Edfeldt & Wistedt, 2009). But it is research in gifted education in mathematics that has had the strongest growth due to the state financed project *Pedagogy
for students with the skills and aptitudes in mathematics* (Edfeldt & Wistedt, 2009;
Wistedt, 2005). This project started in 2004 and is led by Professor Inger Wistedt
at the Linnaeus University and includes in-service training for teachers as well as
research in gifted education. There are currently six doctoral students linked to
the project. Since research in gifted education in Sweden is in its infancy, there
are a lot of open questions. This is noticeable in the diversity of the doctoral students'
research. Some commonalities are however visible in the projects. Firstly, giftedness is considered as giftedness on an individual level, where gifted and/or creative
achievers mentally formulate and manipulate their own models of the reality. The
gifted individuals see and recognize what most of us don't see or recognize. The
gifted are hence considered as what Ziegler (2009) call *Propperian Creatures*.

By comparison, the next step would be the *Spenserian Creatures*, who together in social groups accomplish creative and innovative achievements (*ibid.*). Secondly, the research has its starting point in Krutetskii's study of capable children (1976). Many of the doctoral students' studies include the identification of Krutetskii's abilities in problem solving processes or outcomes of a problem solving process. Krutetskii's list of abilities is also used as a tool for designing or classifying mathematical problems. Thirdly, the studies are mostly qualitative, following the national research tradition.

The research studies are in most cases not yet completed. Among the published results is a case-study following two gifted compulsory school students, of which one was low-achieving. The study highlights the students social and cognitive development that probably partly takes place as a result of the recognition and stimuli of their mathematical abilities (Pettersson, 2008). Another study investigates upper secondary school head-teachers conception of giftedness in mathematics (Mattsson, in press). The results show that Swedish head teachers in particular emphasizes students' creative ability, such as the ability to find multiple solutions to a problem or the ability to find a solution of a problem that they have never seen before, their logical ability and their strong motivation to study the subject. Moreover, head teachers used various indicators to detect giftedness; most common was that the students were detected by their own initiative for engaging in, or pursuing, mathematics. The head-teachers also used several different detection indicators involving quality aspects. The three most frequent were oral mathematical reasoning, test results and types of questions posed. Despite the lack of debate on conceptions of giftedness in Sweden and its long history of egalitarianism in school and society, this study offers findings that are consistent both with international studies of teachers' characteristics of gifted students and with studies focusing on gifted students' character traits. These results underline the relevance of international findings in gifted education for the Swedish discussion in the field and vice versa.

Most Swedish research labeled gifted education in Mathematics is related to the research group at the Linnaeus University. Occasionally there are studies from elsewhere concerning gifted students, like *Students' conceptions of limits, high achievers versus low achievers* (Juter, 2007), where students learning development of limits are studied in terms of concept images. Results show that the learning path of high achievers has similarities with the historical development of the concept of limits, especially concerning abstraction and formality. This was not the case for low achievers. Moreover results show that even high achievers rarely showed a coherent trace of their concept images.

Taking into account that mathematical giftedness internationally often include creativity as a trait (Sriraman, 2005), it is also relevant to highlight other Swedish mathematics educational research. There is a series of studies concerning various types of mathematical reasoning lead by Professor Johan Lithner at Umeå University. The Umeå research is not based on studies of gifted students or their specific educational situation. Nevertheless the studies provide important information about the mathematics culture or mathematics milieu (Brousseau, 1997) of the Swedish schools that affects the gifted students. In an attempt to understand what makes the students fail in mathematics Lithner identified problems with by-heart-learning and developed a research framework to analyze and describe the type of mathematical reasoning needed or used to solve a problem (Lithner, 2008). Lithner identifies two main categories of reasoning, *imitative* and *creative reasoning*. Imitative reasoning is either memorized or algorithmic, and calls for a complete recalling of an answer or a solution algorithm. Creative reasoning, on the other hand, is a mathematically well founded argument that considers the intrinsic mathematical properties of the components involved and asks for novel reasoning as well as clear motivations for choice of strategies (*ibid.*).

Concurrent to the development of this framework the nature of mathematical reasoning required for solving test tasks in secondary school (Boesen, 2006) and at university level (Bergqvist, 2007), as well as textbook tasks (Lithner, 2000a, 2000b, 2003, 2004) were studied. The type of reasoning that students use in individual- or small-group learning situation has also been studied as well as the basis for the type of reasoning which upper secondary school students use when solving mathematical problems (Bergqvist, Lithner & Sumpter, 2008). Altogether these results show a very high frequency of imitative reasoning in textbook tasks, exams and in learning situations, only demanding mathematically superficial strategies from the students. The secondary school students rarely demonstrated mathematically well-founded considerations when answering mathematical questions. Instead they often look for suitable, albeit sometimes randomly selected, algorithms (*ibid*). Furthermore, exams set up by upper secondary school teachers seldom requires students to think in a new way, or consider the intrinsic mathematical properties involved in the tasks (Boesen, 2006). Similarly, studies show that students could pass 15 of 16 reviewed university exams in mathematics by using imitative reasoning alone (Bergqvist, 2006).

Through interviews with teachers the group at Umeå University has investigated why exams tend to emphasize imitative reasoning. The results show that at upper secondary school the teachers had limited awareness of how to pose questions that demand creative mathematical reasoning. Another explanation was that the problem of a packed curriculum in mathematics (Boesen, 2006). The University teachers, on the other hand, were aware of that their questions only required imitative reasoning. However, the university teachers did not find it reasonable to expect creative reasoning from the students, due to the student's insufficient prerequisites (Bergqvist, 2006). In contrast, the studies show that the national exams at upper secondary school require a high degree of creative mathematical reasoning (Palm, Boesen & Lithner, 2005).

There is currently no large-scale, comparative study with control groups on Swedish provision for gifted students. An obstacle for such studies is the lack of well-defined and measurable objectives for the development of mathematical giftedness. Tests such as *Torrance Test of Creative Thinking* (Torrance, 1966), *Raven's Advanced Progressive Matrices* (Raven, Court & Raven, 1993), *Stanford-Binet Intelligence Test* (Thorndike, Hagan & Sattler, 1986), *Wechsler Intelligence Scale* (Wechsler, 1991) etc. have not yet gained approval within the Swedish educational system as ways of measuring desirable abilities. Nor is there in Sweden any obligatory national university enrolment examination such as in for example in China (Phillipson *et al.,* 2009) or as SAT-M in the US (Brody, 2009). To be able to make a national evaluation of the provision for gifted students Sweden needs an officially accepted description of highly-valued expressions of giftedness in mathematics. Mattsson's study (2010) can be considered as a first step in this direction.

In the international research mathematical talent is often discussed in terms of the individual's abilities in mathematical problem solving processes (Sriraman, 2005). Mathematical problem solving has also been the subject or the starting point for a number of Swedish studies (see e.g. Ahlberg 1991; Möllehed, 2001; Taflin, 2006; Wyndhamn, 1993). But none of these studies focuses directly on gifted students or high- achievers but rather on factors influencing the mathematical problem solving of all students in the classroom.

GIFTED EDUCATION IN THE SWEDISH TEACHER EDUCATION

The Swedish Teacher Education is governed by a legislation (Swedish statue-book, 1993) that stipulates goals for all Swedish educational degrees. The legislation also specifies the structure of the teacher education programs. Three areas with a given number of credits are stipulated. The first two areas are subject knowledge and practical training. The third area is a general domain which is the same for all teacher students independent of level or subject at the university. However the content of this part varies from university to university. Gifted students are not mentioned in the legislation. Surprisingly not even "student in need of special support" is an obligatory part of the teacher training programs. However the list of courses at all the 21 universities offering teacher education degrees in mathematics in Sweden in 2010, reveals that Special pedagogy (Specialpedagogik) is available at all of them. Many of them do not only offer courses but also complete specializations, consisting of a number of courses and a thesis, or even a masterprogram in Special Pedagogy.

A thorough search among all available course syllabi in Special Pedagogy in July 2010 reveals however that the gifted students are not explicitly included, according to the syllabus, with very few exceptions. Exceptions are Stockholm University, where there is a course about the gifted students, and at Linnaeus University, where there are courses about students with special needs that also includes topics on gifted education in mathematics and also a course about the mathematically gifted solely. The latter course is a distance course and is, according to T. Biro, who is responsible for the course, taken by in average 70 students per year since the start in 2005 (phone interview, June 2010). The course is divided into three different themes. The first deals with giftedness from an overall perspective, as well as characteristics of mathematics as a subject. On the basis of Krutetskii's (1976) list of abilities characteristics of mathematical abilities are discussed. The second theme highlights the possible organization like e.g. grouping and differentiation, as well as the social context relevant to the learner's mathematical development. The third theme discusses problem solving as a means to stimulate and support the development of mathematical ability. In this part one looks at *Rich Problems* (Taflin, 2007).

Since 2009 there are two full professors (Edfeldt & Wistedt, 2009) with the ordinance to award ECHA-certification. This certificate represents an international recognition of the teacher as a specialist in gifted education within a specific subject. At the moment the only possible subject for an ECHA-diploma in Sweden is mathematics.

Requirements for obtaining a diploma is to have completed the course in gifted education (7.5 ECTS) and to have written a master's degree thesis (15 ECTS), both with the highest possible mark. The first Swedish ECHA-diploma was awarded in October 2009. ECHA-certified teachers are supposed to function as regional support for gifted students and teachers, to design intervention plans for how education and resources should be used to insure the development of the student (Edfeldt & Wistedt, 2009). This idea of ECHA-certified teachers as regional leaders for gifted education around the country is not yet known in the general education system. However the project managers have paved the way for a future organized structure for the work with the local development of individualized teaching for gifted students.

In the international debate on students in need of special support it has been emphasized that gifted students should be included and that particular attention should be given to their needs (see e.g. Recommandation on gifted education from Council of Europe, 1994, and the UNESCO definition of special educational needs in Mitchell, 1995). This has been embraced by several countries such as Israel, Spain, France and Greece (European Commission, 2006; Peyser, 2005). Yet until 2010 there has not, in Swedish teacher education, been much improvement in this direction. This is unsatisfactory as research already in 1998 has shown that Swedish teachers would find it beneficial to learn more about gifted education (Persson, 1998). Luckily there are exceptions like Linnaeus University which is in the fore front in these matters. One can also see a changing attitude at other universities by the increasing number of undergraduate theses treating questions about giftedness, especially mathematical giftedness and provision in schools.

From 2011 Sweden will have a new legislation for teacher education which stipulates that Special Pedagogy must be included in all teacher training programs (Swedish Statue Book, 1993). Gifted students are once again not explicitly mentioned in the legislation, even though the Swedish Government Official Rapport, that preceded the legislation, states that "even gifted students may need to be the subject of special pedagogical efforts" (Swedish Government Official Report, 2008, p. 209).

IMPLEMENTATION OF GIFTED EDUCATION IN SCHOOLS

In 2009 Sweden took the first step towards a State sanctioned gifted education program by launching a five year pilot activity (Swedish statue-book, 2008). Twenty upper secondary schools around the country has been selected to arrange cutting-edge programs focusing on one specific area. The area can either be mathematics, natural sciences, social sciences or humanities. The students follow the regular national program in all other subjects. Four of the selected schools have mathematics as their focus area. At most 30 students per class are allowed, implying that this project involves annually at most 120 new gifted students in mathematics nationally.

The statues for the pilot activity (*ibid.*) says that a cutting-edge education should:

1. include courses with special depth and breadth in the subject or subject area which it is oriented towards, in addition to the compulsory courses in the national program and specialization that most closely correspond to cutting-edge education, and

2. make it possible for students to study courses at a university that run parallel to the studies at upper secondary level.

As a matter of fact there have, since a quarter of a century, been upper secondary schools in Sweden engaged in similar activities as the cutting-edge education is intended to do. These programs have been developed by mathematical very competent teachers. There has been a steady enrollment of approximately 15–25 students per class yearly. Currently Sweden has a number of upper secondary schools with a specific mathematical profile, including Danderyds matematikgymnasium, Ehrensvärdska gymnasieskola, Hvitfeldska gymnasiet, Luleå gymnasieskola, Malmö Borgarskola and Norra Real. The first four of these schools have been selected to participate in the cutting-edge pilot project.

There are advantages for schools participating in the pilot. Firstly the students can be recruited nationally. Schooling in Sweden is free of charge and run by municipalities. The schools are financed by taxes, and money is transferred from the national level to the municipality where the student is registered. If a student is admitted to a school with right to do national admission, money will be transferred from the student's city of origin to the municipality of the school. However in contrast to many countries, where boarding schools are a socially accepted and fairly common option, it is extremely unusual that Swedish families choose to enroll their children at schools if it means that the child has to move away from the family. Looking at the history of, for example, Danderyds matematikgymnasium that has had national admission since more than 20 years, students predominantly comes from the municipality where the school is situated.

The second advantage of the cutting-edge program is that students can be selected for admission by using an admissions test in addition to the average mark. Other-wise Swedish schools can, by law, only select students for admissions by comparing their average marks from primary schools. Hence, selection can only be based on the student's general achievements in all subjects, including subjects such as art, music, sport, home of knowledge and arts and crafts. These admission tests have so far been designed by each school individually, but consist in most cases of two parts, a first part testing the basic knowledge of the mathematics from compulsory school, and a second part with emphasis on problem solving, where the ability to solve problems that require several steps in the solution process is tested. In some cases the students' ability to grasp new mathematical information is examined. Even if these tests give the schools the option to admit students that are gifted in mathematics but not generally high achievers, they have had no significant role in the admission process. So far the tests have only been used to give the students a recommendation to enroll or not. No student has yet, by the merits of the test result, been admitted, taking the place from a student with a higher average mark. So in principle this is self selection among students with high average marks, and there is no specific mathematical competition between the applicants like in for example Israel (Peyser, 2005).

A third advantage of the cutting-edge programs is the media exposure helping the schools in their recruitment work. Since there is no financial support for cutting-edge programs and since the recruitment so far is local, and since the admission test has not played any significant role yet, the extra media exposure might turn out to be the most important advantage both for the individual school and for the implementation of gifted education in Sweden.

At the compulsory school level Sweden has, during the last 130 years, gone from parallel school systems via alternative courses to the classroom that includes all levels of giftedness and in which the teacher shall individualize the teaching according to every student's abilities and level of giftedness. In the teaching of mathematics the individualization has been dominated by an education where all students work at their own pace (Wistedt & Sundström, in press). Theoretically this allows for acceleration, an effective way to meet the need of the gifted students (Kolitch & Brody, 1992; Kulik & Kulik, 1992), specially the profoundly gifted students (Brody, 2009). But in practice the speed-differentiation has meant that all students in the rather quiet classroom work individually with mostly routine tasks and repetitions of the same materials from the textbook (Wistedt & Sundström, in press), and that the individual student's interaction with the teacher is sparse (National Agency for Education, 2003). Moreover, research shows that Swedish teacher do not emphasize creativity in choice of problems and when constructing exams (Boesen, 2006) and a national evaluation shows that the Swedish school leaves talented students in mathematics with few challenges (National Agency for Education, 2003). Hence there is a great need of improvement on the practical level, especially regarding the quality of teaching (Wistedt & Sundström, in press).

There are no state sanctioned activities to back up or complement this in-class differentiation. Some municipalities have started their own projects as for example the project *Maximum development for all – how does the school meet the needs of the students with high academic potential* (Wallström, 2009). The most common kind of support, however, comes from a number of upper secondary schools which offer gifted students at secondary level the opportunity to study mathematics courses at upper secondary level. A very ambitious program is set up at Malmö Borgarskola where the nearby secondary schools and Malmö Borgarskola have coordinated their schedules to facilitate for the mathematically gifted secondary students to participate in the mathematics teaching at upper secondary school. Secondary schools students study at their own speed, and if the student chooses to enroll at Malmö Borgarskola an individual plan is created. The consequence is that Malmö Borgarskola offers highly individualized mathematics teaching throughout upper secondary school.

CHALLENGES FACING SWEDISH GIFTED EDUCATION IN MATHEMATICS

The ultimate goal of gifted education is to give each gifted student access to a stimulating, challenging and developing education. Even though mathematically gifted students may have some common characteristics (Sriraman, 2005; Wieczerkowski, Cropley & Prado, 2000) they might learn in different ways and tempo, have different needs socially as well as emotionally and show their (first sign of) giftedness at different ages. This calls for a varied organization and provisions for gifted students at all ages. In order to act for such a development Sweden needs to face some challenges.

Legal Recognition of Gifted Students

In Sweden there is a strong need to clearly recognize the gifted students and their needs in policy documents. The present formulations about *students in need of special support* have had very limited impact on the situation of the gifted students. The gifted students need to be addressed more directly in the policy documents, as in the law for the education of the gifted in Brazil (Alencar *et al.,* 2009), in Wisconsin Statute 118 (Wisconsin Statute, 2007a) and 121 (Wisconsin Statute, 2007b) in the U.S., or in the Law of Special Education in Taiwan (Phillipson *et al.,* 2009). Such a law puts pressure on the development of gifted education (Shaughnessy & Persson, 2009) and experiences from other countries shows that this often leads to fast-growing gifted education with a variety of measures to provide for the gifted students (European Commission, 2006; Phillipson *et al.*, 2009). The Swedish policy-makers have so far refrained from all forms of labeling, beside the non-specific notion of *students in need of special support*. Even in the policy document about the cutting-edge programs (Swedish statue-book, 2008) there is no mention of the target group and instead the general framework for the activities is described. To label this group could, according to the critics, mean alienation and stigmatization of these students, and could make people believe that they form a homogeneous group. Using a label like high-achievers would for example exclude underperforming students with potential, but include school-smart hard working students with average talent, while a word like gifted would refer too much to what a person is given by nature and not enough to what it can achieve by nurturing. These questions are problematic, but the lack of an accepted terminology that recognizes giftedness and gifted students with special abilities and aptitudes is not fruitful. The avoidance to label the group, has not been a success so far, and has made this group all too invisible in Sweden.

A first, and very important, step in this direction will be taken through the new Education Act that will be in effective from 2012 (Swedish Statue-book, 2010) which states that

> All children and students should be given the guidance and stimulation that they need in their learning and their personal development so that they can develop as much as possible in accordance with educational goals. Students that easily can reach the knowledge requirements, that at least should be achieved, should be given guidance and stimulation in order to achieve further advancement in their knowledge.

Strengthening the Connection between Research and Implementation of Gifted Education

There is a need to strengthen Sweden's foothold in the existing knowledge about the gifted and talented students. Neither before nor after the introduction of the cutting-edge education was there any discussion on what is meant by giftedness or special abilities within an academic subject or how to develop giftedness. In many other countries there are gifted programs that are theoretically founded, and different programs can have different views of giftedness. In Brazil (Alencar *et al.,* 2009), for example, there are programs built on *The Schoolwide Enrichment Model* by

Renzulli (Renzulli & Reis, 1985) as well as on a combination of Gardner's conception of *Multiple Intelligences* (1993), Sternberg's *Triarchic Theory of Intellectual giftedness* (1986), Bloom's *Taxonomy of Educational Objectives* (1956), and Kohlberg's *Psychology of Moral Development* (Kohlberg, 1984). Different models of programs for mathematically gifted students that are founded on diverse views of mathematics are also found around the world. The models used by for example the Center for Talented Youth in the U.S. focus on rapid acceleration in the advanced academic field, whereas the Hamburg Model developed in Germany focus on the creative work of posing, exploring and solving mathematical problems (Sriraman & Steinthorsdottir, 2008). As for now, there is no clear discussion about or formulation of if and how provision for the Swedish gifted students should include special focus on creativity aspects, critical thinking, higher-order thinking, writing skills and communication skills, the ability to learn how to learn, inquiry skills, etc. (Phillipson *et al.*, 2009; Shaughnessy & Persson, 2009). Regardless of which models of giftedness a program is founded on, the theoretical basis makes the views of giftedness as well as the educational goals and measures more visible, coherent and easier to evaluate.

Sweden has had special classes for gifted students in mathematics at upper secondary school for a quarter of a century. However these activities have, from an educational policy perspective, been almost unnoticed. It is probable that these models have been taken into account when developing the cutting-edge education pilot, but it is surprising that these programs have not yet been thoroughly evaluated. Areas that would be important to evaluate are for example the effectiveness of the activities with respect to well-defined objectives formulated as desirable outcomes for participating students (Shaughnessy & Persson, 2009). Another important question is the sustainability of the activities, both considering the teachers' workload and knowledge-transfer. As there today is no financial support for the development of education and material for gifted students the developmental work is mainly done by enthusiasts that spend a huge amount of their own free time to develop the programs and the material used (Mattsson, in prep.). Finally it is also important to study to what extent the backgrounds of the student population fulfils the law that that all students should be given equal access to education regardless of for example gender and socio-economic situation (Swedish statue-book, 1985). The development of gifted education in Sweden is dependent on that it is not in conflict with the ideology of social justice, and might need to involve a "social justice agenda", like the one in the English model (Eyre, 2009).

The research in gifted education is under development in Sweden. Since it has already shown serious shortcomings in the current school education in relation to the operation and development of gifted students' cognitive potential and social situation (Persson, 1998b, 2010; Pettersson, 2008), it is time to take the next step and focus on the design of effective and developing activities/tasks for the gifted students. The cutting-edge programs will be one important object of study the coming years.

Identification of Gifted Students

Sweden has taken the first steps in the direction of separate education for gifted students in form of the cutting-edge education pilot. But while Sweden does this pilot at the upper secondary level, other countries like China and Taiwan started their actions at compulsory school levels. To postpone the differentiation to the non-compulsory school level is more in line with the Swedish egalitarian ideology where all students should be individually taught in the same class room (Axelsson, 2007; Wallby, Carlsson & Nyström, 2001). However it is important also to identify and support gifted children at a much earlier stage of their life, in order to provide them with encouragement and provision so that they can develop according their potential and stay interested all the way to upper secondary school. Otherwise it is a risk that only gifted children, which have families that understand how to stimulate and support them, who will find their way to the cutting-edge education in Sweden.

> Children gain self-confidence through intellectual challenge. The key lies in providing a range of activities that allow all students, including the gifted, to display their fullest abilities (Glass, 2004, p. 28).

So even if this pilot at upper secondary school is successful it needs to be complemented with actions that develop the identification of young children in Sweden that are gifted, and in need of special provision. It is not likely that Sweden, with its strong tradition of egalitarianism, will introduce an identification program for gifted students among the entire population like e.g. Israel (Peyser, 2005). But what is important is that the method also identifies students that have great potential in a limited domain. Giftedness is an exceptional aptitude for something, not for everything (Lohman, 2009). But in light of the limited effect of the admission test to the cutting-edge programs development is needed in Sweden. Today, it is over-all high achieving students that are admitted to cutting-edge programs, exactly as at the other upper secondary schools, with a mathematical profile, that are not allowed to use tests.

Gifted Educa tion in the Swedish Teacher Education

It is likely that the most gifted students in Sweden, at least in the foreseeable future, will not be found in special classes but rather in the regular classrooms. A necessary condition for the fulfillment of the needs of all gifted students is hence that the general teacher is knowledgeable about giftedness, including detection and provision. The teachers also need to understand the dynamic relationship between potential, support and motivation, i.e. that stimulation is required in order for talent to be shown (Krutetskii, 1976) and that fear of rejection by peers is pervasive among many under-achieving gifted students (Lohman, 2009). In other words, we need like in England, to consider "Every teacher a teacher of the gifted" (Eyre, 2009, p. 1053). This calls for an enhanced and mandatory training in gifted education within the teacher training programs and as in-service training, as needed in many countries around the world (Alencar *et al.*, 2009; Phillipson *et al.*, 2009). In this regard an interesting developmental approach is taken by the Australian Government in their national gifted educational Professional Development Package for teachers that started in 2005 (Australian Government, 2005). There is also a need of experts that can support the regular teachers and also arrange out of class activities where the students meet peers and experience advanced learning just for the joy of it and not necessarily for assessment (Eyre, 2009). The establishment of the ECHA-diploma is an important step in this direction.

Coordinating Measures for Gifted Students

Like many other countries Sweden would benefit from coordinating the provision for gifted students. There are however many different ways of coordinating measures for gifted students (see e.g. Alencar *et al.,* 2009; Brody, 2009; Phillipson *et al.,* 2009; Peyser, 2005). For example, some countries have governmental departments, like Israel's special Department for Gifted Pupils (Peyser, 2005), while other countries have major organizations that supply programs for gifted students, like The Center for Talented Youth in USA (Brody, 2009). It would be beneficial if a Swedish coordinating agency, like the Brazilian High Abilities/Giftedness Centers of Activities (Alencar *et al.,* 2009), could coordinate support activities, including extracurricular activities and programs for gifted students, and transfer information about national and international development between schools, parents and others. An infrastructure for the support is also needed for a quality program to be established. The agency should also attempt to influence government policies, research and teacher education.

Social Dimensions of Giftedness

In Sweden there is also a need to recognize that the gifted individual not only have specific intellectual needs, but also special social and emotional needs that come with a precocious thinking. In Brazil there are extracurricular courses where students not only deepen their knowledge in mathematics but also get a better understanding of his or her role in social interaction, personal relationship courses, with the aim to help gifted students to understand themselves, better relate to their peers and accept their individual differences (Alencar *et al.,* 2009). In other countries such as Singapore the course syllabus is extended to include enriched civic and moral education, emphasizing self-awareness, social awareness, and involvement in community. Those with outstanding abilities must also be equipped with the emotional skills that will help them to take on leadership roles (Phillipson *et al.,* 2009). Thus, there is a challenge in Sweden to develop the curriculum to be better suited for the gifted students.

CONCLUDING REMARK

Many societies recognize two arguments for gifted education: education as a means for individual development and education as a means to achieve national targets (Ziegel, 2009). But the concrete representation and interpretation of gifted education is still strongly influenced by the specific culture of the society (Moon & Rosselli, 2000). However, the culture of a country is not fixed and changes over time and it is important not to prevent people from trying to develop to their full potential, also in Sweden. Some very important steps, in the direction toward a strengthened Swedish gifted education, have recently been taken by the government. Now Sweden should embrace the changing conditions in society and be inspired by other countries development in order to stay on track towards a successful gifted education.

REFERENCES

Alencar, E. M. L. S., Fleith, D. S., & Arancibia. (2009). Gifted education in research on giftedness in South America. In L. V. Shavinina (Ed.), *International handbook on giftedness* (pp. 1491–1508). Springer Science+Business Media B.V.

Ahlberg, A. (1992). *Att möta matematiska problem: En belysning av barns lärande* [The meeting with mathematical problems. An illumination of children's learning]. PhD thesis, University of Gothenburg.

Axelsson, R.-M. (2008, October 16). Spetsutbildningar för eliten splittrar eleverna [Cutting-edge programs for the elite disunify the students]. *Sydöstran*, p. 13A.

Axelsson, T. (2007). *Rätt elev i rätt klass. Skola, begåvning och styrning 1910–1950.* [The right student in the right class. School, giftedness and management]. Linköping Studies in Arts and Science No. 379, Department of Thematic Studies.

Australian Government. (2005). *Gifted education professional development package.* Retrieved August 4 from http://www.dest.gov.au/sectors/school_education/publications_resources/profiles/gifted_education_professional_development_package.htm

Bergqvist, E. (2006). *Mathematics and mathematics education – two sides of the same coin: Creative reasoning in University Exams in mathematics.* PhD thesis, Umeå University, Department of Mathematics.

Bergqvist, E. (2007). Types of mathematical reasoning required in University Exams in mathematics. *The Journal of Mathematical Behaviour, 26*(4), 348–370.

Bergqvist, T., Lithner, J., & Sumpter, L. (2008). Upper secondary students' task reasoning. *International Journal of Mathematics Education in Science and Technology, 39*(1), 1–12.

Björklund, J. (2010). *Jan Björklund om höjda ambitioner i skolan* [Jan Björklund on raising the ambition in school]. Retrieved August 20, 2010, from Ministry of Education and Research, http://www.sweden.gov.se/sb/d/12468/a/150537

Bloom, B. S. (1956). *Taxanomy of educational objectives. Handbook I: Cognitive domain.* New York: McKay.

Boesen, J. (2006). *Assessing mathematical creativiy – compairing national and teacher-made tests, explaining differences and examining impact.* PhD thesis, Umeå University, Department of Mathematics.

Brody, L. E. (2009). The John Hopkins talent search model for identifying and developing exceptional mathematical and verbal abilities. In L. V. Shavinina (Ed.), *International handbook on giftedness* (pp. 999–1016). Springer Science+Business Media B.V.

Brousseau, G. (1997). *Theory of didactical situations in mathematics.* Dordrecht: Kluwer.

Council of Europe. (1994). *Recommandation 1248(1994)1 on education for gifted children.* Retrieved August 5, 2010 from http://assembly.coe.int/Main.asp?link=/Documents/AdoptedText/ta94/EREC1248.htm

Edfeldt, Å. W. (2003). *Kunskapsutveckling och/eller socialt främjande. En historisk återblick* [Knowledge Development and/or Social Enhancment. A Historical Review]. No. 70:2003, Department of Educational Science, Stockholm University.

Edfeldt, Å. W., & Wistedt, I. (2009). High ability education in Sweden: The Swedish model. In T. Balchin, B. Hymer & D. J. Matthews (Eds.), *The Routledge international companion to gifted education* (pp. 76–83). London: Routledge.

Engström, A. (2003). *Specialpedagogiska frågeställningar i matematik: en introduktion* [Issues of special education in mathematics: an introduction]. Sweden: Örebro University, Department of Education.

European Commission. (2006). *Specific educational measures to promote all forms of giftedness at School in Europe.* (Working document).

Eyre, D. (2009). The English model of gifted education. In L. V. Shavinina (Ed.), *International handbook on giftedness* (pp. 1045–1059). Springer Science+Business Media B.V.

Gardner, H. (1993). *Multiple intelligences.* New York: Basic Books.

Glass, T. F. (2004). What gift? The reality of the student who is gifted and talented in public school classrooms. *Gifted Child Today, 27*(4), 25–29.

Government Offices of Sweden. (2006). *Regeringsbeslut.* [Cabinet decision] 111:8 (U2006/564/G).

Husén, T., & Härnqvist, K. (2000). *Begåvningsreserven. En återblick på ett halvt sekels undervisning och debatt.* [Talent pool. A Review of Half a Century of Education and Debate]. Uppsala: Föreningen för svensk undervisningshistoria.

Juter, K. (2007). Students' conceptions of limits: High achievers versus low achievers. *The Montana Mathematics Enthusiast, 4*(1), 53–65.

Kohlberg, L. (1984). *The psychology of moral development.* San Francisco: Harpert Row.

Kolitch, E. R., & Brody, L. E. (1992). Mathematics acceleration of highly talented students: An evaluation. *Gifted Child Quarterly, 36*, 78–86.

Krutetskii, V. A. (1976). *The psychology of mathematical abilities in schoolchildren.* Chicago: The University of Chicago Press.

Kulik, J. A., & Kulik, C. C. (1992). Meta-Analytic findings on grouping programs. *Gifted Child Quarterly, 36*, 73–77.

Lithner, J. (2000a). Mathematical reasoning and familiar procedures. *International Journal of Mathematical Education in Science and Technology, 31*, 83–95.

Lithner, J. (2000b). Mathematical reasoning in task solving. *Educational Studies in Mathematics, 41*, 165–190.

Lithner, J. (2003). Student's mathematical reasoning in University textbooks exercises. *Educational Studies in Mathematics, 52*, 29–55.

Lithner, J. (2004). Mathematical reasoning in calculus textbook exercises. *Journal of Mathematical Behaviour, 23*(4), 405–427.

Lithner, J. (2008). A research framework for creative and imitative reasoning. *Educational Studies in Mathematics, 67*(3), 255–276.

Lohman, D. F. (2009). Identifying academically talented students: Some general principles, two specific procedures. In L. V. Shavinina (Ed.), *International handbook on giftedness* (pp. 971–997). Dordrecht: Springer Science + Business Media B.V.

Magne, O. (2001). *Literature on special educational needs in mathematics: A bibliography with some comments* (Educational and psychological interactions 124). Sweden: Malmö University, College of education.

Magne, O. (2006). Historical aspects on special education in mathematics. *NOMAD. Nordic Studies in Mathematics Education, 11*(4), 7–35.

Mattsson, L. (in press). Head teachers' conceptions of gifted students in mathematics in Swedish Upper Secondary School. *Nordic Studies in Mathematics Education.*

Mattsson, L. (in prep). *Gifted education in mathematics in Swedish Upper Secondary School and questions of conception, provision and Egalitarianism.* Gothenburg: University of Gothenburg.

Ministry of Education and Research. (2008). *Inrättande av försöksverksamhet med riksrekryterande gymnasial spetsutbildning.* [Establishing a Pilot Project for Upper Secondary School Level Cutting-Edge Program with National Recruitment] (U2008/3879G). Stockholm: Government Offices of Sweden.

Ministry of Education and Research. (2010). *Spetsutbildningar på gymnasiet.* [Cutting-Edge Programs at Secondary School]. Retrieved August 24, from http://www.regeringen.se/sb/d/12468/a/150578

Mitchell, D. (1995). *Best practices in inclusive education: A basis for needs in Europe.* London: Cassell.

Moon, S. M., & Rosselli, H. C. (2000). Developing gifted programs. In K. A. Heller, F. J. Mönks, R. J. Sternberg, & R. F. Subotnik (Eds.), *International handbook of giftedness and talent* (2nd ed., pp. 499–521). Oxford: Pergamon.

Mullis, I. V. S., Martin, M. O., Robitaille, D. F., & Foy, P. (2009). *TIMSS advanced 2008 International report: Findings from IEA's study of achievement in advanced mathematics and physics in the final year of secondary school.* Chestnut Hill, MA: TIMSS & PIRLS International Study Center, Boston College.

Möllehed, E. (2001). *Problemlösning i matematik: En studie av påverkansfaktorer i årskurserna 4–9.* [Problem Solving in Mathematics: a Study on Impact Factors in Grade 4–9]. PhD thesis, Malmö College of Education, Department of Education.

National Agency for Education. (2003). *Lusten att lära – med fokus på matematik.* Rapport nr 221 [The urge to learn – with focus on mathematics. Report No 221]. Stockholm: Fritzes.

National Agency for Education. (2006a). *Curriculum for the compulsory school system, the pre school class and the Leisure-time Centre, Lpo 94.* Stockholm: Fritzes.

National Agency for Education. (2006b). *Curriculum for the non-compulsory school system - Lpf 94.* Stockholm: Fritzes.

Olsson, L. (2008, May 24). Klart för elitklass på gymnasiet [Time for Elit Classes at Upper Secondary School]. *Svenska Dagbladet,* p. 3A7.

Palm, T., Boesen, J., & Lithner, J. (2005). *The requirements of mathematical reasoning in upper secondary assessments.* Research Reports in Mathematics Education 5, Department of Mathematics, Umeå University.

Persson, R. S. (1998a) *High ability and teacher roles in an Egalitarian context. Research report I. The Jonkoping Urban Giftedness Identification Project (JUGIP).* Sweden: Jönköping University, School of Education & Communication.

Persson, R. S. (1998b). Paragons of virtue: Teachers' conceptual understanding of high ability in an Egalitarian School System. *High Ability Studies, 9*(2), 181–196.

Persson, R. S. (1999). Exploring high ability in Egalitarian settings: Swedish School Teachers and gifted students. *Gifted and Talented International, 10*(1), 6–11.

Persson, R. S., Joswig, H., & Balogh, L. (2000). Gifted education in Europé: Programs, practice, and current research. In K. A. Heller, F. J. Mönks, R. J. Sternberg, & R. F. Subotnik (Eds.), *International handbook of giftedness and talent* (2nd ed., pp. 703–734). Oxford: Elsevier Science.

Persson, R. (2005). Voices in the wilderness: Counselling gifted students in a Swedish Egalitarian setting. *International Journal for the Advancement of Counselling, 27*(2), 263–276.

Persson, R. (2009a). The unwanted gifted and talented: A sociobiological perspective of the societal functions of giftedness. In L. V. Shavinina (Ed.), *International handbook on giftedness* (pp. 913–924). Dordrecht: Springer Science+Business Media B.V.

Persson, R. (2009b). The elusive muse: Understanding musical giftedness. In L. V. Shavinina (Ed.), *International handbook on giftedness* (pp. 727–749). Dordrecht: Springer Science+Business Media B.V.

Persson, R. S. (2010). Experiences of intellectually gifted students in an Egalitarian and inclusive educational system: A survey study. *Journal for the Education of the Gifted, 33*(4), 536–569.

Pettersson, E. (2008). *Hur matematiska förmågor uttrycks och tas om hand i en pedagogisk praktik.* [How Mathematical Abilities are Expressed and Taken Care of in a Pedagogical Practice]. Lic. thesis, Växjö University, The School of Mathematics and Systems Engineering.

Peyser, M. (2005). Identifying and nurturing gifted children in Israel. *International Journal for the Advancement of Counceling, 27*(2), 229–243.

Phillipson, S. N., Kaur, I., & Phillipson, S. (2003). A late developer – Gifted education in Malaysia within a global context. *The Asia-Pacific Education Researcher, 12*(2), 135–175.

Phillipson, S. N., Shi, J., Zhang, G., Tsai, D. M., Quek, C. G., Matsumura, N., et al. (2009). Recent developments in gifted education in East Asia. In L. V. Shavinina (Ed.), *International handbook on giftedness* (pp. 1427–1462). Dordrecht: Springer Science + Business Media B.V.

Raven, J. C., Court, J. H., & Raven, J. (1993). *Manual for Raven's advanced progressive matrices and vocabulary scales: Section 4 advanced progressive matrices.* Oxford: Oxford Psychologists Press.

Renzulli, J. S., & Reis, S. M. (1985). *The schoolwide enrichment model: A comprehensive plan for educational excellence.* Mansfield Center, CT: Creative Learning Press.

MATTSSON AND BENGMARK

Shaughnessy, M. F., & Persson, R. S. (2009). Observed trends and needed trends in gifted education. In L. V. Shavinina (Ed.), *International handbook on giftedness* (pp. 1285–1291). Dordrecht: Springer Science + Business Media B.V.

Sriraman, B. (2005). Are giftedness and creativity synonyms in mathematics? *Journal of Secondary Gifted Education, 17*(1), 20–36.

Sriraman, B., & Steinthorsdottir, O. B. (2008). Mathematics, secondary. In J. A. Plucker & C. M. Callahan (Eds.), *Critical issues and practices in gifted education: What the research says* (pp. 395–408). Wasco, TX: Prufrock Press Inc.

Sternberg, R. J. (1986). A triarchic Theory of intellectual giftedness. In R. J. Sternberg & J. E. Davidson (Eds.), *Conceptions of giftedness* (pp. 223–243). Camebridge: Camebridge University Press.

Ström, S. (2010, August 18). Spetsutbildningar för 13-åringar [Cutting-edge programs for 13 year olds]. *Svenska Dagbladet*, p. 14.

Swedish Government Official Report. (2004). *Att lyfta matematiken – intresse, lärande och kompetens.* [Enhancing the Status of Mathematics – Interest, Learning, Competence] (2004:97). Stockholm: Fritzes.

Swedish Government Official Report. (2008). *En hållbar lärarutbildning.* [Sustainable Teacher Education] (2008:109). Stockholm: Fritzes.

Swedish National Agency for Higher Education. (2005). *Nybörjarstudenter och matematik – matematikundervisningen under första året på tekniska och naturvetenskapliga utbildningar.* [Freshman Mathematics – Teaching Mathematics in First-Year Programmes in Technology and the Natural Sciences] (2005:36 R). Stockholm: Swedish National Agency for Higher Education.

Swedish statue-book. (1985). *Skollag.* [The Education Act] (SFS 1985:1100). Retrieved August 4, from http://www.notisum.se/rnp/sls/lag/19851100.htm

Swedish statue-book. (1993). *Högskoleförordning.* [Higher Education Ordinance] (SFS 1993:100). Retrieved August 4, from http://www.notisum.se/rnp/sls/lag/19930100.HTM

Swedish statue-book. (2008). *Förordning om försöksverksamhet med riksrekryterande gymnasial spetsutbildning.* [Ordinance on a Pilot Project for Upper Secondary School Level Cutting-Edge Program with National Recruitment] (SFS 2008:793). Retrieved August 4, from http://www.notisum.se/rnp/sls/lag/20080793.htm

Swedish statue-book. (2010). *Skollag.* [The Education Act] (SFS 2010:800). Retrieved August 4, from http://www.riksdagen.se/Webbnav/index.aspx?nid=3911&bet=2010:800

Taflin, E. (2007). *Matematikproblem i skolan: För att skapa tillfällen till lärande.* [Mathematical Problems in School: To Create Opportunities for Learning] PhD thesis, Umeå University, Faculty of Science and Technology, Mathematics and Mathematical Statistics.

Thorndike, R. L., Hagan, E. P., & Sattler, J. M. (1986). *Stanford-Binet intelligence scale fourth edition. Technical manual.* Chicago: The Riverside Publishing Company.

Torrance, E. P. (1966). *The Torrance Test of Creative Thinking (TTCT).* Lexington, KY: Personell Press, Grinn and Company.

Wallby, K., Carlsson, S., & Nyström, P. (2001). *Elevgrupperingar – en kunskapsöversikt med fokus på matematikundervisningen.* [Grouping of Students – A Knowledge Review Focusing on Mathematics Education]. Stockholm: Liber.

Wallström, C. (2009). *Maximal utveckling för alla. Hur möter skolan elever med goda studieförutsättningar?* [Maximum development for all. How Does the School Meet the Needs of the Students with High Academic Potential?]. Nacka: C&C Organisation och Ledarskap AB.

Wechsler, D. (1991). *Wechsler intelligence scale for children* (3rd ed.). (Wisc-III). San Antonio, TX: Psychological Corporation.

Wiecerkowski, W., Cropley, A. J., & Prado, T. M. (2000). Nurturing talents/gifts in mathematics. In K. A. Heller, F. J. Mönks, R. J. Sternberg, & R. F. Subotnik (Eds.), *International handbook of giftedness and talent* (2nd ed., pp. 413–425). Oxford: Elsevier Science.

Wisconsin Statute 118. (2007a). *General school operations.* Retrieved August 5, from http://www.legis.state.wi.us/statutes/Stat0118.pdf

Wisconsin Statute 121. (2007b). *School finance.* Retrieved August 5, from http://www.legis.state.wi.us/statutes/Stat0121.pdf

Wistedt, I. (2005). Gifted education in Sweden. *ECHA News, 19*(2), 4.

Wistedt, I., & Sundström, M. (in press). Quality and equity in mathematics education – A Swedish perspective. In B. Atweh, et al. (Eds.), *Modelling quality and equity in mathematics education,* Springer Forlag.

Wyndhamn, J. (1993). *Problem-Solving revisited, on school mathematics as a situated practice.* PhD thesis, Linköping Studies in Arts and Science, Linköping University.

Ziegler, A. (2009). Research on giftedness in the 21st century. In L. V. Shavinina (Ed.), *International handbook on giftedness* (pp. 1509–1524). Springer Science+Business Media B.V.

Linda Mattsson
Department of Mathematical Sciences
University of Gothenburg
Sweden

Samuel Bengmark
Department of Mathematical Sciences
Chalmers University of Technology
Sweden

ROZA LEIKIN AND ORA STANGER

7. TEACHERS' IMAGES OF GIFTED STUDENTS AND THE ROLES ASSIGNED TO THEM IN HETEROGENEOUS MATHEMATICS CLASSES

INTRODUCTION

The present study discusses the opportunities that are available to students with high mathematical abilities in school mathematics. Our focus is on teaching mathematically able students (MAS) in heterogeneous mathematics classrooms. Based on individual interviews with teachers, we describe images that teachers hold of mathematically gifted students. By analyzing multiple classroom observations, we characterized the roles that the teachers assign to MAS in the mathematics classroom and found that the teachers use MAS to help them manage the whole-class discussion fluently. At the same time, we found no special mathematical activities that the teachers prepared for MAS in any of the observed lessons. We suggest that mathematics teachers need special preparation for the education of MAS in each and every type of mathematics class.

NCTM (2000) standards stressed the importance of addressing individual differences between students in various aspects of school mathematics: "...Equity does not mean that every student should receive identical instructions; instead it demands that reasonable and appropriate accommodations be made to promote access and attainment for all students" (p. 12). In the past decade, increased attention has been paid to the mathematics education of gifted students because of the awareness of the danger of talent loss (Milgram, 2009). Mathematics educators have argued that teaching students with high abilities in mathematics (mathematically able students, or MAS[1]) requires a special curriculum, special instructional materials, and special teachers (Evered & Karp, 2000; Karp, 2007; Sheffield, 1999; Vogeli, 1997; Leikin, 2009a).

MAS can achieve a high level of mathematical performance when their potential is realized to the greatest extent (NCTM, 1995; Sheffield, 1999; Leikin, 2009a). Students' mathematical potential is determined by their cognitive, affective, and social characteristics (Goldin, 2009; Subbotnik, Pillmeier, & Jarvin, 2009; Sheffield, 1999; Leikin, 2009a; submitted). The realization of the students' potential is a function of the quality of learning opportunities that are provided to them (Leikin, 2009a; in press, under review). Naturally, teachers must provide mathematical opportunities for all students, including the mathematically able ones.

In the last three decades, many educators have called for teaching gifted students in heterogeneous classrooms. These opinions are based on well-established ideological, social, and psychological arguments, but at the same time, providing MAS with appropriate learning opportunities in a heterogeneous mathematics classroom is a

B. Sriraman and K.H. Lee (eds.), The Elements of Creativity and Giftedness in Mathematics, 103–118.

complex task for any mathematics teacher. We therefore focus our study on the opportunities that are available to MAS in practice in a heterogeneous classroom.

THEORETICAL BACKGROUND

Mathematically able Students

MAS differ from other students in several characteristics. The educational literature makes the connection between high mathematical ability and mathematical problem solving (e.g., Barbeau & Taylor, 2008; Krutetskii, 1976; Leikin, Koichu, & Berman, 2009; Sheffield, 2009; Sriraman, 2003). Krutetskii's (1976) fundamental study of mathematical giftedness in school children stressed the components of high mathematical ability. Krutetskii pointed out the general synthetic component called *mathematical cast of mind* and provided detailed characteristics of mathematical abilities in gifted students: memorizing mathematical objects, schemes, principles, and relationships; grasping formal structures; thinking logically in spatial, numeric, and symbolic relationships; switching from direct to reverse trains of thought; generalizing rapidly and broadly; flexibility with mental processes; appreciation of clarity, simplicity, and rationality. Sheffield (2009) described the continuum of levels of mathematical abilities based on students' performance in problem solving. On this continuum, students move from being innumerate, unable to perform simple mathematical computations, to being able to do some mathematics, to being proficient at computation, to being intelligent consumers.

MAS differ from other students in the level of their creativity, reflected in their ability to raise original ideas, as well as in their mental flexibility and fluency. Creativity in school mathematics differs from the creativity of professional mathematicians: "At the K–12 level, one normally does not expect works of extraordinary creativity; however, it is certainly feasible for students to offer new insights" (Sriraman, 2005, p. 23). Mathematical creativity in school students is considered with respect to their previous experiences and to the performances of other students with similar experiences (Leikin, 2009a, b). Liljedahl and Sriraman (2006) agreed that at school level and undergraduate college level it is feasible for students to offer insights and solutions to mathematics, which are new with respect to the mathematics that the students have already learned and to problems they have solved.

Personality characteristics play a crucial role in the development and the realization of intellectual potential (Shani-Zinovich & Zeidner, 2009). Personality characteristics of MAS include openness, conscientiousness, "teachability," self-evaluation, and mathematical inclination (e.g., Shani-Zinovich & Zeidner, 2009; Subotnik et al, 2009). Teachers should take into account these characteristics when teaching MAS. The complexity of the teachers' work with MAS follows from the variety of types of gifted students. Betts and Neihart (1988) identified six gifted child personality types. For example, children of the *successful type* are usually successful academically, are identified as gifted in school, and seek other people's approval; children of the *challenging type* are highly creative but often frustrated or bored; gifted children of the *dropout type* are angry and depressed because the school system does not recognize their abilities and does not address their special educational needs.

When designing instructional activities for MAS, the teachers should take into account these students' specific characteristics, a complex undertaking.

Teachers of MAS

Based on the works of Cropley and McLeod (2004), Maker (1975), Mills (2003), and Hansen and Feldhusen (1994), teachers of MAS need special knowledge and skills, special personal qualities, openness and flexibility, and must be able to value logical analysis and objectivity. Outstanding teachers of the gifted are usually characterized by enthusiasm and self-confidence, the ability to facilitate, strong achievement orientation, and commitment to the role of educator of the gifted. Karp (in press) stresses the need for the teachers' own creativity in order to develop the mathematical creativity of their students. Leikin (accepted) provides an analysis of the characteristics of teachers of MAS, as seen by an expert teacher of the gifted and by his former students. The study demonstrated that the teachers' genuine interest in the subject and their readiness for any challenge (from the students) result in teaching that is interesting and difficult (in other words, challenging) and develops in students motivation, curiosity, willingness to cope with difficulties, and most important, love of the subject. Teachers' kindness to students and pride in their successes leads to respectful teaching that develops in mathematically promising students respect, kindness, and support for peers, qualities that are often mistakenly perceived as missing in talented students. Teachers' creativeness and deep subject matter knowledge open opportunities to inspiring, open, critical, and creative teaching that develops creative, critical, and independent reasoning in students. Teachers of gifted students should be patient and sensitive and have deep pedagogical, didactic, and psychological knowledge relating to gifted students. Finally, an explicit expression of love of mathematics and a sense of humor allow overcoming difficulties and generating a positive atmosphere of joyful learning that promotes the students' sense of humor and kindness.

This analysis shows that expert teachers of MAS address in their teaching all the components of the students' mathematical potential (intellectual, affective, and social), providing students with multiple opportunities for the realization of their potential. The special qualities of these teachers allow for a differential education based on the realization that even classes of gifted students are heterogeneous with respect to the students' abilities.

Because the majority of elementary school MAS learn in heterogeneous classes, the present study focuses on this setting and asks the following questions: What are the teachers' conceptions of MAS? What role do teachers assign to MAS in heterogeneous classes? What learning opportunities do they provide to MAS?

THE STUDY

Participating Teachers

The paper focuses on three 5th and 6th grade elementary school mathematics teachers (Ilana,[2] Hila, and Anat) who participated in the study. The teachers differed in their school mathematical background. Anat successfully completed high-level studies in school mathematics, Hila excelled in mid-level mathematics in school, whereas Ilana studied low-level school mathematics. All the teachers had B.Ed. degrees in mathematics from teacher education colleges. None of the participants underwent systematic preparation in the education of gifted students.

Procedure

The cases study presented in this paper analyzes the conceptions and practices of elementary school mathematics teachers associated with teaching MAS in a heterogeneous mathematics classroom. The empirical study was performed using a qualitative research methodology based on individual semi-structured interviews with three elementary school teachers and on ethnographic observations of their classes. The interviews were conducted before (Int-A) and after (Int-B) lesson observations. Int-A was directed at identifying the teachers' educational background and their conception of mathematically able and gifted students. At this stage, the teachers were not informed about the precise purpose of the study in order to allow ethnographic nature of the observations. Int-B was aimed at the analyzing the decisions made by the teachers during the observed lessons. Observations were focused on the teachers' interactions with MAS. Each teacher was observed during 4–5 consecutive lessons to allow teacher-students interactions during various types of the lessons, although the variability between the lessons turned out to be minor.

We had information about the students' achievements in mathematics and their success on IQ test they took in 3rd grade as part of a national search for gifted students. This enabled us to focus our attention on the participation of MAS in mathematics lessons in a heterogeneous classroom. The interviews and the lessons were video-taped and transcribed.

Data Analysis

Through the content analysis of the interviews and of the observations, we searched for clear explanations by the teachers about who are the gifted students and how they should be taught. We carried out multiple readings of the transcripts and multiple observations of the video tapes. We also searched for the metaphors the teachers provided when characterizing gifted students. In the class observations we paid special attention to (a) the role that teachers assigned (consciously or unconsciously) to their students and (b) the changes in the level of mathematical discussion in the classroom associated with the participation of the gifted students in the discussion.

FINDINGS

Teachers' Images of Gifted Students

We identified three main images of mathematically gifted students held by teachers. Although the images are not disjoint and have certain features in common, we found them sufficiently different to describe each separately.

High abilities as a gift of god. Ilana believes that high mathematical ability is a gift of God and it is child's responsibility to preserve and develop it. Ilana is aware of such special characteristics of gifted students as perfectionism and persistence:

Ilana: They are *perfectionists*, they are *persistent and responsible*. He feels *responsibility for the gift that God gave him.*

Because the other students did not receive this gift, in Ilana's opinion, it is the teacher's responsibility to help the mid- and low-level students. This opinion derives partly from her own experience as a student, when she belonged to the group of mid-achievers. She is therefore more attentive to this group of students.

Ilana: Since I am not coming from the group of excelling and gifted students I *pay attention to mid-level* students and *do my best to strengthen them.* At the same time I *try to provide* excelling students *with their space in the lesson.*

The main characteristics of gifted students that Ilana mentions in the interview are good analytical thinking, reasoning skills, and willingness to learn. In her opinion, gifted students have a different way of thinking, so that the cognitive abilities of gifted students are at the center of Ilana's attention.

Ilana: They [gifted students] have *good reasoning, like learning, and tend to have high achievements* in many fields of learning. They *think differently.*

A gift is like a jug with a narrow opening. Hila thinks that many good things reside inside a gifted student.

Hila: [A gifted students is] like a *jug that releases slowly* what is needed and when it is needed.

Gifted students know better than others what is important in any given situation and for any given problem. They find solutions to different problems in authentic ways. Affective aspects associated with giftedness are expressed in the students' willingness to use their knowledge at their own pace. Her image of gifted students is based on the abilities, behavior, and mathematical performance of one of her students, Itai:

Hila: Itai represents for me a typical gifted student. He is *not the most popular student* in the class, but he *has several friends*. In my opinion, he is *gifted but not excelling* because *he does not study at all*. He knows without studying, and can excel *without having to make many attempts*. He *has difficulty organizing things.*

Ora: Who is gifted in your opinion?

Hila: One who can use something that he learned a year ago, and now when we talk about a different thing *to connect between things*, between concepts and algorithms. He has the ability *to see beyond things*. He can solve *an exercise he never solved before*, without *prompts about how to do it.*

Gifted students have high abilities in many different fields and usually excel in several of them. The following image of a gifted child is based on her niece, whom she calls "brilliant."

Hila: When I think about the gifted I always think about her: *open to new things and new experiences. She does not necessarily excel* in one particular field, but she sees "beyond."

In contrast to Ilana, who makes no reference to creativity, Hila stresses that creativity is one of the basic properties of gifted students because they can discover things and do things without guidance. At the same time, whereas in Ilana's opinion giftedness is characterized by responsibility and motivation, Hila does not mention these properties as characteristics of gifted students.

A gifted student is a cyclamen with a lowered head. For Anat, gifted students are like a cyclamen: special, beautiful, and different from others, with bright colors. But they are also shy and sensitive, and need protection.

Anat: Cyclamen is a protected flower. It is *embarrassed and strange*. At the same time, it is *very special.*

We learn from this image that for Anat the affective characteristics are central in her reasoning about gifted students. These students are not strong and need protection. They are "strange and not always aware" of what is happening around them.

Anat: I am immediately thinking about *his feelings*. I imagine this child as being *honest and naïve*. He is *very sensitive* and *not exactly strong from the social perspective.*

Among the cognitive characteristics of gifted students, Anat mentions their ability *"to struggle with complex problems and their ability to explain themselves perfectly."*[3] Anat connects creativity and high ability with the *"ability to solve problems in ways that other students do not see."*

Table 1. Profiles of gifted students in the eyes of the teachers

The teacher / Images of MAS MAS characteristics	Ilana	Hila	Anat
"Gift"	High mathematical abilities are a God-given gift		
Intellectual characteristics			
Abilities *Broad knowledge*	Above average abilities	Bright and clever. Critical thinking Sees the most Demonstrates his knowledge at his own pace and in his own time Accumulates knowledge	Many special abilities Knows what to do

Table 1. (Continued)

Reasoning / understanding	Good thinking	Good mathematical understanding and reasoning	
Solving complex problems			Able to cope successfully with complex problems
Connectedness / explaining		Connects – between different topics – between different subjects – between previously learned material and new material	Knows how to explain his ideas;
Creativity			
Different from others	Thinks differently from other students	Able to see things that are "beyond"	Sees ways for reaching solutions that others do not see
Solutions to problems		Finds solutions without prompts and in new ways	Succeeds in solving problems in creative ways
Affect / Motivation / Personality			
Learning attitude	Likes learning	Enjoys new learning, new knowledge	
	Perfectionist		
Responsibility	Responsible for the gift he received		
Openness		Open to new things	
Persistence	Willingness to achieve the highest level in learning skills	Does not need to try hard Does not necessarily excel	
Emotional characteristics			Sensitive Discrepancy between mathematical abilities and affective growth
Self-perception		Strong opinion	Low self-esteem
Social skills		Not the most popular in the class Has several friends	Naïve in his relationship with other students
Working skills	Well organized	Has difficulty organizing things Hyperactive	

109

Table 1 summarizes the findings from the interviews and shows the similarities and differences in the teachers' conceptions of gifted students. Although the three teachers agree that MAS have special cognitive abilities which are higher than in other students, they differ in the amount of intellectual characteristics they mention and in their opinions about the personal and emotional characteristics of MAS.

Students' Roles in the Classroom

During all the observed lessons the teachers presented mathematical tasks to the whole class. All the students, including the gifted ones, were asked to cope with the same tasks. But the lessons developed differently in the various classes. Situations in which MAS participated in the lesson showed three repeating patterns, in all of which the gifted students presented their solutions and ideas to the class. Below we describe these situations and illustrate them with episodes from 5th and 6th grade lessons. The episodes were selected based on the frequency of a particular type of student roles in a particular teacher classroom.

MAS as a catalyst for class discussion. In the first type of situations a MAS presents a solution or answer to the teacher's question immediately after the question is posed. In this situation, the gifted student plays the role of a catalyst in the development of the lesson.

Episode 1: Catalyst-1. In the following situation, Yoav (MAS) helps Ilana (the teacher) explain the task to the whole class.

Ilana: Here is the problem:

There is a new 4-floor apartment building on Polygon street. On each floor in the building there is one apartment. Four quadrilaterals are friends who enter the building. They discuss who will live on which floor. They decide that the lower floor will belong to the quadrilateral that was first among the friends to have a particular property. Who are the friends and who can leave on each of the floors?

Ilana: [immediately] Who can explain what should be done in this problem? **Yoav.**[4]

Yoav: We have a building with 4 floors.

Ilana: Tell us who can live in the building.

Yoav: Parallelogram, kite, rhombus, and square.

Ilana conducts a dialog with Yoav, while the other students are silent. She asks Yoav not only to explain to the class what are the tasks required of them, but also to provide the answers. Although the problem is addressed to the whole class, Ilana considers the task to be a complex one and therefore speeds up the development of the lesson by asking a high-ability student. In this case, Yoav provides the answers but both the problem and the solution remain unclear to many students in the class.

Episode 2: Catalyst-2. In the introductory minutes of a lesson on divisibility principles, the teacher (Ilana) attempted to lead students to formulate the rule of divisibility by 4. As in the previous episode, the class is given no time to think about the question. Immediately after formulating the question, Ilana asks Yotam (another MAS in the same class) to answer the question.

Ilana: I choose a number: 104. I want to know whether it is divisible by 4. It is a three-digit number and is not included in the multiplication table. How can I know that it can be divided by 4? **Yotam?**

Yotam: 100 is divisible by 4, plus 4 is divisible by 4.

Ilana: What I am doing to the number. I separate 100 and 4 and I know that...

Yotam: Both 100 and 4 are divisible by 4.

....

Ilana: How much is it 104 divided by 4?

Yotam: 100 divided by 4 is 25, plus 4 divided by 4 is 1. It is 26.

Ilana: Who can repeat what Yotam said?

Clearly, in these two episodes Ilana uses the gifted students as a tool for managing the lesson. In both episodes, she considers the questions to be complex. In the first episode, the problem requires that students think about hierarchy of quadrilaterals. The first problem can have different solutions based on which isosceles trapezoid lives on the first floor (whether it has a pair of equal or parallel sides), the parallelogram occupies the apartment on the second floor (having two pairs of equal sides), and the rectangle and square are on the third and the fourth floors. Note that the discussion did not develop in this direction because Ilana unconsciously assigned Yoav as a catalyst in this episode. The second episode developed in a similar way, although the question was less complex. Ilana explained that in these two cases she "was not sure that all the students would understand the questions, and therefore asked Yoav and Yotam to explain the problem to the class." But no explanation was actually provided, and the geometry lesson continued without any examination of whether other students understood the solution or maybe had different suggestions. In the divisibility lesson the students were required to repeat Yotam's solution. The repetition allowed other students to hear the solution again, and Yotam was clearly bored during this part of the lesson.

MAS as a scaffold for class discussion. In the second type of situations, MAS were asked by the teacher to present a solution or an answer when some of the students in the class had difficulties of various types. In this case, MAS played the role of *scaffolds* and helped the teacher provide additional explanations to other students in the learning process. Often teachers ask MAS when other students answer incorrectly. The following two episodes demonstrate this tendency.

Episode 3: Scaffold-1. In a lesson focusing on approximation and the time units, the students had to find the approximate value of 1,000,000 seconds. Ron gave an incorrect explanation.

Hila: I am writing on the board:
(a) 12 minutes
(b) 12 hours
(c) 12 days
(d) 12 weeks
Which of these time periods is an approximation of 1,000,000 seconds?

Who thinks it is (a)? [counts] eight students [and writes 8 next to "12 minutes"]

Who thinks the answer is (b)? [counts] sixteen students [and writes 16 next to "12 hours"]

How many think it is (c)? [counts] five [and writes 5 next to "12 days"]

Who chose (d)? [counts] one [and writes 1 next to "12 weeks"]

Let's think. More than half of thirty children in the class think that one million seconds are approximately equal to 12 hours, and about a fourth of the students think it is about 12 minutes. Those who want to check can use the calculator. Who wants to share his thoughts with us?

Ron: (c) is correct.

Hila: How did you find this?

Ron: I did sixty multiplied by sixty and multiplied by sixty and got 216000. [Hila writes on the board 60×60×60=216000]

Hila: Who wants to give another explanation? **Tal?**

Tal: The answer is (c). I did 60 by 60 and got 3600, then I multiplied by 60 and by 12 and got 2592000.

Hila: [Tal multiplied] by 12 (days) to get closer to one million.

In Episode 3 Hila provides the entire class an opportunity to solve the task. She collects the answers, and after she receives an incomplete explanation from Ron she asks Tal (one of the MAS in the class) to help Ron by providing the complete solution. Although she does not indicate to Tal explicitly that she expects a complete explanation, he provides the complete solution as a part of Hila's didactic contract with MAS. But several possibilities for discussion inherent in the task remained unutilized. First, some students still wondered why 1000000 was an approximation of 2592000. Second, a reasonable discussion of why about half the students chose option (b), 12 hours, did not take place. These are missed opportunities for providing clear explanations and enabling both MAS and other students to deepen their mathematical understanding and share their reasoning and conclusions with others.

Episode 4: Scaffold 2. In the following episode, Hila asked the class whether Saar's answer was correct and to explain why it was not correct. Two MAS, Tal and Niv, helped Hila in providing the required explanation to the class.

Saar: $^1/_2 \div ^3/_5 = ^3/_5 \div ^1/_2$

Hila: What do you think? We want to know whether Saar is right or not.

Tal: No, he is not.

Hila: Why? How much is this $^1/_2 \div ^3/_5$?

Niv: $^1/_2 \times ^5/_3 = ^5/_6$ and $^3/_5 \times ^2/_1 = ^6/_5$. These ratios are inverse.

As in Episode 3, one could expect a continuation of the discussion that would elaborate on Niv's observation that the resulting fractions on the two sides of equality are inverse. The discussion could be developed, for example, in the direction of a generalization of the type $a \div b = 1 \div (b \div a)$. Although algebra is learned at a later stage of the curriculum, a verbal formulation of the rule may be achieved through class discussion, enabling MAS to move into a new mathematical territory, more challenging than the regular classroom exercises.

MAS as a springboard for class discussion. In the third type of situation, students played the role of a springboard in the development of the lesson, as they provided an opportunity to raise the level of mathematical discussion. This often happens during the concluding discussion of a task. To create a *springboard* situation, the teacher must be open and provide students with the opportunity to develop their ideas. In episodes 5 and 6 Anat goes freely with the students' ideas and encourages them to explain their answers and solutions, although the class still did not learn the concepts and topics that MAS mentioned in their answers.

Episode 5: Springboard-1

Anat: Here are five numbers: 12, 25, 8, 14, 26. Which one is special?

Adi: 25 is a special number, it is odd.

Anat: Additional options. Noam?

Noam: 8, since it is the only one-digit number.

Anat: OK. Elad?

Elad: Twenty six, since it is composed of two even digits

Anat: I think…

Yuval: 26 since it is the only number that does not appear in the multiplication table. It is divisible by 2, but it is greater than 20.

Anat: Very good.

Anat provides all the students in the classroom the opportunity to present their answers, and MAS join the discussion to add their answers when the other students run out of ideas. It is clear that Anat did not expect Elad and Yuval's irregular answers, but gave them the opportunity to present the answer that " nobody thought about."

Episode 6: Springboard-2. In contrast to the previous episode, in which MAS helped Anat broaden the solution space of the task, in the following episode MAS help Anat develop an understanding of a new concept that is on the agenda for the lesson. Yuval and Elad discover differences between two-dimensional and three-dimensional objects, and introduce concepts related to the three dimensions (length, width, and height). Yuval introduces the concept of parallelepiped to the class, and Anat shows her excitement at his knowledge. Elad provides a clear "definition" of a three-dimensional figure.

Anat: You have a set of figures. Each group should classify the figures according to their preferences.

Elad: We divided the figures according to two dimensions and three dimensions and investigated them.

Anat: For example?

Elad: We measured and searched for different properties.

Anat: What do you call this figure [points to a right parallelepiped]?

Elad: It is a rectangle in three dimensions.

Yuval: No, this is a **parallelepiped**.

Anat: Great! **We have not learned this yet**, but this is very good.

....

Elad: Three-dimensional figures have three measures: length, width, and height. Two-dimensional figure have two dimensions: length and width. One-dimensional figures have only one measure – either length or width.

Anat: Put the figures that I gave to you on the table and choose only the three-dimensional ones. Explain why they are three-dimensional.

Surprisingly, Ofek, a regular-level student, asks a non-trivial question, and Anat encourages a discussion about it: *If we remove one of the faces, will the figure still be three-dimensional?* MAS discuss the question together with the other students. Ido-1 gives an incorrect answer and provides a reasonable "scientific" explanation for it, based on his physical understanding of the concept of volume. Yuval concludes with a mathematical definition of the concept of three-dimensionality.

Ofek: *If we remove one of the faces, will the figure still be three-dimensional?*

Anat: Who will answer Ofek?

Ido -1: If we remove one of the faces, the figure will not be three-dimensional.

Yuval: Can you explain why?

Anat: We still have three measures length, width, and height.

Yuval: Still there is a volume.

Ido - 2: Not really. It does not have a volume. There is a hollow. If you put in water, the water level does not rise. From the scientific point of view [there is no volume].

Anat: What do you think? Remove a face from a cube. Is this figure three-dimensional? Maybe not anymore? Maybe it is two-dimensional?

...

Yuval: If I take a cube, even if I remove this [one of its faces] and compare it with something two-dimensional, it is still bigger. It has three measures.

Although initially Anat's agenda was categorization according to the objects' dimensions, as presented by Yuval and Elad, the question posed by Ofek was unexpected, and Ido's answer advanced the discussion with an explanation that was difficult to refute. The MAS were supported by Anat's questions, which led the discussion to a successful solution.

CONCLUDING REMARKS

The present study focused on teaching MAS in heterogeneous classes. We analyzed teachers' conceptions of mathematically gifted students, the roles that the teachers assigned to MAS in their classes, and the opportunities provided to MAS for raising the level of mathematical discussion in the classroom.

We identified three images of MAS held by the teachers. These images include a variety of teachers' conceptions about mathematically gifted and able students, and describe three types of roles that teachers assign to their students in mathematics lessons. Two of the roles, catalyst and scaffold, are usually initiated by a teacher. In many cases, the gifted students willingly share their ideas with the class and initiate their participation. MAS participation in the role of springboards can be initiated either by the teacher or by the students themselves. Often the answers of MAS have the potential to raise the level of mathematical discussion, and in springboard situations, we found actual changes in the level of mathematics. In catalyst and scaffold situations, however, student answers are predicted by the teacher, and if unpredicted elements appear they are usually overlooked. In springboard situations student answers are often unpredicted by the teachers and serve as an initial point of meaningful mathematical discussion.

We found that every type of situation can occur in every lesson, but their frequency differed for each teacher. We therefore tried to identify the relationships between the teachers' conceptions of gifted students and the roles they assigned to students in classroom discussions. Ilana perceives mathematical ability as a gift of God, and compound of a small number of positive characteristics, both intellectual and affective. Because at the basis of high abilities is a gift of God, Ilana does not see the need to provide special treatment for these students, although she agrees that MAS should be given "space for their learning." In her lessons, MAS often played catalyst and scaffold roles, whereas springboard situations were rare in her lessons.

Hila's conception includes an extensive list of characteristics that testify to the intellectual strength of MAS. She finds that although MAS do not need to make an attempt to succeed in learning, they are not necessarily high achievers because some of them are not well organized. When MAS participated in the classroom discussion at Hila's lessons, it was mainly as scaffolds, but at times they also acted a catalysts and less often as springboards. Anat regards gifted students as expert problem solves, but in her opinion, they have social and emotional problems, which is probably why we almost never found MAS in the role of catalysts. At Ilana's lessons, MAS played primarily the roles of scaffolds and springboards.

Generally the teachers provided MAS with opportunities to exhibit their mathematical knowledge and abilities in the classroom. But we rarely found classroom situation specifically designed by the teachers for the benefit of these students. In other words, whereas MAS helped the teachers in lesson management, they did not receive special treatment in any of the observed lessons. This finding contradicts our conception that it is necessary to provide special tasks for MAS to promote the realization of their intellectual potential (Milgram, 2009; Leikin, 2009).

None of the study participants had systematic knowledge (acquired at teacher development courses) in the field of gifted education. When teachers talked about their conception of gifted students, they clearly based their reasoning on their mathematical experiences as students and on their experience in teaching MAS. For example, in her interview, Ilana connected her conception of giftedness with her own experience as a student: "Because I'm not coming from the group of excelling and gifted students I *pay attention to teaching mid-level* students." Hila referred to one of the children she knows to be gifted ("Itai represents for me a typical gifted student...") and described the characteristics of MAS by reference to him.

The findings of this study stress the importance of teacher awareness about the ways in which they work with MAS and the opportunities they miss in their lessons that could advance MAS effectively. These findings highlight the importance of systematic knowledge in the field of mathematically gifted students, and of awareness of students' intellectual, personality, and affective characteristics. Mathematics teachers must be equipped with instructional materials for working with MAS and with the skills needed for teaching these students.

The set of teachers' images of MAS and the types of MAS roles identified in this study are clearly not exhaustive, and broader studies, involving a larger number of teachers both in elementary and secondary school, could identify additional images and types of roles. Finally, taking into account the teachers' different mathematical backgrounds, we claim that the level of the teachers' mathematical knowledge may affect their conceptions of MAS and their approach to teaching gifted students, which is yet another topic for future investigation.

NOTES

[1] As in Leikin (2009, accepted) we use the terms *mathematically able* students, *mathematically promising* students, and *highly able* students, together with the term *mathematically gifted*. All three groups are characterized by high mathematical potential.

[2] All names of teachers and students are pseudonyms.

[3] Some of the quotations from the interviews with teachers are incorporated in the body of the text, others are given as excerpts.

[4] The names of MAS appear in bold.

REFERENCES

Barbeau, E., & Taylor, P. (Eds.). (2009). *Mathematical challenge in and beyond the classroom: ICMI Study-16 Volume*. Springer.

Betts, G., & Neihart, M. (1988). Profiles of the gifted and talented. *Gifted Child Quarterly*.

Betts, G. T. (1991). Autonomous learning and the gifted. In G. Davis (Ed.), *Handbook of gifted education*. NeedhamHeights, MA: Allyn and Bacon.

Cropley, A., & McLeod, J. (1986). Preparing teachers of the gifted. *ZDM-International review of education, 32*, 125–136.

Davis, G. A., & Rimm, S. B. (2004). *Education of the gifted and talented* (5th ed.). Boston: Pearson Education Press.

Goldin, G. A. (2009). The affective domain and students' mathematical inventiveness. In R. Leikin, A. Berman, & B. Koichu (Eds.), *Creativity in mathematics and the education of gifted students* (pp. 149–163). Sense Publishers (in press).

Hansen, J. B., & Feldhusen, J. F. (1994). Comparison of trained and untrained teachers of gifted students. *Gifted Child Quarterly, 38*, 115–121.

Karp, A. P. (in press). Teachers of the mathematically gifted tell about themselves and their profession. *Roeper Review*.

Karp, A. P. (Ed.). (2007). A. R. Maizelis: In Memoriam [Pamiati A. R. Maizelisa]. St. Petersburg: SMIO Press. (In Russian)

Krutetskii, V. A. (1976). *The psychology of mathematical abilities in schoolchildren*. (J. Teller, Trans., J. Kilpatrick & I. Wirszup, Eds.). Chicago: The University of Chicago Press.

Leikin, R. (accepted). Teaching the mathematically gifted: Featuring a teacher. *Canadian Journal of Science, Mathematics and Technology Education*.

Leikin, R. (in press). Teaching mathematically gifted. *Gifted Education International, 27*(2).

Leikin, R., Koichu, B., & Berman, A. (2009). Mathematical giftedness as a quality of problem-solving acts. In R. Leikin, A. Berman, & B. Koichu (Eds.), *Creativity in mathematics and the education of gifted students* (pp. 115–127). Rotterdam, the Netherlands: Sense Publisher.

Leikin, R. (2009a). Bridging research and theory in mathematics education with research and theory in creativity and giftedness. In R. Leikin, A. Berman, & B. Koichu (Eds.), *Creativity in mathematics and the education of gifted students* (pp. 383–409). Rotterdam, the Netherlands: Sense Publishers.

Leikin, R. (2009b). Exploring mathematical creativity using multiple solution tasks. In R. Leikin, A. Berman, & B. Koichu (Eds.), *Creativity in mathematics and the education of gifted students* (pp. 129–145). Rotterdam, the Netherlands: Sense Publisher.

Liljedahl, P., & Sriraman, B. (2006). Musings on mathematical creativity. *For The Learning of Mathematics, 26*, 20–23.

Maker, C. J. (1975). *Training teachers for the gifted and talented: A comparison of models*. Reston, VA: The council for exceptional children.

Mills, C. J. (2003). Characteristics of effective teachers of gifted students: Teacher background and personality styles of students. *Gifted Child Quarterly, 47*, 272–281.

Milgram, R. & Hong, E. (2009). Talent loss in mathematics: Causes and solutions. In R. Leikin, A. Berman, & B. Koichu (Eds.), *Creativity in mathematics and the education of gifted students* (pp. 149–163). Rotterdam, the Netherlands: Sense Publishers.

National Council of Teachers of Mathematics (NCTM). (1995). *Report of the NCTM task force on the mathematically promising*. NCTM News Bulletin, 32.

National Council of Teachers of Mathematics (NCTM). (2000). *Principles and standards for school mathematics*. Reston, VA: NCTM.

Sheffield, L. J. (Ed.). (1999). *Developing mathematically promising students.* Reston, VA: National Council of Teachers of Mathematics.

Sriraman, B. (2003). Mathematical giftedness, problem solving, and the ability to formulate generalizations. *The Journal of Secondary Gifted Education, 14,* 151–165.

Sriraman, B. (2005). Are giftedness & creativity synonyms in mathematics? An analysis of constructs within the professional and school realms. *The Journal of Secondary Gifted Education, 17,* 20–36.

Shani-Zinovich, I., & Zeidner, M. (2009). On being a gifted adolescent: developmental, affective, and social issues. In R. Leikin, A. Berman, & B. Koichu (Eds.), *Creativity in mathematics and the education of gifted students* (pp. 195–219). Rotterdam, the Netherlands: Sense Publishers.

Subotnik, R. F., Pillmeier, E., & Jarvin, L. (2009). The psychosocial dimensions of creativity in mathematics: Implications for gifted education policy. In R. Leikin, A. Berman, & B. Koichu (Eds.), *Creativity in mathematics and the education of gifted students* (pp. 165–179). Rotterdam, the Netherlands: Sense Publishers.

Roza Leikin
Faculty of Education
Research and Advancement of Giftedness and Excellence (RANGE) Center
University of Haifa

Ora Stanger
Faculty of Education
University of Haifa

BHARATH SRIRAMAN, NARGES YAFTIAN
AND KYEONG HWA LEE

8. MATHEMATICAL CREATIVITY AND
MATHEMATICS EDUCATION

A Derivative of Existing Research

INTRODUCTION

In this chapter, we address the notion of mathematical creativity by taking into account specific research findings from contemporary literature. We do not attempt a summative review or a meta-synthesis of what is known, instead we focus on findings related to what it means to solve a problem in mathematics, and unpack different constituent ideas in mathematical creativity, such as "incubation". The chapter is a derivative of what is known at this point in time. and builds heavily on Gontran Ervynck's (1991) influential contribution on mathematical creativity.

Various chapters in this book have alluded to the fact that there isn't a conventional definition per se of mathematical creativity or there are various definitions for it (Mann, 2005; Sriraman, 2005). In this regard, some questions come to the mind, For instance:

- When students solve a problem whose solution is known previously, is this considered creative work?
- Does creativity occur in a mathematical activity when students solve an old problem in a new way? Or,
- Does creativity refer to just finding an authentic, new idea?

The challenges in the identification and development of mathematical creativity and answering these questions are due to the large variety in definitions and characteristics of mathematical creativity found in the literature. Even though describing the structure of mathematical creativity and its characteristics is difficult, numerous definitions are available and in fact compatible.

The two well-known French mathematicians Hadamard and Poincaré believed that creativity is a process by which the mathematician makes choices between questions that are fruitful, i.e., leading to the results rather than those that lead to nothing new (Sriraman, 2005). Creativity is not only related to the original work of mathematicians but is also discovering something not already known by one- even if the result is hitherto known to others (Sriraman, 2004).

Ervynck (1991) points out, that creativity is a human activity, which acts upon and generates new mathematics. He asserts it plays a vital role in the full cycle of advanced mathematical thinking[1] and works towards possible conjectures made in developing mathematical theories. It is an essential factor when new ideas are formulated or when an old idea is presented in a new manner. According to him, formulating the definition of a new valuable concept using previous concepts is an example of creative activity, as is solving an old problem in a new way. We discuss these ideas further in the next section of the paper.

In a conversation about the notion of mathematical creativity (Liljedahl & Sriraman, 2006), Sriraman proposed a differentiation be made between creativity at the professional and school levels. He suggested that at the professional level mathematical creativity be defined as:

1. *the ability to produce original work that significantly extends the body of knowledge (which could also include significant syntheses and extensions of known ideas)*
2. *opens up avenues of new questions for other mathematicians (p. 18).*

And at the school levels as:

1. *the process that results in unusual (novel) and/or insightful solution(s) to a given problem or analogous problems, and/or*
2. *the formulation of new questions and/or possibilities that allow an old problem to be regarded from a new angle (p. 19).*

This differentiation is consistent with the view of Hadamard (1945) that:

> Between the work of the student who tries to solve a problem in geometry or algebra and a work of invention, one can say that there is only a difference of degree, a difference of level, both works being of a similar nature (p. 104).

Answering questions about identifying and developing mathematical creativity would help us to develop appropriate teaching methods. In this chapter some approaches to identify and develop mathematical creativity are discussed in addition to the constructs that constitute mathematical creativity.

IDENTIFICATION AND DEVELOPMENT OF MATHEMATICAL CREATIVITY

According to Ervynck (1991), mathematical creativity cannot occur in a vacuum and needs a context in which the individual moves forward through previous experiences. Previous experiences provide an appropriate environment for creative development. For instance, Zhong et al. (2008) state that the capability to relate vaguely associated components underlies many originalities and creations in fields such as physics and mathematics. There is almost little or no literature related to the synthetic abilities of "ordinary" individuals, except for literature that examines polymathy (Sriraman, 2009a). However, synthetic abilities are commonly found in eminent samples of creators. Recently psychologists have put forth the view that creativity is domain general as opposed to domain specific (Plucker & Zabelina, 2009).

Poincaré (1948) highlighted that discovery in mathematics is combination of ideas. He believed that there are a lot of these combinations but only a few of them are fruitful. Before finding these useful combinations, a large number of them are constructed and then meaningful combinations are distinguished from meaningless ones. This process even though explicitly formulated by Poincaré is by and large unconscious. Creating is to form, recognize and choose important and useful combinations. The rules about how to make the choice among possible combinations are not necessarily formulate-able; it is mostly felt rather than formulated, and in that sense is more related to affect than to cognition.

In the words of Hadamard (1945), there is no sieve to make the choice rather it is influenced by individual's emotional sensibility. The affective relationship is not surprising given the correspondence between aesthetics and creativity among mathematicians (Brinkmann & Sriraman, 2009). However contrary to the reflective writings of eminent mathematicians where one often encounters a direct variation between aesthetics and creativity, Brinkmann and Sriraman (2009) report that many working mathematicians often convey a reciprocal relationship between aesthetics and creativity, particularly when mathematical results and proofs are arrived at with considerable strain and stamina.

The ability to create an object in mathematics is an example of mathematical creativity. For analyzing mathematical creativity at a level of generating new mathematics in new contexts, it is essential that one considers the nature of different branches of mathematics (Ervynck, 1991). For instance, the nature of mathematics in geometry is different from mathematics in algebra, in the sense that a certain aptitude for visualization plays a vital role in generating geometry. The nature of proof in geometry is also very different from algebra (Moreno & Sriraman, 2005). Recent studies in the philosophy of mathematics have shown that visualization has played an important historical role in some remarkable mathematical discoveries in the field of Analysis and is an integral part of mathematical practice (e.g., Bråting & Pejlare, 2008).

Ervynck (1991) views a mathematical theory as a network consisting of concepts and the relations among them, in which concepts are considered as nodes and relations are arrows which connect the concepts. One can hypothesize that one of the key components in mathematical creativity can be an insight into constructing and developing such a network. Thus, a synthetic view of a creative act in mathematics could consist of: creating a new fruitful mathematical concept through- combining concepts or relations; discovering an unknown relation; and reorganizing the structure of a mathematical theory. In the above described sense, a creative work of mathematics could even be making a change or modification in the network of concepts. For instance, in the majority of calculus books, the concept of integral is introduced after the derivative but one could think it is better and more historically congruent to teach derivatives after integrals. Thus, when a person decides or thinks about reforming a network of concepts to improve it even for pedagogical reasons, though new mathematics is not produced the person is engaged in a creative mathematical activity. Therefore, another tentative definition of mathematical creativity building on Ervynck's (1991) definition might be:

Mathematical creativity is the ability to solve problems and/or to develop thinking [cognitive] structures about a mathematical concept or set of concepts considering both the historical development of a concept as well as its logico-deductive framework.

Rickart (1996) gives a structural description to Poincaré's famous use of the Gestalt metaphor of *preparation-incubation-illumination*. He writes

"Mathematical creativity consists in replacing a given familiar mathematical structure with a larger one that is a previously unknown good mathematical structure. Just as for Poincaré, the extensions are unplanned aside from things learned in the preliminary work on the problem, and good extensions are the beautiful ones, which are forced into the consciousness by their beauty" (Rickart, 1996, p. 296)

Ervynck (1991) further unpacks components of mathematical creativity by breaking it down into the constituent elements of understanding, intuition, insight and generalization. These elements were emphasized by the Gestaltists as well. As stated earlier, a creative person needs to understand the structure, concepts, relations and nature of the branch of mathematics they are working within. However, understanding alone is not sufficient for creating and this understanding needs to be coupled with insights (and intuition) about the concepts and their relations, in order to make a meaningful change or contribution. The role of insight in creative mathematical activities is vital because it is essentially detailed knowledge within the domain they are situated in. In Lakatos's (1976) view, intuition in mathematics plays a vital role not only in creating concepts but also in proving truth or falsity of the conjectures. Even though intuition alone is insufficient, it creates a pathway to help a person to form the concept image which is adequately close to its formal definition. Consequently, it leads to present plausible conjectures and then test these conjectures. As a consequence, deeper insight and more accurate hypothesis are reached which ultimately lead to generalization, in cases where the person generalizes into other domains or contexts. Thus, generalization is a form of creative mathematical activity (Sriraman, 2003). It may be useful to keep in mind Polya's (1962) statement, "Thus all human cognition begins with intuitions, proceeds from thence to conceptions, and ends with ideas (p. 103).

THE PROCESS OF CREATIVE MATHEMATICAL ACTIVITY

Is mathematical creativity the result of accidental phenomena or chance? The role of chance cannot be denied. There are numerous historical anecdotes of Archimedes, Kekulé, Pasteur and others stumbling upon remarkable discoveries as a result of chance. But it is unfair and incorrect to attribute remarkable discovery solely to chance and ignore the other stages. The Gestaltists introduced a four-stage process for problem solving[2] consisting of: preparation, incubation, illumination and verification (Wallas, 1926). At the first stage, preparation, one forces oneself consciously to work hard on a new problem or an idea. When no solution is forthcoming, the problem is put aside, and one's mind needs to relax to make the necessary connections. In other words incubation starts. Rickart (1996) comments this is a more frequent occurrence than is acknowledged. He gives instances of temporarily forgetting the name of a person when meeting them, only to remember it moments later. However these "incubatory" moments occur with such rapidity each day (forgetting where keys are placed etc) that not much attention is given to them. On a macroscopic scale, we can say that ideas are related in a quiet and unforced manner at the incubation stage, finally resulting in a "Eureka" moment (which means "I have found it"). In other words, illumination occurs. Polya (1945) also believed that sometimes, after hard work, it was better to leave the problem to rest, with the possibility of gaining a better result with less endeavor after a period of time has elapsed. The final stage, verification, consists of expressing the results in mathematical language and justifying in a formal manner. As Tall (1991) states "the results of the illuminative break-through are subjected to the cold analysis of the light of day, refining the assumptions so that the deductions will stand analytic scrutiny" (p. 15). The product of a mathe-matically creative act needs acceptance from the mathematical community. Sriraman (2004) conducted a qualitative study involving five creative mathematicians to determine whether the Gestalt model was still valid and reported that, in general, the mathematicians' creative processes followed the four-stage model of Wallas and this model is still applicable today. We further discuss this model in the next section of the chapter.

THE WALLAS MODEL OF PROBLEM SOLVING

Preparation, the first stage of the Wallas' model of the process of creative problem solving, emphasizes the individual's experience when struggling consciously and voluntarily with the problem for a period of time. The problem solver is interested and is actively searching and gathering necessary information and facts related to the task. At this stage there are some gaps and inconsistencies in existing facts, which led to mental impasses and dead ends. After a period of hard work on solving the problem and no gained progress in this initial effort, the problem is laid aside intentionally without conscious attention towards the problem and this is the beginning of second stage, namely incubation. As stated in the previous section, most of us have had this experience either in our everyday life or in academic problems. At this stage one leaves the unresolved problem and takes a break as an unconscious step directed to the solution, so that some beneficial insight is achieved. In other words, incubation allows the solution to come to mind after a temporary shift of attention to other domain. The existence and effects of incubation are confirmed in a meta-analysis of past empirical studies on incubation (Sio & Ormerod, 2009).

Although mechanisms underlying incubation are vague and complex (Chamorro-Premuzic, 2009), literature reports many scattered hypotheses to explain the role of incubation period in creative problem solving: hypotheses such as
- fatigue[3] hypothesis (Christensen, 2005; Sio & Ormerod, 2009a; Sio & Ormerod, 2009b; Vul & Pashler, 2007, Ellwood et al., 2009),
- unconscious work (Hadamard, 1945; Christensen, 2005: Liljedahl, 2004; Sio & Ormerod, 2009a; Sio & Ormerod, 2009b; Kim, 2009; Wallas, 1926), and
- forgetting fixation (Christensen, 2005; Davidson, 1995; Liljedahl, 2004; Seabrook & Dienes, 2003; Vul & Pashler., 2007; Zhong et al., 2008).

The fatigue hypothesis offers the idea that incubation effects are due to the fact that during a hard work on the problem, one becomes exhausted mentally. Incubation is essentially the recovery process from mental fatigue that allows for the solution to burst into the mind. "The role of incubation may be to dispel fatigue, or to help problem solvers disperse the effects of prior directions that set them on a rigid path" (Kim, 2009, p. 189). The unconscious work hypothesis states that one releases active attention to the problem which leads to unconscious processes in solving the problem. Incubation provides the opportunity to shift attention from the problem to other issues and leads to an insight or a feeling or an "Aha!" experience. After making large initial attempts at solving the problem leading to seeming dead ends or impasse, the period of incubation leads to providing the additional and necessary insight for seeing the problem differently, towards an unanticipated and sudden realization about either the solution or a hint on the path to solve the problem. Another popular hypothesis of incubation is forgetting fixation. This hypothesis states that during numerous initial attempts to reach the solution of the problem under consideration or the plausible pathways of solution, often one has concentrated too much on some strategies and relationships with unrelated facts or ideas that have acted as blockers or conflicts or barriers to provide creative insights into an unsolved problem. To persist towards a solution, one acts inappropriately on these blockers and causes further incorrect paths towards the solution. Setting aside the problem for a period of time and doing something unrelated may lead to break the fixation on this past experience. And this may result in the required insights to the surface to approach the problem in a new direction. In the history of discoveries, there are several success- ful problem solvers not essentially engaging in the problem when a solution came to their mind (Kim, 2009).

If incubation stage results in accomplishment, in the third stage, illumination, one experiences an "Aha!" moment, which is an unanticipated and unforeseen flash of insight. An "Aha!" experience is "a moment of sublime clarity that brings an intuitive awareness of the answer to a problem with which one has been struggling. In other words, it is an effective experience that yields an insight into a hitherto unsolvable problem" (Sriraman, 2009b, p. 37). A literature review has reported that often the "Aha!" experience has a helpful and strongly transformative effect on a student's beliefs and attitudes towards mathematics and their capability to do mathematics (Liljedahl, 2004, p. 213).

After getting through these three stages, there is a last stage, verification, where the final product is worked out in closer detail to get approval from the mathematical community. That is, the aim of verification is to confirm the accuracy of results of the "Aha!" experience and includes checking, refining, expressing, evaluating, confirming, writing out, editing, convincing and finally publishing the results. In other words, the final product is polished and survived.

In summary, mind illuminations never occur except after a conscious and voluntary attempt in a period of time. Therefore, with no endeavor, one should not expect an inspiration of solution. It is important to make conscious efforts that may seem useless or unsuccessful, even if chosen paths may seem to lead us completely astray. Poincaré (1948) states that these efforts are not barren as the person thinks and they can make the unconscious machine move. This machine without those efforts can neither move nor create anything.

Thus, although the role of chance in creativity should be considered, attributing it to a pure chance is not correct and chance consists of numerous stages. For example, in the case of Archimedes before that special moment in which he cried

"I have found it!" and ran into to the streets naked, he had completed the preparation, was under undue pressure which led him to put the problem aside and slip into incubation in the bath tub (pun intended).

As mentioned above, Wallas (1926) proposed a four-stage process for problem solving consisting of preparation, incubation, illumination, and verification. The incubation phase has been somewhat vague, and has been less accessible to scientific inquiry until recently. However, the preparation and verification stages have been the subject of considerable research inside both cognitive and differential psychology (Ellwood et al., 2009). Incubation phases are now the subject of investigation of researchers working on the neuroscience of mathematical thinking, in which brain activity in an orchestrated Aha! moment can in fact captured via physiological evidence[4].

MORE REMARKS ON INCUBATION

Incubation as one of four primary stages of creative thought is a term introduced by Wallas (1926) to refer to the period of time away from conscious problem solving after attempting to solve the problem which needs wider knowledge and insight. It represents the idea that a solution is more achievable if work on the problem is interrupted, instead of continuing without interruption (Vul & Pashler, 2007). The problem solver benefits from an incubation period and it gives an opportunity either to relax or to recover from mental fatigue so that one becomes mentally fresh and ultimately resolves the problem.

A number of studies have examined the role of an incubation period in creative problem solving. For instance Sio & Ormerod (2007) conducted a meta-analytic[5] review of empirical studies that have investigated incubation effects on problem solving. They noted that one theoretical reason for studying incubation is because it is closely associated with insightful thinking. According to this report and others similar to it (Vul & Pashler, 2008), understanding the role of incubation period may also allow us to make use of it more efficiently to foster creativity in problem solving, classroom learning, and working environments. Educators try to incorporate incubation periods in classroom activity in temporal pauses during classroom discourse (Barnes, 2000) or extended time periods for project related learning (Sriraman, 2003), and positive incubation results in positive effects in promoting students' creativity (Sriraman, 2004, Sriraman, 2005) and evident for the mathematicians (Kaufman & Sternberg, 2006). Incubation should not be neglected in the classroom. Students should be encouraged to engage in challenging problems and experience this aspect of problem solving, till a flash of insight results in the "Eureka" or "Aha!" moment and the solution is born (Sriraman, 2009b; Sriraman & Lee, 2010). The benefits of a period of incubation are completely evident for mathematicians (Kaufman & Sternberg, 2006).

Incubation should not be neglected in the classroom. Students should be encouraged engaging in challenging problems and experience this aspect of problem solving, till a flash of insight bursts accompanying "Eureka" or "Aha!" and the solution is born.

FALLIBILITY AND CRATIVE MATHEMATICAL ACTIVITY

One of the characteristics of creative mathematical activity is fallibility (Ervynck, 1991). Mathematical creativity is a human being activity, so it may be accompanied by human error. From Lakatos's (1976) point of view, mathematics does not proceed in a step by step and systematic manner. As a result, errors exist and cause deficiencies and flaws. In other word, creative mathematical activities may be accompanied high insights but there may be flawed proofs, such as initial proofs of Four Color Theorem[6], the various proofs of the fifth postulate of Euclid and, the diverse proofs of the Poincaré Conjecture[7].

Although creative mathematical activity is fallible, this probability of fallibility leads to eventual major successes. For instance, the various proofs of the fifth postulate of Euclid presented with flaws, resulted in discovery of non-Euclidean geometry. The other example is the Poincaré Conjecture that mathematicians made efforts to prove for almost one century and finally in 2003, after 99 years, it was proved by the Russian mathematician Grigory Perelman. We dare say that Perelman's proof was the result of creative attempts of group of mathematicians for about 100 years, though their proofs consisted of flaws and deficiencies. Fallibility of creative mathematical activity is a characteristic which some people may find hard to accept. Because it does not lead to the necessary certainty for them, they prefer to seek algorithms that provide the assurance to solve a given set of problems (Ervynck, 1991). The reason may go back to their mathematical training and may also be due to the fact that they are not familiar with the real work of mathematicians.

THINKING AS MATHEMATICIANS[8]

One of the goals of mathematics educators is to foster students to become familiar with real work of mathematicians and to think as mathematicians. Intentionally or unintentionally, most students are taught mathematics in a manner, that they imagine mathematics is just logical, provable, sure, clear, checkable, reasonable, precise, exact, neat. These students are not aware of mathematics' back stage (Hersh, 1991), of how mathematics is developed. "In the words of *Richard Skemp* current approaches to undergraduate teaching tend to give students the product of mathematical thought rather than the process of mathematical thinking" (Tall, 1991, p. 3, italics added by authors).One may have observed some instructors who have forgotten a theorem's proof or a solution to a problem during their teaching sessions and turning their back on the class, writing something in the corner of the board secretly, and immediately, erasing it after reaching the answer, and not allowing students to look at this necessary work. As opposed to these instructors, we are interested in revealing the back stages of mathematics (Hersh, 1991), the necessary intuitions and the process of reaching the answers. This way, learners do not think of mathematics as a neat, clear, and explicit subject at the beginning and they may dare to take risks, make mistakes, efforts to be a creative person in mathematics and, able to play their role in generating new mathematics and taking part in active mathematics learning.

Students should understand that there is a large difference between the way in which a mathematical idea is created and the way in which it is offered. This dichotomy between creating and learning has been investigated by the late Leone Burton (e.g., Burton, 2004). It is necessary to emphasize that during the creation of mathematical ideas, mathematics is sometimes fallible and mathematicians encounter mistakes and dead ends in the pathways leading to new ideas. It is generally accepted that, it is not easy to think as mathematicians and there is not definitely any formal procedure or magical algorithm that one follows them to be able to do mathematics. Stillman et al. (2009) suggest: "[t]he use of a student-centered inquiry approach that encourages students to think like mathematicians, asking questions that enable them to make sense of mathematics" (p. 16). During the process of posing, answering fundamental questions such as: "who, what, when, where, why and how" students think deeply and investigate, create and extend mathematical challenges (Stillman et al. 2009).

Stillman et al. (2009) offer the following model which can influence the design of instruction in ways that result in improving students' understandings and give deeper insight into mathematical processes so that students are encouraged to think like mathematicians and construct mathematical ideas for themselves. They believe that students of all ages can learn to deepen their mathematical reasoning and enjoyment by asking themselves these questions. During creative mathematical activities students can utilize the following heuristic model.

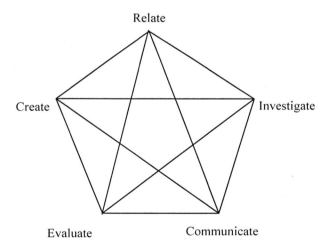

Figure 1. Heuristics used whilst solving challenges (Stillman et al. 2009, p. 17).

"They might do the following:
– Relate the problem to other problems that they have solved.
– Investigate the problem. Think deeply and ask questions.
– Evaluate their findings.
– Communicate their results.
– Create new questions to explore" (Stillman et al. 2009, p. 19).

It appears that this model is a backbone of the path in mathematician's mind when doing creative mathematical activities. There are close relationships between this model and the Wallas model and that many of the processes mentioned in the Wallas model correspond to the above model. For instance, in the Wallas model, one searches and gathers required facts related to the issue which is analogous to "Investigate". Checking, refining and editing in the verification stage are analogous to the component of "Evaluate". In the Wallas model, one requires to express, confirm, convince and publish the results for the purposes of approval from mathematical community which is encapsulated in "Communicate".

CONCLUSION

Human beings are naturally adept at learning from birth until death- it is a biological and evolutionary response to our changing environment. Therefore, one of the goals of any educational system should be fostering creative people to be able to make well informed and critical decisions and choices in unexpected conditions. Although dependency of creativity to intelligence has often been assumed, most mathematics educators recognize cognitive processes, their components and characteristics which constitute creativity. Therefore, they do not attribute creativity simply to intelligence (Sriraman & Kyymaz, 2009). Educators believe that creativity can be fostered if its constituent components are considered. "Mathematics as an intellectual domain stands at or near the top of any hierarchical list of intellectual domains ordered according to the extent to which creativity is evident in disciplinary activity or production "(Silver, 1997, p. 75). Hence, creativity should be considered during mathematics curriculum development at any level of study including university. Further, providing suitable learning environments and by giving confidence to students during creative learning activities to think like mathematicians can only benefit the community of mathematicians.

NOTES

[1] Tall (1991) remarks that Gontran Ervynck coined the usage "advanced mathematical thinking" in the 1980's.

[2] Since problem refers to an unknown situation, problem solving can be considered as a creative mathematical activity.

[3] Other names of this hypothesis are *relieve fatigue* (Vul & Pashler, 2007) or *fatigue dissipation* (Christensen, 2005).

[4] Personal communication with Stephen Campbell, founder of Engrammetron- Educational Neurosciences laboratory at Simon Fraser University.

[5] There were 117 studies included in this meta-analysis that most of them support the existence of incubation effects on problem solving.

[6] "The four color theorem—first conjectured in 1853 by Francis Guthrie—states that every plane separated into regions may be colored using no more than four colors in such a way that no two adjacent regions receive the same color. This theorem was proved in 1977 using a computer-assisted proof" (Calude, 2009, p. 1).

[7] This conjecture is: "every 3-manifold with trivial fundamental group is homeomorphic to the 3-sphere" (Thurston, 1982, p. 358).

[8] For a more detailed treatment of ambiguity and paradoxes in mathematics, see Byers, W. (2007). How Mathematicians Think. Princeton University Press.

REFERENCES

Barnes, M. (2000). Magical moments in mathematics: Insights into the process of coming to know. *For the Learning of Mathematics, 20*(1), 33–43.

Bråting, K., & Pejlare. (2008). Visualizations in mathematics. *Erkenntnis, 68*(3), 345–358.

Brinkmann, A., & Sriraman, B. (2009). Aesthetics and creativity: An exploration of the relationship between the constructs. In B. Sriraman & S. Goodchild (Eds.), *Festschrift celebrating Paul Ernest's 65th Birthday* (pp. 57–80). Information Age Publishing.

Burton, L. (2004). *Mathematicians as enquirers*. The Netherlands: Kluwer Academic Publishers.

Calude, C. S., & Calude, E. (2009). *The complexity of the four colour theorem*. CDMTCS Research Report, 368. Retrieved from http://www.cs.auckland.ac.nz/CDMTCS//researchreports/368cris.pdf

Chamorro-Premuzic, T. (2009). Creative process. In B. Kerr (Ed.), *Encyclopedia of giftedness, creativity and talent* (pp. 188–191). Thousand Oaks, CA: Sage Publications.

Christensen, B. T. (2005). *Creative cognition: Analogy and incubation*. Unpublished doctoral dissertation, Department of Psychology, University of Aarhus, Denmark.

Davidson, J. E. (1995). The suddenness of insight. In R. J. Sternberg & J. E. Davidson (Eds.), *The nature of insight* (pp. 125–155). Cambridge, MA: MIT Press.

Dubinsky, E. (1991). Reflective abstraction in advanced mathematical thinking. In D. Tall (Ed.), *Advanced mathematical thinking* (pp. 95–123). New York: Kluwer Academic Publishers.

Ellwood, S., Pallier, G., Snyder, A., & Gallate, J. (2009). The incubation effect: Hatching a solution? *Creativity Research Journal, 21*(1), 6–14.

Ervynck, G. (1991). Mathematical creativity. In D. Tall (Ed.), *Advanced mathematical thinking* (pp. 42–52). New York: Kluwer Academic Publishers.

Hadamard, J. (1945). *The psychology of invention in the mathematical field*. Princeton University Press.

Hersh, R. (1991). Mathematics has a front and a back. *Synthese, 88*(2), 127–133.

Kaufman, J. C., & Sternberg, R. J. (Eds.). (2006). *The international handbook of creativity*. Cambridge: Cambridge University Press.

Kim, K. H. (2009). Creative problem solving. In B. Kerr (Ed.), *Encyclopedia of giftedness, creativity and talent* (pp. 188–191). Sage Publications.

Lakatos, I. M. (1976). *Proofs and refutations: The logic of mathematical discovery*. Cambridge University Press.

Liljedahl, P. (2004). *The AHA! experience: Mathematical contexts, pedagogical implications*. Unpublished doctoral dissertation, Simon Fraser University, Burnaby, British Columbia, Canada.

Liljedahl, P., & Sriraman, B. (2006). Musings on mathematical creativity. *For The Learning of Mathematics, 26*(1), 20–23.

Mann, E. L. (2005). *Mathematical creativity and school mathematics: Indicators of mathematical creativity in middle school students*. Unpublished doctoral dissertation, University of Connecticut.

Moreno, L., & Sriraman, B. (2005). Structural stability and dynamic geometry: Some ideas on situated proofs. *ZDM- The International Journal on Mathematics Education, 37*(3), 130–139.

Poincaré, H. (1948). *Science and method*. New York: Dover.

Polya, G. (1962). *Mathematical discovery: On understanding, learning and teaching problem solving*. New York: Wiley.

Polya, G. (1945). *How to solve it*. Princeton, NJ: Princeton University Press.

Plucker, J., & Zabelina, D. (2009). Creativity and interdisciplinarity: One creativity or many creativities? *ZDM- The International Journal on Mathematics Education, 41*(1&2), 5–11.

Rickhart, C. (1996). Structuralism and mathematical thinking. In R. Sternberg &T. Ben-Zeev (Eds.), *The nature of mathematical thinking* (pp. 285–330). Mahwah, NJ: Lawrence Erlbaum.

Seabrook, R., & Dienes, Z. (2003). Incubation in problem solving as a context effect. In R. Alterman & D. Kirsh (Eds.), *Proceedings of the 25th annual meeting of the Cognitive Science Society* (pp. 1065–1069). Austin, TX: Cognitive Science Society.

Silver, E. A. (1997). Fostering creativity through instruction rich in mathematical problem solving and problem posing. *Zentralblatt für Didaktik der Mathematik, 29*(3), 75–80.

Sio, U. N., & Ormerod, T. C. (2009a). Does incubation enhance problem solving? A meta-analytic review. *Psychological Bulletin*, (135)1, 94–120.

Sio, U. N., & Ormerod, T. (2009b). *Mechanisms underlying incubation in problem-solving: Evidence for unconscious cue assimilation, 2009 annual meeting of Cognitive Science Society.* Retrieved from http://csjarchive.cogsci.rpi.edu/Proceedings/2009/papers/73/index.html

Sriraman, B. (2003). Mathematical giftedness, problem solving and the ability to formulate generalizations. *The Journal of Secondary Gifted Education, 14*(3), 151–165.

Sriraman, B. (2004). The characteristics of mathematical creativity. *The Mathematics Educator, 14*(1), 19–34.

Sriraman, B. (2005). Are giftedness & creativity synonyms in mathematics? An analysis of constructs within the professional and school realms. *The Journal of Secondary Gifted Education, 17*, 20–36.

Sriraman, B. (2009a). Aha! Experiences. In B. Kerr (Ed.), *Encyclopedia of giftedness, creativity and talent* (pp. 37–39). Thousand Oaks, CA: Sage Publications.

Sriraman, B. (2009b). Paradoxes as pathways into polymathy. *ZDM-The International Journal on Mathematics Education, 41*(1&2), 29–38.

Sriraman, B., & Kýymaz, Y. (2009) Relationship of creativity to intelligence. In B. Kerr (Ed.), *Encyclopedia of giftedness, creativity and talent* (Vol. 2, pp. 726–728). Thousand Oaks, CA: Sage Publications.

Sriraman, B., & Lee, K. (2010). Review of creativity in mathematics and the education of gifted students. In R. Leikin, A. Berman, & B. Koichu (Eds.), Rotterdam, the Netherlands: Sense Publishers. *The International Journal on Mathematics Education, 42*(5), 507–510.

Stillman, G., Kwok-cheung, C., Mason, R., Sheffield, L., Sriraman, B., & Ueno, K. (2009). Classroom practice: Challenging mathematics classroom practices. In E. Barbeau & P. Taylor (Eds.), *Challenging mathematics in and beyond the classroom*, ICMI Study 16 (pp. 243–284). Springer Science & Business. Page numbers in this chapter refer to preprint retrieved from http://www.math.umt.edu/sriraman/ICMI16_Stillmanetal.pdf

Tall, D. (Ed.). (1991). *Advanced mathematical thinking* (pp. 3–21). New York: Kluwer Academic Publishers.

Thurston, W. P. (1982). Three dimensional manifolds, Kleinian groups, and hyperbolic geometry. *Bulletin of the American Mathematical Society, 6*(3), 357–381.

Vul, E., & Pashler, H. (2007). Incubation benefits only after people have been misdirected. *Memory and Cognition, 35*(4), 701–710.

Wallas, G. (1926). *The art of thought.* New York: Harcourt Brace.

Zhong, C., Dijksterhuis, A., & Galinsky, A. D. (2008). The merits of unconscious thought in creativity. *Psychological Science, 19*, 912–918.

Bharath Sriraman
Dept of Mathematical Sciences
The University of Montana
USA

Narges Yaftian
School of Mathematics
Iran University of Science & Technology
IRAN

Kyeonghwa Lee
Dept of Mathematics Education
Seoul National University
KOREA

ALEXANDER KARP

9. GIFTED EDUCATION IN RUSSIA AND THE UNITED STATES

Personal Notes

Comparisons between different countries' approaches to education in general, and to gifted education in particular, are a matter of extreme difficulty, since comparisons are meaningful only if the objects being compared have, on the whole, some degree of similarity. One can discuss which soccer team is better, Spain's or Netherlands'; but to compare Spain's soccer team to Russia's chess team would be nonsensical. Unfortunately, many comparative studies in education, despite making all kinds of pronouncements about cultural distinctiveness, are nonetheless based on the assumption that by and large everyone is striving after the same thing. That this is so, however, is by no means obvious.

While I understand the desire to find out how "our team did," which spurs us to analyze the charts of results from international studies such as TIMMS or PISA, I would nonetheless hazard to suggest that the scientific usefulness of such results is quite limited (their usefulness for public policy is a different matter, since they can sometimes help to increase funding for education, which is a good thing in any event). It appears far more useful systematically to collect various data about one or another system of education; studies of this kind can facilitate a better understanding of the given system, which in turn can facilitate a new understanding of the system in which the researcher lives and works. The process in this case is complex and has many stages.

In other papers, I have attempted to sketch something like a history of mathematics gifted education in Russia (Soviet Union) and the United States (Karp, 2009). This work is certainly not finished; or more precisely, it would be better to say that it has barely begun—very many processes and aspects of education in both countries still await their historians. The aim of the present paper, however, is different. I will make no attempt to offer an objective history, but on the contrary, I will describe my own thoughts and impressions, without attempting to form a complete and absolutely objective picture. The picture offered below will be deliberately subjective and limited.

ABOUT MY EXPERIENCE

First, however, I must describe my own experience of working with the mathematically gifted. Someone once compared such descriptions with school compositions about "what I did last summer," but without this information the reader will unlikely

B. Sriraman and K.H. Lee (eds.), The Elements of Creativity and Giftedness in Mathematics, 131–143.
© 2011 Sense Publishers. All rights reserved.

be able to understand the perspective on which the author's reasoning is based and how exactly this perspective is limited (the fact that any individual's life experience is limited is not itself open to doubt). For example, readers of Toom's (1993) article, which attracted considerable attention, would have benefited from understanding in what kinds of educational institutions its author worked in Russia and the United States, and consequently, how typical and characteristic what took place in these institutions was for each of these countries in general.

For 18 years, I worked as a mathematics teacher (and for 12 of them, in addition, as head of the mathematics department) at school no. 30 with an advanced course in mathematics in Leningrad (St. Petersburg). The literature dealing with schools with an advanced course in mathematics is not small (for example, Vogeli, 1968, 1997; Karp, in print, a). Most Russian (Soviet) mathematicians of any note did indeed pass through these schools. However, very different kinds of educational institutions may lurk behind the term "school with an advanced course in mathematics": "advanced" may mean many different things (Donoghue, Karp, Vogeli, 2000). School no. 30 is one of the oldest and most famous mathematics schools in the country: the list of its graduates who became winners in all kinds of mathematics Olympiads, including international ones, or who became professors at prestigious universities, is quite long and impressive.

My experience of working with the gifted in Russia is in one way or another connected with this school. Specifically, observing the successes of my students and helping them as far as I was able, I became acquainted with the system of mathematics Olympiads, in particular, serving for several years as team leader for a team at the *Baltic Way* International Olympiad. Together with students from my school, I travelled to various conferences for gifted schoolchildren, at which students could report on problems that they had solved (ideally, problems that had not been solved earlier). In the capacity of school teacher I visited mathematics schools in other cities and had the opportunity to become acquainted with how they worked. My experience at school no. 30 was probably the main reason for my being invited, starting in the late 1980s, to work at the St. Petersburg Institute of Continuing Education, where I began to work on the professional development of teachers, overseeing work with teachers from schools with an advanced course in mathematics, that is, with teachers who are expected to work mainly with mathematically gifted schoolchildren. This experience in turn (again, together with the experience of working at the school) spurred me to start writing books for schools with an advanced course in mathematics (for example, Karp, 1992, Karp, 1999, Karp, 2006). It also formed a foundation for my research in the area of mathematically gifted education (the ideas that I had at the time became the basis, for example, for the works Karp, 1998, Karp, 2003).

My American practical experience of working with the gifted is far more limited. I have repeatedly taught courses and workshops for graduate students interested in working with the mathematically gifted. These workshops and courses were also attended by teachers from various schools for mathematically advanced students, with whom I discussed, both during the courses and outside them, the specific conditions and distinctive features of their work. I have also had occasion to visit various schools of this type, in particular, observing student teachers whose practical training I was supervising. Also, while living in the United States I have extensively studied the existing international literature on the teaching of the mathematically gifted and on research in this field (let me say at once, however, that below I will not discuss the differences between research on mathematical giftedness in Russia and the United States, but will concentrate specifically on educational teaching practice, as I see it).

ON TECHNOLOGY IN MATHEMATICS GIFTED EDUCATION

At a certain point, the word "technology" became quite popular in Russian teaching practice (see, for example, Stefanova and Podkhodova, 2005); it was employed in a different sense than the one commonly attributed to it in the United States, where it is usually understood to mean information technology, or simply put, the use of computers. In Russia, the word had a meaning similar to the one used by the prominent Sovietologist Avtorkhanov (1959) in his book, *Stalin and the Soviet Communist Party; a Study in the Technology of Power*; Avtorkhanov wrote about the specific way in which government operates, and in education the issue is how precisely education is *made*, that is, the totality of the techniques and actions employed within the educational system.

How exactly the education of the mathematically gifted is made in different places is indeed a very interesting question. How are Olympiads organized? How are courses constructed? How are tests conducted? All of these questions can and should be studied.

American tests or even Olympiads aimed at highly-gifted schoolchildren contain quite large numbers of problems, but the problems are not very difficult. This changes only at the highest levels: the United States of America Mathematical Olympiad (USAMO) is designed in a different way. But different versions of the American Mathematics Competitions (AMC) contain dozens of problems each, with not very much time being allotted for solving each problem. It is assumed that a gifted person will know how to react quite quickly to the problems given, but, probably, will not be capable of thinking about one question for an extended period of time.

Russian tests (and even more so, Olympiads) usually contain a substantially lower number of problems, but the problems are more difficult. As an example, consider the following test aimed at checking to see how well students in schools with an advanced course in mathematics have assimilated the topics "Polynomials." (It must be pointed out here that this test was designed to be given to students at "ordinary" schools with an advanced course in mathematics, so to speak. As we have already stated, specialized schools vary, some being more selective, others less so; the test below was addressed to schools of the latter variety).

1. Check to see whether following assertion is correct:

   $(x^2 - 4)^n - (2x - 1)^n$ is divisible by $x - 3$ for any positive integer n.

2. Find the remainder of the polynomial $P(x) = x^{11} - 16x^7 + x - 3$ when it is divided by the polynomial $Q(x) = x^2 - 3x + 2$.

3. Solve the following equation: $2x^3 + 3x^2 - 29x + 30 = 0$.

4. Given that the number $1 + \sqrt{3}$ is a root of the polynomial $P(x) = x^3 + ax^2 + bx - a$ with rational coefficients, find the numbers a and b.

5. The numbers x_1, x_2, x_3 are roots of the polynomial $x^3 - 3x - 1$. Find $x_1^2 + x_2^3 + x_2^3$.

6. Determine whether a real number a exists such that the equation $\dfrac{x^3 + (a-1)x^2 + ax - 2}{x - 1} = 0$ has no real roots (Karp, 2006, p. 94).

It was recommended that students be given 45 minutes to complete this test, with the highest score (the equivalent of an "A") being given for correctly solving any five of these problems.

It is easy to notice that the test presupposes a rather high level of algebraic skills. The first problem could practically be an oral one (it is enough to substitute 3 into the first expression and to see that it becomes zero); but the third problem, which is based on an algorithm for searching for rational roots, already known to the students, and the fifth problem, which based on the connection between symmetric expressions related to the roots and the coefficients of an equation, also familiar to the students, require a certain degree of precision in carrying out computations. In the second problem, the students may also rely on precise computations, of course, in dividing polynomials based on an algorithm, but it would be better to notice that the remainder must be a first-degree polynomial ($mx + b$), whose values when $x = 1$ and $x = 2$ are equal to $P(1)$ and $P(2)$, respectively, after which the coefficients are not difficult to find. Problem 5 amounts to substituting the number $1 + \sqrt{3}$ into the given polynomial, after which, since the number $\sqrt{3}$ is irrational, it remains to solve a system of linear equations relative to a and b. Finally, in the last problem, the students must determine for what value of the parameter a the number 1 will be a root of the polynomial in the numerator (obviously, for other a the equation has real roots), and to solve the equation obtained with the given a. As we can see, although these problems are not very difficult, all of them involve many steps (possibly with the exception of the first).

It would be difficult for me to imagine so-called *zachety* (which may be translated as "oral interviews" and which were regularly conducted at school no. 30) in the American context. In essence, these were oral exams, but ones that lasted practically an entire day: they could begin at 9:00 a.m. and end at 5:00 p.m. In this time, students would answer questions about a very large amount of material: they would solve several problems, demonstrate their ability to prove the basic theorems that they had covered and their knowledge and understanding of the basic definitions that they were using. But far more important than all of this was the manner in which the oral interviews would take place. They were usually conducted with the assistance of students who had already graduated from the school and were studying at the city's universities. Consequently, the oral interview constituted less a formal test of schoolchildren's knowledge and abilities than a dialogue of several hours between the schoolchild and a more mathematically experienced individual. This dialogue launched off, of course, from the problems that were assigned to the school-children, but it went far beyond them: the discussion could concern the theorems on which the proofs being carried out were based, the entire sequence of assertions leading up to the assertion that was being examined, other proofs of the same theorems, possibilities for making them stronger, the reasons why these theorems are important, and much else besides. The oral interview turned out to be extremely important not so much as a test of students' knowledge, but more as an educational learning activity.

I know of a similar approach being used, for example, to teach the course in calculus at Moscow's school no. 57, where such "dialogue-oriented" teaching practices are used in the vast majority of classes (see, for example, Karp, in print, a). Organizing education in this way requires the participation of the requisite number of highly-qualified mathematicians who are prepared to work with schoolchildren systematically and practically for nothing (teachers of calculus classes at school no. 57 are helped by 5–6 teaching assistants).

On the other hand, it would be difficult for me to imagine, in those Russian schools with which I was familiar (and it does not appear that they have changed so much in this respect during the time that I have been working in the United States), such work on applying mathematics as is carried out in some American schools with more demanding requirements in mathematics. This is not just a matter of information technology, although American schoolchildren, according to my observations, usually begin performing tasks on computers or calculators far more easily than Russian ones, but has to do more with the range of topics discussed in school. The book *For All Practical Purposes*, published by COMAP (2000) and to some extent used in schools, gives an impression of problems and courses that are quite different from traditional Russian ones.

I can also list other forms and technologies used in educating the mathematically gifted which are at present quite different and probably will remain different for a long time, if only due to differences in living conditions. At the same time, quite a few technologies are similar and becoming more so. Information about the way in which educators work with the gifted in other countries is becoming accessible, thanks to correspondence among colleagues, new books, and simply immigration. For example, the book by Fomin, Itenberg, Kirichenko (1996), translated by Mark Saul, introduced many foreign readers to the way in which mathematics circles are organized in St. Petersburg and to many other formats for working with gifted students (for example, math battles), and these formats are gradually becoming popular in other countries.

As I have already stated, I have never had occasion to work with American participants of international Olympiads; nonetheless, I strongly doubt that the techno-logies used to prepare them for Olympiads are all that different from what is done with future Russian participants—at the very least, they have to solve the same problems. On the other hand, the process of studying mathematics as a whole will very likely be different for Russians and Americans. But this difference cannot be described simply by indicating the specific way in which one or another educational activity is organized in the two respective countries; rather, one would also have to address the rationale behind the activity and more generally to go beyond the discussion of technologies (although such a discussion is of interest to any working teacher) into the far more ambiguous realm of understanding the distinctive features and values of each educational system.

ON THE PLACE OF TEACHING THE MATHEMATICALLY GIFTED IN THE EDUCATION SYSTEM

Russian mathematics education began in earnest during the reign of Peter I, when the new czar, striving to strengthen his autocratic rule and to conquer new territories, ordered that a select number of his subjects be taught military science, for which mathematics was indispensable. The purpose of mathematics education was thus straightforward: it was necessary to prepare qualified specialists-mathematicians. Not that the purpose of mathematics education in other countries during the eighteenth century was entirely different: of course, no one was even thinking about "mathematics for everyone" at that point. Yet mathematics education on the whole in many Western countries during both the eighteenth and nineteenth centuries occupied a different place in relation to the teaching of other subjects, particularly the humanities (see, for example, Howson, 2010). In the 1880s, Dmitri Tolstoy, Russia's minister of education and subsequently minister of internal affairs, wrote in his historical articles with indignation about the fact that some German who had been invited to Russia in the eighteenth century had claimed that the Russians were supposedly an insufficiently developed people to engage in genuine science (that is, the humanities), and that they should therefore devote themselves to lower subjects, namely, mathematics (Tolstoy, 1885). However, the special love for mathematics that was prescribed by the government ensured that it developed in a special way as an academic subject (Karp, 2007), which in turn ensured that it developed in a sufficiently successful manner as a science (Vucinich, 1963).

The Revolution of 1917, or more precisely, the transformation of Soviet education that followed in the 1930s, introduced significant additions: education became accessible to millions. As in the times of Peter I, the purpose of mathematics education was seen to lie in preparing qualified specialists, but now the possibility to become such a specialist was offered to an incomparably greater number of people. The term "highly gifted," just like other psychological terms that had entered the country during the 1920s on the wave of revolutionary experiments, was not officially used, but effectively it was the identification of gifted students and their subsequent utilization that was given priority. The goal was to satisfy practical needs—qualified engineers and mathematicians were in demand—and therefore roles of the highest importance were assigned to specialists in mathematics and mathematics educators.

In other countries, above all in the United States, where mass education (if not universal education) had also been established sufficiently long ago, the role of mathematics was different. Expert engineers, of course, were also in demand, but the logic embodied in popular Soviet slogans that began with the words "Let's direct all efforts to …!" (where necessary continuation like crushing the most recent enemy or building another factory or something else could be easily supplied) was fundamentally alien to American thinking. "All efforts" went to different pursuits without any overarching commands. Consequently, mathematics, too, turned out to be a less important subject, nor was it taught basically exclusively in order to prepare engineers and mathematicians.

The fact that people possess different aptitudes became a commonplace in the United States very early. But determining the level of students' aptitudes—to which the evaluation of all other differences between them was largely reduced—became mainly the prerogative of psychologists, who developed various tests for this purpose. These psychologists included outstanding scientists, but when the tests developed by them were applied on a mass scale, details that were too subtle often turned out to be useless. The outstanding Russian psychologist and educator Blonsky (1919) lamented that "all kinds of directors" distort and pervert everything. American "directors" built a system whose distinctive feature was what Diana Ravitch (2000) has characterized as "brutal pessimism." Everything came down (perhaps not always, but sufficiently often) to using one or another test to determine whether or not a person was gifted, and after that both poorly-gifted and highly-gifted students were not given all that many chances to develop their giftedness: each student was what he or she was, and if giftedness was lacking, then nothing more could be done; the system saw no possibility of giving it to students.

Such views were already criticized many years ago. In particular, the Russian psychologist Vadim Krutetskii (1976) remarked that the abilities to which Edward LeeThorndike referred are actually not innate abilities, but skills that are successfully formed in the process of education. Soviet educators inveighed against what was happening in the United States, seeing it as a manifestation of the class struggle— gifted students, indeed, generally belong to the wealthier and more educated sections of society (although in the USSR, too, as far as can be judged, better results were achieved in teaching children from educated families than in teaching children from poorly educated families).

In any event, what is important is that the contemporary movement of "mathematics for everyone" very often perceives the education of the gifted as something opposed and even inimical to it. Tannenbaum (2000) has remarked that "American society is never interested in teaching both the most and the least successful achievers at the same time." Today, in the minds of some (and perhaps even in the minds of many) "gifted" students are equated with privileged students, and consequently concern with them becomes a form of elitism or even something worse.

SOME PRACTICAL OBSERVATIONS

The preceding comments are based, naturally, not so much on my observations, as on my thoughts and attempts to explain what I have observed. By sketching a (deliberately simplified) picture of the historical development of mathematics education above, we did not by any means wish to act as judges determining which approach was better. One can talk for a very long time about the "victims" of each of the systems described above, just as one can list their respective achievements.

Let us sum things up, however, by saying that the education of the mathematically gifted is viewed differently in Russia and the United States, and that this difference is manifested in different ways.

Public Opinion

I have more than once discussed with my students the question of whether schoolchildren who wish to acquire a more advanced mathematics education should be offered the possibility to do so (on the condition, naturally, that they will be able to manage it). Very often I have heard the response that this should not be done, since it leads to elitism; it has also been pointed out to me that the population of the leading American schools with an advanced course in mathematics by no means reflects the overall population of the United States (which is, of course, true). In response to my questions about what then should be done with schoolchildren who are bored in class, I was told that it was necessary to arrange for team work, in the course of which strong students would explain the material to weak ones, which would engage them and develop their social skills.

It is noteworthy that it usually does not occur to anyone to suggest to those children who want to play baseball to play chess instead—yet the development of social skills instead of mathematical skills is considered a viable substitution, and no one sees in it any curtailment of the rights of the child. Again, the fact that various sections of the populations are not sufficiently represented among the winners or even participants of Olympiads or among the students of various schools with an advanced course in mathematics seems extremely important and an indication of the fact that even many years after Brown v. Board of Education there is no equity in education. But what this means is that intensive efforts must be made to offer more opportunities to those who lack them, not to deprive of opportunities those students who already have them. At this point, however, it turns out that the "achievement gap" is often understood to mean (at least in actual school practice) a gap at the lower end of the spectrum of results, not at its higher end.

Russian (Soviet) teachers were, of course, first and foremost required to work with failing students, but it was assumed that special work would be conducted with strong students as well. Schoolchildren were not officially required to take part in district rounds of mathematics Olympiads, but if the schoolchildren from some school actually failed to participate, the district mathematics supervisor would not fail to call the attention both of the school's director and of the district educational authorities to this fact, and most likely the school's teachers would be strongly advised to devote some serious thought to improving their work. The Institute of Continuing Education in St. Petersburg systematically conducted classes with teachers, giving them recommendations about working with strong students.

Does anything similar exist in New York? I do not know. But I am afraid that public opinion does not exert the necessary pressure on the educational authorities in this respect. Educated and enterprising parents naturally have opportunities for improving their own children's education. But public opinion appears to be less up in arms in this respect when other people's children are concerned.

Opportunities for Children

When people talk about mathematical talent, they often mean talent on the level of Gauss's. Not by accident, therefore, did Sheffield (1999), the editor of a book published by NCTM, prefer a more neutral term: mathematical promise. And indeed, despite the fatalistic views mentioned above, what we are dealing with is promise, which may be realized, but which may also turn out to be deceptive. Moreover, even promise can be absent initially and appear only later. Zalman Usiskin (2000) once spoke about "developing students into the next level of abilities." Giftedness or the kernel of giftedness can develop under favourable conditions. But such conditions must be created.

I have said above that my own history as a teacher was first and foremost connected with the teaching of those whose interest in and gift for mathematics had in one way or another already manifested itself. A teacher of such children faces many important and challenging problems, but it seems to me that in the American context it is no less important to address the preceding stage: the awakening of interest in mathematics.

I remember how the drop in the general level of mathematics education in Russia during the 1990s, brought about first and foremost by economic problems, immediately made selecting students for specialized schools more difficult. To be sure, the top five or ten students in the city remained visible and perhaps among them no drop was observable; but the number of "average" gifted schoolchildren clearly decreased. Nor was this surprising: they had fewer opportunities to develop.

Elsewhere (Karp, 2010a), I have already written about the fact that many Russian textbooks offer schoolchildren material of several levels of difficulty, so that every schoolchild has something to get interested in and something to practice on. Often a teacher will try to find special materials for working with stronger students in class as well. All of this is supported by the system of extracurricular work, to which we have already referred, and which, although it may be developed to very different degrees in different schools, is usually nonetheless present everywhere to some extent (or, because in recent years I have visited Russian schools far less frequently and know them less well than I used to, let us say: which *used to be* present everywhere).

The standard Russian course in mathematics, despite all of the curtailments, nonetheless contains numerous proofs and examples of substantive arguments. Moreover, the value of mathematics as such—arguments, theorems, proofs, and so on— is constantly highlighted.

Do American schoolchildren always have the opportunity to acquire even a minimally adequate notion of mathematics? How often is their attention directed to the beauty of proofs; or more to the point, how often do they even encounter proofs? It must be acknowledged that without this, it is difficult to expect an awakening of interest in mathematics and success in working with potentially gifted students.

In response to these questions, we might say that such things do in fact happen: theorems are proved, and interesting problems are solved. To see this, all that one has to do is visit the classroom of a good teacher. But at this point the issue of teacher preparation arises.

On Teachers

The fact that people are needed who are capable of working with mathematically gifted students has long been stressed (Stanley, 1987). In Russia, in schools with an advanced course in mathematics, a special culture evolved out of interactions between research mathematicians and teachers, which nurtures deep knowledge of many areas of school mathematics, the ability to pose and solve problems, and to conduct substantive and educational discussions with schoolchildren. A new teacher coming to such a school in one way or another comes under the influence of this culture (Karp, in print, b). Moreover, this culture, of course, also exerts an influence on the process of teacher education, at the very least through the problem books and textbooks that are published for schools with an advanced course in mathematics, which are to one or another degree analyzed in the process of teacher education.

American teachers are supposed to acquire the requisite knowledge (let us call it, following Lee Schulman (1986), "pedagogical content knowledge") on their own and during their studies in college. But even leaving aside teachers for schools with an advanced course in mathematics, is the knowledge of teachers always sufficient to give a potentially gifted middle school student an interesting problem? Is the future teacher taught in college to work with strong and interested students, or, more precisely, to work in such a way as to make as many students as possible become strong and interested? Or should we really take differentiated education, which is discussed more and more often today, to mean exclusively the ability to work with students of different degrees of underachievement? (Of course, no one denies the importance of such work; the only point is that all education cannot be reduced to such work.)

I know many wonderful American school teachers of mathematics, but I know many times more people who teach mathematics in schools and who, while possessing excellent social skills (which is important), know no mathematics. In saying this, I do not mean that they are unfamiliar with some lofty regions of the discipline, but that they literally do not understand what is written in the textbook that they use in class, and that they do not love the subject that they are teaching. And without this, it will not be possible to awaken mathematical talent in schoolchildren.

Let us say more. Nowhere and at no point in history have mathematics teachers been recruited from among mathematical geniuses. Mathematical geniuses have usually gone into other fields. Successful teachers of mathematics start out as "average" mathematically gifted students, as it were. Reducing attention to such students means that after a certain period of time there will be fewer teachers who are capable of adequately teaching mathematics, which in turn will lead to a reduction in the number of students who love and understand mathematics, and so on. It is not difficult to extend this line of reasoning and to imagine the ultimate situation to which such a development would lead.

CONCLUSION: SO WHAT SHOULD WE DO?

I do not by any means wish to be taken to mean that the state of mathematics education is wonderful in Russia and terrible in the United States. First, mathematics education does not consist exclusively of the education of the gifted or even of the preparation for such education. We have been discussing that side of education which has traditionally been Russia's strength, but there are also other aspects, which we are not addressing here. Second, since this article makes no claim to any comprehensive examination, I have talked about the Russian school system in which I myself worked; what is actually taking place in Putin's Russia is not examined here, and the processes going on there do not by any means seem beneficial, above all because they are arguably undermining the foundation of general education, without which, as we have said, the education of the gifted is impossible.

But in terms of American education, one would like to set one's sights on the best models, rather than console oneself with the fact that good things used to exist in other places, but have been ruined. The problems discussed in this article have been noticed not by me alone: much has been written about the fact that attention must be paid not only to the number of students who achieve the minimal level of requirements, but also to those who strive for higher results, by noting and studying there successes (see, for example, Walker, 2006). So what can be done on a practical level, in addition to the everyday work of educating future teachers or preparing educational materials, etc., to promote the principles and objectives discussed above?

The author of this article would not have started his career as a school teacher if he did not believe in education. In terms of the issues discussed above, it is important to demonstrate to as large an audience as possible that the education of the mathematically gifted and the education of everyone are problems that are inter-connected, not opposed to one another. It is impossible to identify all mathematically gifted children and to get them involved in learning as long as the opportunity to see genuine mathematics is not offered to everyone; it is impossible to introduce everyone to mathematics as long as there is not a sufficient number of people who are capable of introducing mathematics to children, in other words, who are sufficien-tly gifted themselves (without even mentioning other sides of the issue, such as the fact that introducing everyone to mathematics implies recognizing the value of mathematics, which in turn is also important for the education of the gifted and hardly possible without recognizing the importance of the gifted students' successes).

I would argue that it is precisely explaining this indissoluble connection to everyone, including those individuals who are responsible for regulating education, that constitutes the main task for the mathematical and mathematics education community.

REFERENCES

Avtorkhanov, A. (1959). *Stalin and the Soviet Communist Party; a study in the technology of power.* New York: Praeger.

Blonsky, P. (1919). *Trudovaya shkola* [The Labor School]. Moscow: NARKOMPROS.

COMAP. (2000). *For all practical purposes. Mathematical literacy in today's world.* COMAP, Inc.

Donoghue, E., Karp, A., & Vogeli, B. (2000, January). Russian schools for the mathematically and scientifically talented: Can the vision survive unchanged? *Roeper Review, 22*(2), 121–122.

Fomin, D., Genkin, S., & Itenberg, I. (1996). *Mathematical circles (Russian experience)*. Imprint Providence, R.I. American Mathematical Society.

Howson, G. (2010). Mathematics, society, and curricula in Nineteenth-Century England. *International Journal for the History of Mathematics Education, 5*(1), 21–53.

Karp, A. (1992). *Daiu uroki matematiki...* (Math Tutor available....) Moscow: Prosveschenie.

Karp, A. (1998). *Pis'mennye vypusknye eksameny po algebre v Rossii sa 100 let.* (Russian Written Examinations in Algebra over 100 Years). St. Petersburg University of Education.

Karp, A. (1999). *Sbornik zadach dyia 8-9 klassov s uglublennym izucheniem matematiki* (Mathematics problems for 8-9 grades of the schools with an advanced course of study in mathematics). St. Petersburg: SMIO-PRESS.

Karp, A. (2003). Thirty years after: The lives of former winners of mathematical Olympiads. *Roeper Review, 25*(2), 83–87.

Karp, A. (2006). *Sbornik zadach dlya 10-11 klassov s uglublennym izucheniem matematiki.* (Mathematics problems for Grades 10-11 in schools with advanced course of study in mathematics). Moscow: Prosveschenie.

Karp, A. (2007). 'We all meandered through our schooling...' Notes on Russian mathematics education during the first third of the nineteenth century. *British Society for the History of Mathematics Bulletin, 22*, 104–119.

Karp, A. (2009). Teaching the mathematically gifted: An attempt at a historical analysis. In R. Leikin, A. Berman, & B. Koichu (Eds.), *Creativity in mathematics and the education of gifted students* (pp. 11–30). Rotterdam: Sense publishers.

Karp, A. (2010). Inspiring and developing student interest: Several examples from Foreign Schools. In M. Saul (Ed.), *Peak in the middle* (pp. 171–186). Reston: NCTM.

Karp, A. (2010). Reforms and counter-reforms: Schools between 1917 and the 1950s. In A. Karp, B. Vogeli (Eds.), *Russian mathematics education. History and world significance* (pp. 43–85). London-New Jersey-Singapore: World Scientific.

Karp, A. (in print, a). Teachers of the mathematically gifted tell about themselves and their profession. *Roeper Review*.

Karp, A. (in print, b). Schools with an advanced course in mathematics and schools with an advanced course in the humanities.

Krutetskii, V. A. (1976). *The psychology of mathematical abilities in schoolchildren* (J. Kilpatrick & I. Wirszup, Eds., J. Teller, Trans.). Chicago: University of Chicago Press.

Ravitch, D. (2000). *Left back. A century of failed school reforms.* New York-London: Simon & Schuster.

Stanley, J. C. (1987). State residential high schools for mathematically talented youth. *Phi Delta Kappan, 68*, 770–773.

Sheffield, L. J. (Ed.). (1999). *Developing mathematically promising students.* Reston, VA: NCTM.

Shulman, L. (1986). Those who understand: Knowledge growth in teaching. *Educational Researcher, 15*(2), 4–14.

Stefanova, N., & Podhodova, N. (Eds.). (2005). *Metodika i technologiia obucheniia matematike. Kurs lekzii.* (The Methodology and Technology of Mathematics Teaching. A Course of Lectures). Moscow: Drofa.

Tannenbaum, A. J. (2000). A history of giftedness in school and society. In K. A. Heller, F. J. Mönks, A. H. Passow (Eds.), *International handbook of giftedness and talent* (pp. 23–53). Amsterdam; Oxford: Elsevier.

Tolstoy, D. (1885). Akademicheskaya gimnazia v XVIII stoletii, po rukopisnym dokumentam Arkhiva Akademii nauk [The Academy Gymnasium in the eighteenth century, based on manuscript documents from the Academy of Sciences archive]. *Sbornik otdeleniya russkogo yazyka i slovesnosti Imperatorskoy Akademii nauk*, XXXVII, # 5.

Toom, A. (1993). A Russian teacher in America. *Journal of Mathematical Behavior, 12*, 117–139.

Vogeli, B. R. (1968). *Soviet secondary schools for the mathematically talented.* NCTM.

Vogeli, B. R. (1997). *Special secondary schools for the mathematically and scientifically talented. An International Panorama.* New York: Teachers College Columbia University.

Vucinich, A. (1963). *Science in Russian culture. A history to 1860.* Stanford, CA: Stanford University Press.

Usiskin, Z. (2000). The development into the mathematically talented. *Journal of Secondary Gifted Education, 11*(3), 152–162.

Walker, E. N. (2006). Urban high school students' academic communities and their effects on mathematics success. *American Educational Research Journal, 43*(1), 43–73.

Alexander Karp
Program in Mathematics
Teachers College, Columbia University
New York, USA

HAN HYUK CHO, MIN HO SONG AND JI YOON LEE

10. SEMIOTIC MICROWORLD FOR
MATHEMATICAL VISUALIZATION

INTRODUCTION

With the advent of a knowledge-based society, social demand for nurturing creative talents has increased. Gifted education has also been strengthened in relation to creativity education. The present selection system mainly relies on tests to assess students' abilities. However, gifted education features multi-dimensional considerations such as observation and performance assessment to evaluate the students' abilities, and a teacher training program for the purpose of giving guidance for the selection process of gifted students is also offered. This transformation from teachers' instruction-directed learning to students' self-directed learning highlights constructionism, which allows students to explore and gain knowledge by themselves. Thus, an environment in which students obtain knowledge and develop creativity needs to be provided.

This study aims to discuss how to introduce three-dimensional objects in an educational system based on constructionism in terms of mathematical creativity which can be utilized in a computer-based multimedia environment. We suggest a 3D representation system that can decompose three-dimensional objects into basic modules such as cubes and regular polygons, and the system is similar to the turtle command of LOGO. Based on this 3D representation system, students can construct three-dimensional objects by themselves and communicate with others; also, learners' thought processes can be analyzed. In order to emphasize mathematical expressions rather than LOGO programming, we developed a three-dimensional object expression system through a semiotic approach which was based on action symbols rather than the turtle command. Meanwhile, in this study, we mainly examine the expression system and developed examples. Under the slogan of "learning by making," the creative learning activities and thought processes are also investigated.

MICROWORLD TOOLS FOR MATHEMATICAL VISUALIZATION

According to Nemirovsky and Noble (1997), a lot of research has been conducted since visualization began receiving a great deal of attention by researchers, and a wide range of definitions of the term also have been used. The term "visualization" means mental visualization and manipulative activity in psychology. Zimmermann and Cunningham (1991) stated that mathematical visualization differs from a wide

B. Sriraman and K.H. Lee (eds.), The Elements of Creativity and Giftedness in Mathematics, 145–159.
© 2011 Sense Publishers. All rights reserved.

range of fundamental meanings of visualization, which is more appropriate for mathematical education. They write:

> From the perspective of mathematical visualization, the constraint that images must be manipulated mentally, without the aid of pencil and paper, seems artificial. In fact, in mathematical visualization what we are interested in is precisely the student's ability to draw an appropriate diagram (with pencil and paper, or in some cases, with a computer) to represent a mathematical concept or problem and to use the diagram to achieve understanding, and as an aid in problem solving. In mathematics, visualization is not an end in itself but a means toward an end, which is understanding.... mathematical visualization is the process of forming images (mentally, or with pencil and paper, or with the aid of technology) and using such images effectively for mathematical discovery and understanding. (1991, p. 3)

In Zimmermann and Cunningham's (1991) study, they emphasized the importance of the process of constructing visual objects using the term 'appropriate diagram' and 'process of forming images'. For visualization, the image of an object is mainly focused on in common psychology. However, the 'process of forming images' is highlighted more in mathematical visualization. Dreyfus (1993), for instance, claimed that it is necessary for mathematical objects to have mental representations by distinguishing external representations and mental representations, and external representations could also influence the process of forming mental representations. However, Zazkis, Dubinsky, and Dautermann (1996), unlike Dreyfus, take on this issue and offer a more precise definition that takes into account the range of possible processes:

> Visualization is an act in which an individual establishes a strong connection between an internal construct and something to which access is gained through the senses. Such a connection can be made in either of two directions. An act of visualization may consist of any mental construction of objects or processes that an individual associates with objects or events perceived by her or him as external. Alternatively, an act of visualization may consist of the construction, on some external medium such as paper, chalkboard, or computer screen, of objects or events which the individual identifies with object(s) or process(es) in her or his mind. (1996, p. 441)

As the above quotation stated, Nemirovsky and Noble (1997) emphasized the importance of the connection between internal and external factors using the term "transitional objects." In a related matter, Healy and Hoyles (1996) also proposed that visual representations and symbolic representations of the same mathematical notions should be connected. LOGO, developed by using turtle metaphors, is a representative example to express internal representations with symbolic representations and express the visual representations connected to the external representations. LOGO's turtle, as a transitional object, has been studied in light of constructionism. It aimed to help learners explore two-dimensional geometry through a command system. Learners can use turtle commands such as 'forward' or 'rotate' for self-guided learning by encountering the turtle-virtue object to construct knowledge.

LOGO expresses two-dimensional geometry by decomposing it into two basic mathematical modules: the segment and angle. LOGO has been successfully introduced into classroom teaching and been helpful in the making of great achievements in two-dimensional learning and teaching. Thus, a number of researchers attempted to apply LOGO to three-dimensional object exploration. For example, Kynigos and Latsi (2007) tried to express the three-dimensional geometrical object with a two-dimensional turtle movement trace using MaIT, which is shown in Figure 3.a. Also, Yeh and Nason (2004) used VRMath (Figure 3.b) to present a virtual reality learning environment to form three-dimensional objects by drawing lines along the edges of three-dimensional objects and painting the sides of the figures.

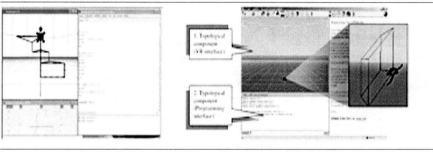

| a. MaLT | b. VRMath |

Figure 1. Three-dimensional LOGO-based microworld.

Figures should preferably be embedded in the text (rather than supplied separately). If you are unable to embed the figures, supply them as glossy prints (for photographs) or good quality black line drawings, or as electronic files in TIFF, EPS or JPEG format only. The resolution of photographs should be 300 dpi and line drawings at least 600 dpi. We cannot accept images in formats such as CorelDraw, Harvard Graphics or Abode Illustrator.

Although the process of using the turtle metaphor to express three-dimensional objects has some positive effects on learning, it still may add cognitive burden for students to trace turtle movement within a three-dimensional context. In Morgan and Alshwaikh (2008), the authors mentioned that students were having difficulty understanding turtle movement within a three-dimensional context relating to everyday gestures. In addition, using a segment and angle whose functions are basic modules of two-dimensional objects to express three-dimensional objects may confuse students due to the manner of the axis in three-dimensional objects. Providing a more familiar command system: turtle commands rather than programming language, LOGO helped significant achievements to be made when it was firstly developed; however, the use of programming languages such as 'repeat', 'forward' and 'rotate' triggered learners' cognitive burden (Hoyles and Noss, 2003).

Some other studies, on the other hand, have been attempted to explore three-dimensional objects using three-dimensional cubes as basic modules. They are quite different from LOGO based studies, which use two-dimensional basic modules to explore three-dimensional objects. That is to say that a three-dimensional object can be constructed by applying a three-dimensional cube as a basic building module. In fact, Korean students are quite familiar with building blocks because this activity is introduced in the curriculum of Korean elementary schools. There is some evidence that early block building skills are related to spatial skills, and that they correlate with later math achievement (Casey et al., 2008). These notions indicate that it is meaningful to explore three-dimensional objects through basic building block activities. As a matter of fact, it is not against our belief of 'learning by making', so we believe that the ability to deal with three-dimensional objects can be achieved as long as one can manipulate environments and experiences. Besides, similarities can be found between prime numbers and building blocks: any integer can be expressed as the product of its prime factors, which is called prime factorization; also, building blocks can serve as modules to express three-dimensional objects. This means that basic three-dimensional objects can be decomposed into polygon tiles or building blocks that serve as their basic building modules. Several 3D geometry programs have been developed in order to examine three-dimensional objects which consist of basic building modules. As shown in Figure 2.a, NCTM (2010) developed software which provides an experimental environment to explore solids and planar figures by using a mouse. What is more, Wisweb (Figure 2), developed by Freudenthal Institute (2010), created a web-based learning environment where students can explore and conduct experiments with three-dimensional objects. Wisweb enables teachers to implement a variety of mathematical activities for classroom teaching. For example, they can do building block activities with mouse manipulation actions, which are very similar to using actual teaching aids (Figure 2.b).

However, the above mentioned 3D-object manipulation activities are not effective enough to understand the process of three-dimensional object configuration. It seems that mouse actions and manipulation activities are convenient from a holistic point of view, whereas they tend to focus too much on the ultimate shape, instead of the whole process of construction. In other words, there is some difficulty for students in analyzing the 3D object construction process, reflecting on what they have done, and modifying the errors they made during the process since the construction process should be parallel processing rather than sequential processing.

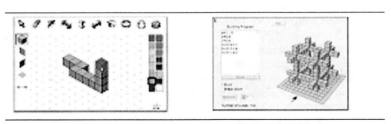

a. block software   b. WisWeb

Figure 2. Mouse-based three-dimesional microworld.

In conclusion, both current 2D-based and 3D-based software are not sufficient to enhance students' effective learning of three-dimensional objects. In particular, as we previously presented, there are basically two reasons why students have difficulty dealing with three-dimensional object exploration by using a 2D-based LOGO program. The first reason is, it is confusing to express three-dimensional objects with two-dimensional folding nets. The other one is, LOGO provides a programming language environment in which students have difficulty dealing with as its mathematical expression. Moreover, 3D-based programs provided by NCTM and Freudenthal Institute also cannot meet learners' requirements since they do not provide mathematical expression in the process of constructing an environment and they cannot perfectly reflect the construction process. Consequently, those transitional objects are not sufficient to be mathematical visualization tools. Based on the 3D module and turtle metaphor of LOGO, we developed a three-dimensional Microworld for 3D mathematical visualization that can construct three-dimensional objects with mathematical expressions. In this study, therefore, we propose a transitional object which can reflect mental operation activity by representing visualizing processes. For this purpose, the turtle metaphor has been extended to 3D, and three-dimensional objects can be represented with turtle expressions. In the manner of this concept, three features of turtle expression are summarized. Firstly, it still uses the idea of the turtle commands of LOGO. Secondly, it utilizes a 3D module as thebasic unit. Finally, the expression is not a turtle programming command, but an action symbol. In the following chapter, the process of how to develop the original LOGO environment using turtle expression will be reviewed.

SEMIOTIC TOOLS FOR MATHEMATICAL VISUALIZATION

Visualization has always been emphasized in relation to mathematics education, particularly with the advent of computer technology that allows the possibility of a wide range of visual displays. Presmeg (2006a) stressed that both symbolic information and visual information are important for understanding spatial visualization. She explained that 'mathematics is a subject that has diagrams, tables, spatial arrangements of signifiers such as symbols, and other inscriptions as essential components'. According to her argument, visualization plays an important role in mathematical education especially when visual components are combined with symbolic components. When designing a computer-based learning environment, it is not enough to simply emphasize mouse manipulation or menu selection. Rather, in order to facilitate students' learning, designing a symbolic operation environment in which students can easily manipulate symbols is needed. Therefore, this study aims to develop a semiotic approach which can enhance students' three-dimensional learning using LOGO-based action symbols.

Along with visualization, semiotics also has been an area of interest for a number of researchers. There are two divergent traditions in semiotics stemming respectively from **Saussure** and **Peirce**. **Peirce** and **Saussure** used the term 'symbol' differently: Saussure defined a sign as being composed of a two-dimensional structure: the signifier and signified. Unlike Saussure, Peirce's concept of a sign is a relation between three signifying dimensions: represents, representamen and interpretant in which the three dimensions are irrevocably connected. In Peirce's theory of signs, knowledge does not consist of objects or entities, but it is thought of as knowing, or a process. They way people build knowledge is though their experiences in the world (Uden et al. 2001). Thought processes take place in semiotic chains, where individual signs connect to each other and mutually interact. It is clear that semiotic chains can enhance knowledge building, and a number of researchers drew their attention toward semiotic chains. According to Presmeg (2006b), "Using a semiotic chain, a sequence of abstractions is created while preserving the important relationships from the everyday practices of the students." The importance of situational knowledge has been emphasized by De Jong and Monica (1996), and they claimed that having situational knowledge is beneficial to students for good understanding. Noss, Hoyles and Pozzi (2002) also pointed out the situated abstract and they argued that abstraction is not decontextualization; they believed instead that students not only organize structure and relation but also enlarge the situation within the situation and context. More-over, Van der Meij and De Jong (2006) examined the representation activities through various ways to support learners in the translation between representations in simulation-based learning environments. The results of their study stressed that a learning environment with integrated representations could lead to better under-standing about an abstract concept. Taking on the issue of a semiotic chain, Hall (2000) developed a general model of a semiotic chain as shown in Figure 4. He claimed that students can expand the 'signifier' to the 'signified' as long as they make a connection between their experiences and proper situation. In other words, a situation which links activities from the lives of students should be provided.

As stated above, most research tends to focus on the semiotic approach in the field of mathematics education. Although mathematical activity such as symbol (eg., equation) operation is pivotal in mathematics classroom teaching, providing an environment which deals with primitive operating symbols seems necessary. This way, students are not only able to develop embodied activities to mental activities through primitive symbols provided with meaning, but also they can construct semiotic chains through construction activities by combining primitive symbols.

An entire activity that serves as partial material of the next activity can be an example of a semiotic chain. In Table 1, the turtle activity on the left is used as partial material of the next turtle activity, which means the first entire activity is compressed into a sign and functions as a partial sign in the next activity. This semiotic chain shows the process of how to construct a whole configuration using partial signs. Meanwhile, the use of symbolic characters can be considered as the process of

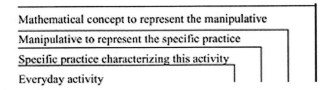

Figure 3. A general model of a semiotic chain between practices (Hall, 2000, p. 174).

Table 1. Turtle actions and semiotic chain

Def QuaterCircle {
repeat 9 {
fd 3;
rt 10;
}
}
	Def Petal {
	repeat 2 {
	QuaterCircle;
	t 90;
	}
	}
		Def Flower {
		Petal; rt -90;Petal;
		rt 90; fd 40;
		repeat 8 {
		Petal;
		rt 360/8;
		}
		fd -40;
		}
			Def Garden {
			repeat 3 {
			Flower;
			rt 90;
			fd 40;
			rt -90;
			}
			}

Table 2. SOLO's taxonomy (Biggs & Collis, 1982)

Pre-structural	Unistructural	Multistructural	Relational	Extended abstract

forming partial signs into the whole configuration. As can be seen in Table 1, in the complete picture, three flowers stand for the units, and each of them is a six-petalled flower with two leaves. Also, their leaves are made up of symmetrical curved lines to form the shape of zygomorphic flowers. This analysis is closely related to mathematical thinking, which finds and organizes rules or patterns from a holistic point of view. Symbolic expressions with signs reveal three-dimensional configurations of objects, as well as analytical thinking, and a number of researches have been carried out in this manner. For instance, Olive (1991) examined the signs which students made to construct polyhedrons with LOGO, and Biggs and Collis (1982) set out SOLO's Taxonomy as a means of evaluating the quality of students. According to the level of students' understanding, the taxonomy classified them into five stages: prestructural, unistructural, multistructural, relational and extended abstract. In fact, SOLO taxonomy can be used as a useful tool To evaluate LOGO. The five levels identified by Biggs and Collis are explained briefly in Table 2.

Figure 4 presents the evolution process of the tool that was developed through evolving the same (or similar) turtle action commands and compressing complex objects into symbols. The more detailed evolution process can be seen in Figure 4.a and Figure 4.b. Taking a close look at the evolution process, the turtle commands

a. Turtle in LOGO	b. Turtle in L-system	c. Turtle net	d. Turtle block
		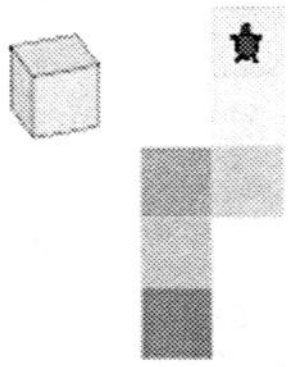	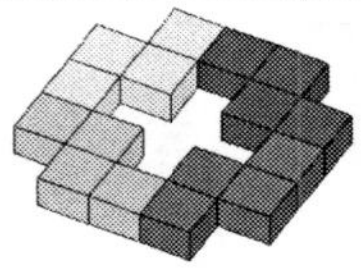
fd : go forward rt : turn left	f : make 1D line L : turn left R : turn right	m : make 2D rectangle L : turn left R : turn right	s : make 3D cube L : turn left R : turn right

repeat 4 {
fd 30 ; rt 90;
}
	f L f L f L f L	mmm R m L mm	repeat 4 {
			ssRsLs R
			}

turtle commands	action symbols and turtle expressions		
turtle goes forward to draw 1D line		turtle makes 2D faces	turtle makes 3D blocks

Figure 4. Turtle symbols and semiotic chain.

(Figure 4.a) such as 'forward' and 'rotation' had been compressed into 'F', 'L', and 'R' (Figure 4.b). In Figure 4.c, the polygon (square in this case) was constructed with the turtle movement which was generated form Figure 4.a and Figure 4.b.In Figure 4.d the turtle is moving and making blocks, and these blocks resulted from blocks made in Figure 4.c by attaching polygons and folding the nets together to construct blocks. This study, therefore, aims to propose a transitional object whose turtle commands like 'forward' and 'rotation' function as action symbols which are generated from three-dimensional objects and nets, as it simultaneously uses 3D modules such as blocks and tiles as basic units of three-dimensional objects. As can be seen in Figure 4.c and Figure 4.d, footing metaphors and elevator metaphors are introduced as storytelling materials. In this study, the former and the latter are called a turtle net and turtle block, respectively.

As the turtle puts together the blocks using elevator metaphors, a three-dimensional object is generated and the entire turtle blocks become a thinkable object. The turtle also is constructing 3D blocks around it in elevator metaphors while it is moving forward. In other words, the turtle is constructing a block with three action symbols- s(moving forward), **L**, and **R**(rotating from side to side with 90 degrees)- on the same floor. As long as the turtle is constructing blocks in 3D space, turtle commands which can help the turtle move from floor to floor are required. The authors, thus, developed two action symbols- **u**(going up one floor) and **d**(going down one floor)- as a complementary measure, and this measure enables the turtle to move from floor to floor to construct blocks, just like taking an elevator. An example of constructing three-dimensional objects with these two symbols is shown in Figure 5, and the arrow indicates the initial location and direction of the turtle.

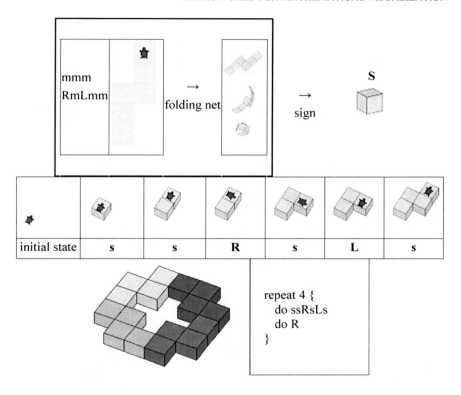

Figure 5. A tetracube and its turtle expression.

MATHEMATICAL VISUALIZATION WITH TURTLE BLOCKS

The authors introduced the turtle block to the teacher training classes and gifted school classroom teaching. In the teacher training classes, we pointed out the potential connection between the theoretical factors of the turtle block and mathematical knowledge and also introduced the turtle block as a tool which can function as creative mathematical activity. While in gifted school classes, we utilized the turtle block to do mathematical exploration and made creative works. For example, we only provided a basic manual in which we explained the action symbols - **u**, **d**, **s**, **L**, and **R**- in teacher training classes. However, we gave a ten-minute lecture to explain the function of turtle blocks, and after that we also did an activity with turtle blocks as well. As a result, a number of various creative works (Figure 6) were developed. From the perspective of 'learning by making', we can conclude that students are not only able to produce a sense of three-dimensional objects while they are making various creative works, but also can develop structural understanding about three-dimensional objects.

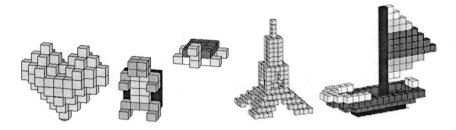

Figure 6. Mathematical visualization with turtle blocks.

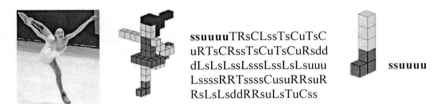

ssuuuuTRsCLssTsCuTsC
uRTsCRssTsCuTsCuRsdd
dLsLsLssLsssLssLsLsuuu
LssssRRTssssCusuRRsuR
RsLsLsddRRsuLsTuCss

ssuuuu

Figure 7. Physical objects and their commands.

It is noteworthy that the structural characteristics of the target three-dimensional object should receive attention in order to express three-dimensional objects with turtle blocks. In this section, we will review how the turtle block represents students' thought processes by giving examples which are made of turtle blocks. The example below is intended to express the figure skating starYuna Kim by using turtle blocks. This work was made by a teacher who attended a teacher training program, and she was just shown a simple manual explaining action symbols such as **s, u, d, R, L** and did not attend any extra lectures. A more detailed analysis on the symbolic system of the turtle block in this work will be discussed.

Looking at the beginning part of the turtle command –ssuuu (Figure 7)-, this work was constructed from its bottom to its top to express 'Yuna Kim'. In other words, the teacher used the feet as a central axis to construct the entiwork from its toe to its head, a method often used in building block activities. According to the command, the order of the construction can be guessed. In this case, the order is as follows: right foot, left foot, left arm, skirt, body, right arm and head. For the skirt, the command - **LsLsLssLssLssLsLs**- shows it starts from the middle and spirals upward.

In this sense, our 3D representation program can be applied to creativity education for math-talented students since turtle blocks, as basic modules, can construct three-dimensional objects; also, symbolic analysis can reflect students' thinking. Therefore, we conducted 3D creative design activities which have extended LOGO to 3D.

As shown in Figure 9.a, students are given basic figures to make as many unique stories as they can. This type of question has been frequently used in some activities relating to creativity such as Torrance Test Creative Thinking (TTCT) (Figure 8.a)

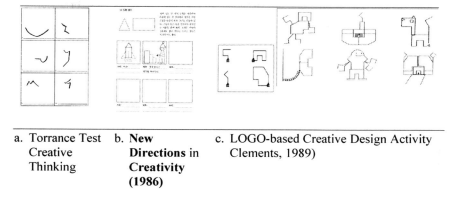

| a. Torrance Test Creative Thinking | b. **New Directions** in **Creativity (1986)** | c. LOGO-based Creative Design Activity Clements, 1989) |

Figure 8. Creativity question.

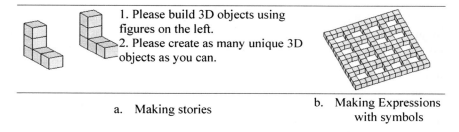

1. Please build 3D objects using figures on the left.
2. Please create as many unique 3D objects as you can.

| a.   Making stories | b.   Making Expressions with symbols |

Figure 9. Creative activity with turtle blocks.

or 'Renzulli's New Directions in Creativity (Figure 8.b)'. Moreover, Clements (1989) proposed a LOGO-based creativity activity as a means to test creativity (Figure 8.c). Figure 9.a presents a new type of creativity activity which has extended the existing activities to the 3D level-activity. On the one hand, this new activity promotes divergent thinking; on the other hand, it also requires convergent thinking and spatial visualization abilities which precisely express one's own ideas with symbols. Therefore, this activity can be considered as a mathematical creativity activity since it requires systematic thinking and spatial sense, which are necessary in mathematics, along with common creativity.

The students each made four or five works with the given materials, and each student developed a story by making connections between two pieces at a time. Figure 10 displays one of the examples of students' works. This student chose a recent hot issue-the Chun an hum incident- as a story and built up blocks to depict the story with vivid turtle block figures. The reason why his work is so impressive is because he describes the story well with a minimal number of blocks. Also, he used an emoticon which expresses "sad" to make his work seem simple but impressive. It seems, therefore, this kind of activity can be evaluated based on the creativity test criteria.

	story	object		story	object
1	When I heard about the Chun-An-Hum incident,		3	The whole nation flies to Baeknyeong Island,	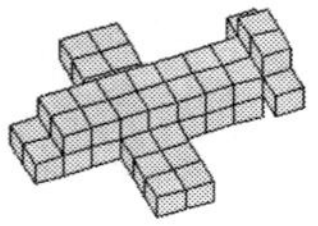
2	I felt ㅠ.ㅠ (sad)		4	make a line to try our best to pull our sailors out of the water. Cheer up~!! Please come back to us.	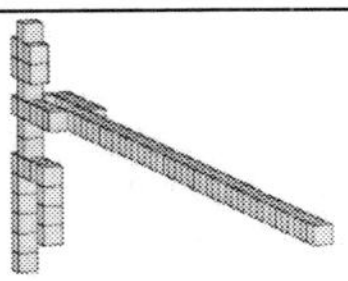

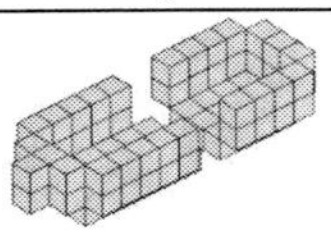

Figure 10. Students' work using turtle blocks to make a story.

Unlike the above activity, Figure 9.b displays an activity which can be used to analyze students' thinking by examining the symbols made by students. This activity requires students' ability to find patterns and develop their ideas, skills which are useful in mathematical creativity, to build the given objects. It was noted that students were able to express the command "promise" in a simple and organized manner.

Table 3 shows an example of describing students' performance in each of the different levels based on the semiotic chain. As can be seen, students only focused on building objects without finding out any structures in the pre-structural phase, while they could figure out the structures as the units of the whole object in the uni-structural and multi-structural phases. Especially, students applied the 'promise' command, which was used in the previous phase, to the next stage in the multi-structural phase, indicating that a semiotic chain had been created.

This level of taxonomy provides the basis of a more developed creativity assessment which is different from the present subjective and ambiguous one, so that it will be a little more accessible and objective. Therefore, creativity can be tested using turtle block activities in terms of configuration and analysis.

Table 3. Analysis on symbols with SOLO taxonomy

	Use of "promise" command	Example	Command structure
Pre-structural	To avoid simple repetition	Promise A { do sssssssssssss } do sARARARA do RsssRALsssLARsssRALsssLARRsss do RALsssLARsssRALsssLARRsss	s — A s L R

Table 3. (Continued)

Uni structural	As one Structure unit	Use 'Promise' command once	Promise A {do ssssLssssLssssLssss} do AAAAsssssssssAAAALsssssss AAA ALsssssssAAAA	s > A L s L
		Use 'Promise' command twice	Parallel structure	Promise 만{do 4sL3sL3sL3sL2s} Promise 해{do LL11sTsR3sCR} do 만만만만만해만만만만만해만만만 만해 만만만만	s > 만 L s → 해 L R
Multi structural	Hierarchy structure with more than two structure units		Promise A {do sssRsssRsssRsss} Promise B {do AAAA} do BssssssBRssssssBRssssssB	s > A — B R s
			Promise A {do sssL} Promise B {do sss} Promise X {do AAAA} Promise Y {do XBXBXBXBL} do YYYYBBLYLY	s > A — X > Y L s — B B

CLOSING REMARKS

The transitional object in the present study has been developed with the goal of facilitating students' learning, and aims to compensate for other programs' shortcomings. According to Zazkis and Liljedahl (2004), "Prime numbers are often described as building blocks of natural numbers" (p. 164). Hence, turtle blocks were viewed as prime numbers of a three-dimensional object in this study. In a related matter, a certain command system is necessary to express the three-dimensional object using basic building blocks since it is identical with using prime numbers to show prime factorization when we study integers in mathematical education. That is why we introduced the command system related to the LOGO-based action symbols. As a matter of fact, we used proper metaphors in developing these action symbols in our aim to provide students with a concrete situation to facilitate their learning. Meanwhile, it is notable that the complicated situation should be expressed in a simple way in order to be a students' exploration environment. Thus, we tried to provide students with a few action symbols and related metaphors to make a concrete situation. Since both building block activities and the LOGO environment are included in the curriculum of Korean elementary schools, students eventually consider both building blocks and action commands as concrete objects because of their familiarity with them.

Moreover, using turtle symbols makes it possible to understand of students' thinking processes by analyzing the commands which students used. Also, it is one of the important factors to enhance algebraic analysis ability. Spatial visualization ability is the ability to mentally manipulate two-dimensional and three-dimensional figures, and it is considered to be an important ability in many different fields. In addition to spatial visualization ability, building blocks are often used in various tests such as MRT (Mental Rotation Test, Vandenberg and Kuse, 1978) or WISC (Wechsler Intelligence Scale for Children, Wechsler, 2003) for the purpose of estimating spatial visualization ability.

In sum, in this study, we developed turtle expression, which is a transitional object like a turtle block, by introducing building blocks and footing in the semiotic microworld. We also introduced footing metaphors and elevator metaphors for the turtle block. Then, we discussed creative activities and mathematical activities which applied to turtle expressions in terms of the turtle block.

Moreover, this study may contribute to the further development of various mathematical creativity activities using turtle blocks since it provides a Microworld Turtle Block environment which requires the method of creativity assessment to be counted into consideration. Finally, the turtle block can be utilized in special education for gifted students regarding mathematics. As previously described, the turtle block can be a thinkable object, because it is the basic module of a 3D object and it has a polyhedral shape as well; however, more investigations, just like on-going explorations about Euler characteristics, are needed. In addition, the turtle block can be investigated in relation to Graph Theory in Discrete Mathematics since the generation process of blocks is a sequential process in which each block is created as a symbol is added onto it. And thus, one block corresponds to the endpoint of the graph and the turtle movement trace likewise corresponds to a line segment of the graph. We believe the proposed Microworld Turtle Block will provide a significant implication not only for mathematics but also creativity education.

REFERENCES

Biggs, J. B., & Collis, K. F. (1982). Evaluating the quality of learning: The SOLO taxonomy (Structure of the Observed Learning outcome). New York: Academic Press.

Casey, B. M., Andrews, N., Schindler, H., Kersh, J. E., Samper, A., & Copley, J. (2008). The development of spatial skills through interventions involving block building activities, *Cognition and Instruction, 26,* 269–309.

Clements, D. H. (1989). *Computers in elementary mathematics education.* New Jersey: Prentice-Hall, Inc. A Division of Simon & Schuster Englewood Cloffs.

De Jong, T., & Monica, G. F. (1996). Types and qualities of knowledge, *Educational Psychologist, 31*(2), 105–113.

Dreyfus, T. (1993). Didactic design of computer-based learning environments. In C. Keitel & K. Ruthven (Eds.), *Learning from computers: Mathematics education and technology, NATO ASI Series* (Vol. F 121, pp. 101–130). Berlin: Springer-Verlag, 1993.

Freudenthal Institute. (2010-present). *"WisWeb", Freudenthal Institute and APS-wiskunde.* Retrieved from http://www.fi.uu.nl/wisweb/

Hall, M. (2000). *Bridging the gap between everyday and classroom mathematics: An investigation of two teachers' intentional use of semiotic chains.* Unpublished Ph.D. Dissertation, The Florida State University.

Healy, L., & Hoyles, C. (1996). Seeing, doing and expressing: An evaluation of task sequences for supporting algebraic thinking. In L. Puig & A. Gutierrez (Eds.), *Proceedings of the 20th PME international conference* (Vol. 3, pp. 67–74).

Hoyles, C., & Noss, R. (2003). What can digital technologies take from and bring to research in mathematics education?. In A. J. Bishop, M. A. Clements, C. Keitel, J. Kilpatrick, & F. K. S. Leung (Eds.), *Second International Handbook of Mathematics Education* (pp. 323–349). Dordrecht: Kluwer Academic Publishers.

Kynigos, C. & Latsi, M. (2007). Turtle's navigation and manipulation of geometrical figures constructed by variable processes in a 3d simulated space, *EuroLOGO*, 2007.

Morgan, C., & Alshwaikh, J. (2008) Imag(in)ing three-dimensional movement with gesture: 'Playingturtle' orpointing? *Proceedings of the British Society for Research into Learning Mathematics*, *28*(3).

NCTM (2010-present). *Isometric drawing tool.* National Council of Teachers of Mathematics. Retrieved form http://illuminations.nctm.org/activitydetail.aspx?id=125

Nemirovsky, R., & Noble, T. (1997). On mathematical visualization and the place where we live. *Educational Studies in Mathematics*, *33*, 99–131.

Noss, R., Hoyles, C., & Pozzi, S. (2002). Abstraction in expertise: A study of nurses' conceptions of concentration, *Journal for Research in Mathematics Education*, *33*(3), 204–229.

Olive, J. (1991). Logo programming and geometric understanding: An in-depth study. *Journal for Research in Mathematics Education*, *22*(2), 90–111.

Presmeg, N. (2006a). Research on visualization in learning and teaching mathematics. In A. Gutierrez & P. Boero (Eds.), *Handbook of research on the psychology of mathematics education: past, present and future.*

Presmeg, N. (2006b). Semiotics and the "Connections" standard: Significance of semiotics for teachers of mathematics. *Educational Studies in Mathematics*, *61*, 163–182.

Uden, L., Liu, K., & Shank, G. (2001). Linking radical constructivism and semiotics to design a constructivist learning environment, *Journal of Computing in Higher Education*, *12*(2), 34–51.

Vandenberg, S. G., & Kuse, A. R. (1978) Mental rotations, a group test of three dimensional spatial visualisation. *Perceptual and Motor Skills*, *60*, 343–350.

Van der Meij, J., & de Jong, T. (2006). Supporting students' learning with multiple representations in a dynamic simulation-based learning environment. *Learning and Instruction*, *16*, 199–212.

Wechsler, D. (2003). *Technical and interpretive manual of the Wechsler intelligence scale for children-IV.* New York: Psychological Corporation.

Yeh, A., & Nason, R. (2004). *Toward a semiotic framework for using technology in mathematics education: The case of learning 3D geometry.* International Conference on Computers in Education, Melbourne, Australia.

Zazkis, R., Dubinsky, E. & Dautermann, J. (1996). Using visual and analytic strategies: A study of students' understanding of permutation and symmetry groups. *Journal of Research in Mathematics Education*, *27*(4), 435–457.

Zazkis, R., & Liljedahl, P. (2004). Understanding primes: The role of representation. *Journal for Research in Mahtematics Education*, *35*(3), 164–186.

Zimmermann, W., & Cunningham, S. (1991). Editors' introduction: What is mathematical visualization? In W. Zimmermann & S. Cunningham (Eds.), *Visualization in teaching and learning mathematics*, (pp. 1–7).

Han Hyuk Cho, Min Ho Song and Ji Yoon Lee
Seoul National University in Korea

VIKTOR FREIMAN

11. MATHEMATICALLY GIFTED STUDENTS IN INCLUSIVE SETTINGS

The Example of New Brunswick, Canada

INTRODUCTION: CONTEXT AND ISSUES

In many countries including Canada, an inclusive view of mathematics education
aims to reach all students in mathematics classroom allowing everybody to make
progress at her own pace. When we say 'all students', this also includes the gifted
ones. Or, research shows that an appropriate mathematical provision for the most
able students is still an unsolved task. For example Diezmann and Watters (2002)
argue that in mathematics education, the focus is now put on numeracy with the
emphasis on 'minimums' of mathematical capability and lacking of attention to the
'maximums'.

Why is it important to care about those 'maximums'? Example of Canada can be
an interesting case to analyze because despite its global economic leadership (Finances
Canada, 2010), there are growing concerns about lack of highly qualified human
resources able to meet challenges of several sectors, such as digital economy, that
are seen as crucial for maintaining this position (Government of Canada, 2010). In
a certain way, we can see some interesting parallels between historically first wave
of particular attention to gifted and talented students in Canada as in other Western
countries that appears to be related to the Soviet Sputnik in the late 1950s. However,
this attention, especially related to the area of science did not last and education of
the gifted was somewhat neglected (Bortwick, Dow, Levesque and Banks, 1980).

Nowadays, in 2002, it was a well-established fact that while Canada wants to
keep the highest level of economic growth and social prosperity, it has to care of
brightest young citizens in all areas but especially in science and technology where
the gap between the need for high qualified professional and enrolment in university
programs is the most striking. With its recently developed strategy for innovation,
the Canadian government stresses the need to double a number of highly qualified
professionals through the development, attraction and retaining of talented and highly
skilled task force as a crucial condition of a successful global economy of the
knowledge-based modern society (Government of Canada, 2002). This policy has a
direct impact on educational system that must provide the better education in the
world, especially at the post-secondary level forming better scientists and managers.
There is no surprise that one of the direct outcomes of this strategy should be a
particular attention to the educational needs of the most gifted and talented population.
Again, areas of mathematics, science, along with reading become priorities focus

B. Sriraman and K.H. Lee (eds.), The Elements of Creativity and Giftedness in Mathematics, 161–191.

in this new trend which is also seen in attention given by Western governments to comparative studies, such as PISA (Freiman and Lirette-Pitre, 2007; Organization for Economic Co-operation and Development, OECD, 2000).

GIFTED EDUCATION IN CANADA: A BRIEF PORTRAYAL

Education is a very complex system in the modern Canadian society since it is governed autonomously by provinces that may develop different policies and legislations related to education, in general, and gifted education, in particular; this can lead to substantial disparities in what kind of educational services will be provided to the whole population and to particular groups with specific needs and how these specific needs will be met.

Goguen (1989) recalls results of the survey conducted in 1980, the Canadian Education Association (CEA) has conducted a survey, which indicated that the school acts of only two provinces, namely Ontario and Saskatchewan, specifically provided for education of gifted students. The author asked whether those legislation provisions have been revised since 1980. He found that disparities still existed with 4 provinces without any specific policy on gifted education (Newfoundland, Prince Edward Island, Manitoba and Yukon) and 6 others (Nova Scotia, New Brunswick, Quebec, Alberta, British Columbia and the Northwest Territories) where specific Ministry-level administrative policy statements on education of gifted children were adapted, in addition to the mentioned above Ontario and Saskatchewan where provincial legislations already existed in 1980 (Goguen, 1989).

These disparities in gifted education result in diversity of approaches for identifying and educating gifted students, so it becomes possible that an individual can be gifted in one province but "not gifted" in another; the differences could also be at the school district level as noted by Lupart et al. (2005).

Among others, New Brunswick has a unique school system because of its duality in providing separate education services in two official languages French and English which adds more complexity to these issues because of several substantial differences in a school culture, school structure and functioning, teaching and learning approaches as well as curriculum. These differences may also affect education of gifted students. For example, one of latest studies reports that the French sector is more concerned about issue with gifted students (Mackay, 2006).

In an educational system where all students are attending all school levels from Kindergarten to Grade 12 with a very low drop-out rate and no state regulation in- and beyond-school programs for gifted, it is not surprising that the provision of mathematically gifted relies mostly on particular classroom conditions (school leadership, teacher engagement and qualification, resources, methods of teaching) as well as beyond-school support (family, community, job market, university). In fact, the recent study of the inclusive school system in New Brunswick produced a report in which the situation with gifted is being portrayed as lacking of a clear policy and resources (Mackay, 2006). The report points at the gifted students as one of the most often neglected groups of students with special needs. One reason given is that labelling a student as gifted is not appropriate because every student is gifted in certain way. Another reason is a lack of a clear definition of enrichment policy in the school curriculum.

Following recommendations of the report, the New Brunswick government has launched a new initiative 'Kids come first' (MENB, 2007). The text of the document has six entries for the word 'gifted' which witness a particular political (and financial) attention given to this specific category of learners. First, it expresses a *concern* that a child who loses a natural interest and curiosity towards Grade 3 may drift this attitude all way through the high school. Therefore, a two million $ Innovation Fond will be provided to the organization of activity that would challenge gifted students.

Second, the government plan to make its curriculum more *flexible* to let bright high school students pursue their interest in special subjects through joint programs with universities. Third, teachers will be encouraged to use innovative teaching methods and co-curricular activities to *energize* gifted students. Fourth, special *services* are to be provided for inclusive school settings making them better suitable for all learners with special needs including the gifted ones. Finally, the document sees an evolutional approach to make necessary changes building on existing *models* and practices that have already been experimented with the gifted population.

What does this policy mean for mathematically gifted students? In the next section, we will analyze new trends in mathematics school curriculum.

NEW TRENDS IN MATHEMATICS EDUCATION: WHAT DOES IT BRING TO GIFTED STUDENTS?

During the last twenty years, school systems of many countries have been looking for changes in their curriculum that would help each student to meet challenges of modern complex world but have been doing it in a different way. The school reform undertaken in New Brunswick, Canada aims to follow these tendencies aiming to ensure that each child receives the best possible education and to reach the highest possible level of self-realisation (MENB, 2003).

According to this, the learning shall be differentiated in order to meet the educational needs on the basis of respect of individual differences. Thus, a particular attention will be brought to each student helping him/her to fully use his/her personal resources and taking into consideration his/her knowledge and interests. New trends in making mathematics classroom more student-centred appeal to the intensive use of so-called new methods of teaching: project-based learning, group work, social oriented teaching based on the student's real life experience, which is believed to help students to understand mathematics better.

However, it remains an open question, to what extent these innovations provide a harmonious passage to more abstract levels of mental development and are sufficiently helpful to form a student's theoretical thinking. For example, our comparative study of Russian and German schools conducted in the early 90s revealed substantial differences in mathematics curricula and teaching approaches (Freiman, 1995). We found that while the German Middle School curriculum was more student-oriented and diversified, and its mathematical content was much simpler in terms of formal and abstract mathematics; therefore we asked in what way this difference would affect students' access to more advanced mathematics courses (Freiman, 1995).

Several researchers express similar concerns, as for example Pareja-Heredia (2008), by saying that mathematics contents are degrading with time and we are probably teaching less mathematics now than a century ago:

We are creating a great volume of mathematics nowadays, as it can be verified through the web and through the many mathematical journals all around the world. This great amount of mathematics, of course, cannot go directly to the classroom. However, after some decantation, some parts of it would be suitable to be taught either at high school or at college level. There are no enough pedagogical or scientific reasons for not teaching at high school, for example, either Riemannian geometry, or non-Euclidean geometries, after almost two centuries since these topics were discovered (Pareja-Heredia, 2008: 4).

According to the author, this approach might create a gap between school and higher levels of education, such as college and university. Some students would have difficulties in following advanced mathematics and science courses. The most able students would lose their interest in mathematics and diminish their high intellectual potential. Similar observations were made by Tall (1995) who argues that mathematics taught in school and at the university are very different:

Now mathematics educators involved with mathematics in school are operating in an age of democratic equality of opportunity which is predicated on a broad curriculum suitable for the needs of the wide population. There are signs that the curriculum in elementary mathematics is producing students less ready to study mathematics at university (Tall, 1995: 14).

The author makes suggestions that 'it would be pertinent for a proportion of the mathematics education community to focus on the learning of those students in elementary mathematics who might develop the potential for advanced mathematical thinking, to analyse whether their learning environment is suitable for their long-term development' (Tall, 1995: 14).

At the same time, the new curriculum gives schools and teachers a real opportunity to develop classroom situations that meet needs and interests of all students.

Already in 1990s, a strong tradition of teaching challenging mathematics curriculum has been developed in New Brunswick with the implementation of the *Challenging Mathematics* textbooks (Lyons and Lyons, 1989) at the elementary school (Grades 1–6). In addition to more traditional curriculum content, the discovery approach emphasized by the textbooks offered possibility to all students to investigate in more depth mathematical concepts and relationships already taught and to study some topics earlier than in other textbooks.

For example, already in Grade 5, solving of system of linear equations with two variables was introduced. One chapter of Grade 6 textbooks was devoted to the study of *Konigsberg Bridges* problem to investigate graphs. At the same school level, students were asked to make geometric constructions with compass and straightedge. These topics as well as additionally taught set theory, logic and chess were accompanied by solving challenging contest-like problems, puzzles and enigmas allowed teachers to construct open-ended enriched in-class activities which we found suitable for identification and fostering early mathematical giftedness (Freiman, 2006, 2010). Locally conducted study with 437 fifth graders about the impact of chess on problems solving found increased gains in math problem-solving and comprehension proportionate to the amount of chess in the curriculum (Gaudreau, 1992). However, this program was found as difficult to teach to all students, had no continuation in the Middle Grades, and the effort to bring some elements of discovery-based and problem-based learning in the high school using the Math IMPACT text book series has failed.

As result, the mathematics curriculum had to be replaced in early 2000s with a new one which was a response to several issues and trends. Many features of the discovery-based learning and enrichment mentioned above had to disappear living place to more standard-based (referring to the Standards of the National Council of Teachers of Mathematics, NCTM, 2000) compatible with other provinces (there was an agreement between Atlantic provinces to keep learning outcomes intact to facilitate students' mobility, Council of Atlantic Ministers of Education and Training, CAMET, 1996), and reflecting trends towards numeracy development and connecting mathematics to the real-life making problem-solving more contextualized and putting emphasis on development of abilities in mathematical reasoning and communication while solving problem situations (situations-problèmes).

Moreover, this shift puts also more pressure on teachers as solving complex contextual real-life related problems is becoming part of mandatory provincial exams, so some of them may opt for instruction focused on only getting good scores on tests of performance instead of using more problem-based learning approaches (Roh, 2003). Also, it may force them to reduce the use of enriched materials, recreational mathematics, in-depth investigations, and more abstract mathematical content that was part of the previous *Challenging Mathematics* curriculum and to increase the use of performance-based tasks that may affect the interest of gifted learners in pursuing study of pure mathematics.

Today's mathematics curriculum in New Brunswick French schools does not specify any concrete content or approach addressed to the needs of mathematically gifted students. However, in its common part with other subjects, it recognises individual differences in students and sees the diversity of learning styles and abilities as richness (MENB, 2005). Differentiation is thus seen as an angular stone of the pedagogical model that aims to create a rich and stimulating learning environment for all students. Among other, the curriculum stresses the necessity to enrich sometimes the required curriculum adjusting it to the small number of students who have particular forces.

Research suggests to the caring teacher a variety of methods to differentiate teaching making it suitable for gifted students like the use of multiple resources, inquiry-based, discovery learning approaches, higher-order questioning, flexible and differentiated assessment tools, create opportunities for participation in different contests along with content which extends curriculum requirements mentioned by

Johnson (2000) or several concrete examples from the more recent work of Reed (2004) who points at three types of differentiation: extension, open-ended investigation, and self-selection of topics for in-depth study.

Renewed curriculum brings also some additional more real-life related inter-disciplinary problem-based focus (situation-problème) with emphasis on mathematical communication and reasoning abilities. While mathematical content fixed in learning outcomes in four main study domains: numbers, algebra, space and statistics and in learning principles: problem solving, reasoning, communication and making links is the same for all students, the high school program establishes four competence levels with the highest one labelled as 'above average' thus expecting some students going beyond prescribed minimum (*MENB*, 2005).

Although this level describes a concrete mathematical content and skills related to this level, it leaves to the teacher to decide how to develop in her brightest students this superior capacity to analyse, synthesize and conceptualize abstract mathematical ideas as well as develop higher order thinking abilities allowing gifted individuals to solve complex, ill-defined non-routine problems. Therefore, along with the major shift in the school curriculum which is already a 'revolution' in terms of approaches to teaching and learning mathematics, teachers have to deal with an inclusive classroom in which the appropriate resources have to be found or created for all type of learners.

INNOVATIVE PROJECTS AND NEW OPPORTUNITIES FOR GIFTED

Looking for new opportunities to enrich mathematics teaching and learning in regular classrooms, we started implementing and investigating problem-based learning scenarios within a New Brunswick Individual Laptop Initiative (2004–2006) in which we measured an impact of laptops in learning mathematics, science, and literacy, as well as organizational skills and ICT competence in Grades 7 and 8 (ADOP, 2006).

Gifted learners were not studied specifically in this project. However, our findings suggest that teachers using laptops in their classed can cover mandatory curriculum faster than without technology. Remaining time can be spent on in-depth study of some topics, as well as go beyond curriculum. Another finding suggests that students learn different skills and in a different way which makes possible to almost individualize learning making it suitable to all students' needs (Freiman et al., 2010). Also, our data show that when learning to solve problems using technology students become more autonomous learners, become curios in learning more and make unusual knowledge transfers which may have an impact on their creativity, inventiveness, questioning and investigation. Working with laptops, students get easier access to the Internet-based resources such as home-made problem solving website CAMI (www. umoncton.ca/cami).

Our previous publications suggest that this online resource is suitable for challenge (Freiman et al., 2009), enrichment (Freiman, Manuel, and Lirette-Pitre, 2007, Freiman, 2009), and creativity (Manuel, 2009). The site CAMI is a part of a larger research project on informal learning, the main theme of the Center for Research in Youth, Science Teaching and Learning for the Atlantique Canada (www. crystalatlantique.ca, Sullenger and Freiman, 2010, in press). It has now an extension called Virtual Mathematical Marathon, an online mathematics summer competition for mathematically promising students interesting in more challenge that we run since 2008 (Freiman and Applebaum, 2009) thanks to the support of the Canadian Mathematical Society and Canadian Natural Sciences and Engineering Research Council (Promoscience Program). The latest program helps in realisation of the idea of the marathon as bilingual (French and English) year-around competition using newly created website www.umoncton.ca/umcm-mmv).

Concepts of community of practice, community school, and professional learning communities become popular in the provincial educational system. As university-based community, CAMI begins to attract school teachers willing to innovate in their practices using expertise of the project team which becomes partner in the government initiated programed called Innovative Learning Funds. Openness of the innovation to the gifted population is one criterion in this program. Together with teachers, we developed and implemented robotics-based scenarios (Blanchard, 2009).

In another project that looked how to involve gifted students from two local Middle schools (Grades 6–8) identified by their teachers as gifted basing on school marks and 'good' behaviour. Parents' agreement was also asked. Students became part of the CAMI team participating in the developing and integrating new problems on the website, and analyzing solutions submitted by other students to these problems. In certain problems, students decided to integrate audio and video clips aiming to help others to understand the text better by listening and visualizing.

Some of these students participated also in workshops for teachers demonstrating their work and sharing experiences. Others took part in international workshops organized by VMM team and MACAS team one of which helped them to explore in-depth the Golden Ratio (Manuel, in press). The last project to be mentioned was developed for Grade 10 students allowing them exploring links between mathematics, technology and architecture. Results from this study show that majority of students appreciate activity as meaning-making, enjoyable and enriching (Cormier, in press).

EXAMPLES OF EXTRACURRICULAR INITIATIVES

While in the regular school settings, provision for mathematically gifted remains on the shoulders of innovative teachers, supportive school administrators and collaboration with the university, more enthusiastic efforts are needed to organize extracurricular in- and after-school activities when mathematics competes with other traditionally attractive fields like sports and arts. Few examples of successful practices can be mentioned.

First, the provincial bilingual Middle School mathematics contest organized jointly by the University of New Brunswick (UNB) and Université de Moncton with the support of the provincial Ministry of Education is also to be mentioned. In the last 2010 contest, 1189 students participated: 374 at UNB-Fredericton, 245 at UNB - Saint John, and 147, 285 and 138, respectively, at the Edmundston, Moncton and Shippagan campuses of l'Université de Moncton. Students represented 157 schools from all 14 school districts.

According to the website of the Department of Mathematics at the UNB (http://www.math.unb.ca/mathcomp/), the competition provides a valuable opportunity for interaction between universities and schools. Teachers meet with competition coordinators while their students are busy solving problems. Teachers and students enjoy the afternoon tours and demonstrations. The competition rewards Grades 7, 8 and 9 students for academic excellence. While cited above activities had popularization of mathematics and science as main goal, gifted learners could also benefit from such forms (Bicknell, 2008).

Second, francophone students have another opportunity to participate at the Opti-Math national contests open to students aged 12 to 18, providing them with an opportunity for nearly 100,000 francophones across Canada to demonstrate their problem-solving ability. The last one was won by a student whose problem-solving abilities were identified by his teacher (with 32 years of teaching experience) as exceptional according to the Ministry of Education (http://www.gnb.ca/cnb/news/edu/2010e1037ed.htm)

Third, a new type of extracurricular activities that may attract gifted can be organized by school Districts with help of parents and enthusiastic teachers like, for example, 'Mathematical nights' (*Nuit de mathématiques*) when more than hundred students from several schools spending a night at school competing in chess, mathematics and science.

These local examples illustrate innovative opportunities in university-school collaboration that helps making the inclusive mathematics classroom more open to the gifted students a reality. However, a lot of issues related to the education of mathematically gifted remain unsolved. Already, the word 'giftedness' can be interpreted in different ways that may affect tools and criteria used to select students for special programs and activities. What instruments should be used and in which situation? Should be created provincially accepted uniform system of identification? What role could play parents in supporting programs for gifted (in case, their own children are identified as gifted or when other children from their child's class are selected)?

CONCLUSIVE REMARKS ON UNSOLVED ISSUES

With not enough research data available, it is difficult to dress a more complete portray of mathematical giftedness and judge about efficiency of cited programs and activities. As mentioned by some authors, classrooms do not always provide intellectually stimulating environments for gifted and talented students which can lead to situation when not only high potential of mathematically gifted may remain uncovered and underexplored, those students who do not fit into the school routine, are left on their own, and may became bored and even disturbing in terms of behaviour (Maccagnano, 2007; McCoach & Siegle, 2008).

On the other side, there are many types of giftedness and methods suitable for one student may not suit or even contradict to the other. It is very difficult and may be even impossible to find appropriate solution in all cases. A lot relies on teachers, their professionalism, devotion and enthusiasm. The teacher training is becoming crucial.

Survey data reported by Bajard (2009) allows drawing a profile of teachers to work with gifted. According to her,

> these teachers need to be enthusiastic and show a strong desire for intellectual growth. They need to seek excellence in themselves and others. They are self-confident and not threatened by those who learn with surprising speed. They need to demonstrate flexibility and a tolerance of ambiguity. They need to take creative risks, and to maintain intuitive and emotional relationships with the students. They need to believe in the importance of individual differences and to respect them. Teachers in these circumstances need to facilitate and guide rather than direct learning. They are positive, well-organized and methodical. Above all, they must have a sense of humour (Bajard, 2009, p. 2).

How to prepare such teachers? Recently, we conducted two studies comparing teachers and pre-service teachers' views of the mathematically promising students and their needs in Canada and Israel, as well as their readiness to work with them in the classroom. Far from generalizing our findings, it is interesting to mention that whereas teachers in both countries find they need learn more about psychological traits of mathematically gifted, there is less agreement in what kind of mathematical knowledge should teachers possess. Namely, 100% of Israeli participants agreed or strongly agreed that teachers need to learn how to solve investigation problems compared with only 60% of their Canadian colleagues who seem to share this point of view at the same level of agreement (Applebaum, Freiman, and Leikin, in press).

Another study with pre-service teachers' enrolled in mathematics education courses in Quebec and New Brunswick looked at their perceptions about the CAMI project and their ability to analyze multiple strategies and communication styles employed by students in solving complex, contextualized and sometimes open-ended problems posted on the website. We found that while majority of participants found useful having opportunities to solve rich mathematical problems online, as well as analyze students' solutions as a part of their didactic courses, they showed less competences in seeing flaws in students' solutions and giving students appropriate comments (LeBlanc and Freiman, in press).

The last issue to be mentioned but one of the first by its importance is related to the specificity of the French linguistic minority context in which we are working. Especially, shortage of resources and stimulation may force gifted Francophone students to move to the English schools that will give them more challenge, according to the findings reported by Bajard (2009). She found, among others that in the absence of accurate statistics on the identification of giftedness in minority communities, there is a fear that gifted students in Francophone minority communities are simply not identified because of a shortage of resources (Bajard, 2009).

REFERENCES

Applebaum, M., Freiman, V., & Leikin, R. (in press). Prospective teachers' conceptions about teaching mathematically talented students: Comparative examples from Canada and Israel. *Montana Mathematics Enthousiast, 8*(1–2).

Bicknell, B. (2008). Gifted students and the role of mathematics competitions. *Australian Primary Mathematics Classroom, 13*(4), 16–20.

Borthwick, B., Dow, I., Lévesque, D., & Banks, R. (1980). *The gifted and talented student in Canada: Results of a CEA survey.* Toronto: The Canadian Education Association.

CAMEF. (1996). *Foundation for the Atlantic Canada mathematics curriculum.*

Cormier, M. (in press). Bâtissons une ville géométrique ensemble: Apprentissage par projet en mathématiques des élèves de 10e année. In.

Diezmann, W. (2002). Summing up the education of mathematically gifted students. In *Proceedings 25th annual conference of the Mathematics Education research Group of Australasia* (pp. 219–226). Auckland.

Gaudreau, L. (1992). *Étude Comparative sur les Apprentissages en Mathématiques 5e Année.* June manuscript.

Finances Canada. (2010). *Canada's global economic leadership: A report to Canadians. Government of Canada.*

Freiman, V. (2006). Problems to discover and to boost mathematical talent in early grades: A challenging situations approach. *The Montana Mathematics Enthusiast, 3*(1), 51–75.

Freiman, V. (2009). Mathematical E-nrichment: Problem-of-the-week model. In R. Leikin, A. Berman, & B. Koichu (Eds.), *Creativity in mathematics and the education of gifted students* (pp. 367–382). Rottrerdam: Sense Publishing.

Freiman, V., & Applebaum, M. (2009). Involving students in extra-curricular school mathematical activity: Virtual mathematical marathon case study. In M. Tzekaki, M. Kaldrimidou, & H. Sakonidis (Eds.), *In search for theories in mathematics education: Proceedings of the 33th conference of the International Group for the psychology in mathematics education* (Vol. 1, pp. 203–205).

Freiman, V., Kadijevich, D., Kuntz, G., Pozdnyakov, S., & Stedoy, I. (2009). Challenging mathematics beyond the classroom enhanced by technology. In E. Barbeau & P. Taylor (Eds.), *The 16th ICMI study. New ICMI Study Series* (Vol. 12). *Challenging mathematics in and beyond the classroom.* Springer.

Freiman, V., Manuel, D., & Lirette-Pitre, N. (2007). CASMI virtual learning collaborative environment for mathematical enrichment. *Understanding our Gifted,* summer 2007, 20–23.

Freiman, V., & Lirette-Pitre, N. (2007). PISA2000 case study: New Brunswick. In Arbeitsgruppe Internationale Vergleichstudie (HRSG), *Schullleistungen und Steurung des Schulsystems in Bundesstaat: Kanada und Deutschland im Vergleich* (pp. 336–362). Muenster, New-York, Muenchen, Berlin: Waxmann.

Goguen, L. (1989). The education of gifted children in Canadian laws and ministerial policy. *Canadian Journal of Education, 14*(1).

Government of Canada. (2002). *Canada's innovation strategy.* Retrieved from http://www.innovation strategy.gc.ca/gol/innovation/site.nsf/en/in04113.html

Johnson. (2000, April). *Teaching mathematics to gifted students in a mixed-ability classroom.* ERIC EC Digest #E594.

Lupart, J. L., Pyryt, M. C., Watson, S. L., & Pierce, K. (2005). Gifted education and counselling in Canada. *International Journal for the Advancement of Counselling, 27*(2).

Lyons, R., & Lyons, M. (1989). *Challenging Mathematics-3.*

Maccagnano. (2007). *Identifying and enhancing the strength of gifted learner, K-8.* Corwin Press.

Mackey, A. (2006). *Connecting care and challenge: Tapping our human potential.* Report for the New Brunswick Ministry of Education.

McCoach, D. B., & Siegle, D. (2008). Underachievers. In J. A. Plucker & C. M. Callahan (Eds.), *Critical issues and practices in gifted education: What the research says* (pp. 721–734). Waco, TX: Prufrock Press.

MENB. (New Brunswick Ministry of Education, 2005). Programmes d'études M-12.

MENB. (New Brunswick Ministry of Education, 2007). Kids come first.

NCTM. (2000). *Principles and standards for school mathematics.* Reston, VA: NCTM.

OECD. (2000). *Program for international student assessment.* © OECD.

Reed, C. (2004). Mathematically gifted in the heterogeneously grouped mathematics classroom: What is a teacher to do? *The Journal of Secondary Gifted Education, 15*(3), 89–95.

Viktor Freiman
University of Moncton
New Brunswick
Canada

YASEMIN KIYMAZ, BHARATH SRIRAMAN
AND KYEONG HWA LEE

12. PROSPECTIVE SECONDARY MATHEMATICS TEACHERS' MATHEMATICAL CREATIVITY IN PROBLEM SOLVING

A Turkish Study

The main aim of this study was to extend the framework developed in Sriraman's (2004) study on mathematical creativity and to determine the characteristics of creative thinking skills developed by secondary mathematics prospective teachers' during the process of mathematical problem-solving. The study was motivated by the fact that although research mathematical activities are nested within creativity, schools provide insufficient experiences related to creativity in mathematics. The main aim of the study was to determine pre-service secondary mathematics teachers' creative thinking skills when presented with different mathematical problem-solving situations. Creative thinking was made operational in terms of fluency, flexibility and originality, and examined using qualitative research methodology. Twenty two pre-service secondary mathematics teachers participated in this study during their optional course called 'Selected Topics in Mathematics'. In order to obtain in-depth knowledge, and triangulation criteria, data included classroom observations, pre-service teachers' journals, and semi-structured interviews. Coding techniques from grounded theory were used in the data analysis. The results of this study pointed out a number of issues related to mathematical creativity. It was found that pre-service teachers developed various problem-solving behaviors in different mathematical problem situations but also encountered various difficulties due to the types of algorithmic strategies used and the dead ends that some of these strategies led to. The research findings also pointed out that creative thinking skills in terms of fluency, flexibility and originality (Guilford, 1959, 1962) mainly depended on personal and extra cognitive factors.

CONCEPTUAL FRAMEWORK

Creativity is a universal construct and in spite of its everyday presence, much of the scholarly literature focuses on creativity in eminent individuals. While it is important to distinguish between domain specific creativity and everyday acts of creativity (Craft, 2002, 2003), most studies on mathematical creativity have by and large focused on eminent persons (Sriraman, 2005). Leikin (2009) in her synthesis of studies in the last decade that have explicitly addressed creativity and/or giftedness found only six out of around a thousand published articles in the main journals of the field, dealt with mathematical creativity!

We adopt the view that everybody has creativity, what is termed as little "c" (Weisberg, 1988, 1992) which allows one to believe that creativity can be developed in the classroom in terms of the five principles posited by Sriraman (2005) and that everyone can live a more productive life (Houtz, 1994). The main aim of this study was to determine the characteristics of creative thinking skills developed by secondary mathematics prospective teachers' during the process of mathematical problem-solving. In particular, the study attempted to answer the following questions:

(1) What kinds of problem-solving behaviors are developed by prospective teachers during the process of mathematical problem-solving?
(2) What are the difficulties faced by prospective teachers in finding solutions?
(3) Which factors are effective in creative thinking skills (fluency, flexibility and originality)?
(4) Is there any relationship between creative thinking skills?

THE STUDY

This study was carried out in one of the largest state universities in Ankara during the spring term of 2006–2007 academic year. Twenty two secondary prospective teachers from the Department of Secondary Science and Mathematics Education participated to this study. The data was collected during an optional (elective) course called 'Selected Topics in Mathematics'. In the optional course, prospective teachers were given information about creativity, and explicitly introduced to the notions of fluency, flexibility, and originality. In the lessons where the problem solving activities were held, prospective teachers were required to solve the problems in consideration of fluency, flexibility, and originality. Since creativity as introduced as part of the day to day instruction, unlike previous studies where these constructs are implicitly found in coded student artifacts, the goal was to enhance student's creative abilities and promote a metacognitive awareness of these characteristics of creativity. In other words, students were
– encouraged to find different solutions or ideas.
– prospective teachers' different and original solutions/ ideas were presented to the other prospective teachers.

THE PROBLEMS[1]

The problems selected for this study were typical of math Olympiad and other related contest math problems with the caveat that they were accessible to the students that participated in this study, given their undergraduate mathematics background. Many of the problems that required proof were rephrased or adapted so as to make them seem ambiguous. The problems meet the criteria of what might be construed as challenging problems (Barbeau & Taylor, 2009), and allowed for a variety of approaches. The data was collected through a variety of sources, namely classroom observations, journal work, and semi structured interviews.

Problem 1. What can you say about the following equations?
a) $x!+y!=z!$
b) $x!y!=z!$

Problem 2.
a) Prove that there are no integers $x>1$, $y>1$, $z>1$ with $x!+y!=z!$.
b) Find infinitely many integers $x>1$, $y>1$, $z>1$ with $x!y!=z!$.
    (Erickson & Flowers, 1999: 30)

Problem 3. Let $n\geq2$ be an integer. What can you say about the integer $5^n+6.7^n+1$?

Problem 4. Let $n\geq0$ be an integer. Show that the integer $5^n+6.7^n+1$ is divisible by 8?

Problem 5. What can you say about the sequence 9,99,999,…?

Problem 6. The hexagon is inscribed in the circle, which means that each vertex of the hexagon lies on the circle and all of the other points of the hexagon lie inside the circle. The six corner points of the hexagon have been labeled A, B, C, D, E and F, and so the hexagon can be named hexagon ABCDEFG. As you examine this drawing, you will observe certain things about it. As ideas come to your mind while you are making these observations, write them in the space provided beneath the drawing. Write even those things that seem very obvious to you, and try to express just one idea in each of your statements. Do not take any measurements; write your statements according to how things appear. Thus, if certain parts of the figure appear to be equal in size, say so if you want to. The O near the centre of the circle is just the letter O and is given as a label to name the centre of the circle. Write as many ideas as you can about the figure shown. Two examples of possible statements you might write about observations you make are: (Imai, 2000)

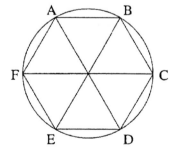

(1) Each vertex of the hexagon lies on the circle
(2) The center of the circle is also the centre of the hexagon.

Problem 7. Assume that the following assertions hold for the set $M\subset Q$:
a) If a and b are the members of M then a+b and ab are the members of M.
b) For every $r\in Q$, only the one of the following assertions is true.
    $r\in M$, $-r\in M$, $r=0$.
So what can you say about the set M?
(Formed from Karakaş & Aliyev (2003b: 150))

Problem 8. If a function f satisfies $f(x^2 +f(y))=y+(f(x))^2$ for all real numbers x,y, then what can you say about the function f?
(Formed from Karakaş & Aliyev (2003a: 216))

Problem 9. Find which of these two numbers was greater, the sum of $\sqrt{10} + \sqrt{17}$ or $\sqrt{53}$?
(Hekimoglu, 2004)

Problem 10. In square ABCD, M is the midpoint of $\overline{AB}$. A line perpendicular to $\overline{MC}$ at M meets $\overline{AD}$ at K. Prove that $\hat{BCM} \cong \hat{KCM}$.
(Posamentier & Salkind, 1988: 54)

Problem 11. Prove that any peripheral angle (subtended angle) standing over the diameter is equal to 90. (Baki, 2006)

Problem 12. Given a square ABCD with $m \angle EDC = m \angle ECD = 15$, prove $\hat{ABE}$ is equilateral. (Posamentier & Salkind, 1988: 56)

Problem 13.

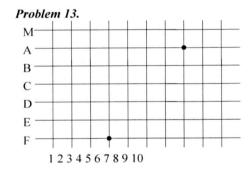

1 2 3 4 5 6 7 8 9 10

A map of a local town is shown in the following figure. Akın lives at the corner of 4th Street and F Avenue. Betül lives at the corner of 8th Street and A Avenue. Akın decides that he will visit Betül once a day until he has tried every different route to her house. The streets only run East and North. How many different routes can Akın get to Betül's house?

(Posamentier & Krulik, 1998: 46)

Problem 14. Suppose $a_1, a_2, \ldots, a_{17}$ are integers and $b_1, b_2, \ldots, b_{17}$ is a permutation of these integers'. Show that $S= (a_1- b_1)(a_2 - b_2) \ldots (a_{17} - b_{17})$ is an even number?
(Karakaş & Aliyev, 2003b:19)

Problem 15. Let a,b,c be odd integers. Show that there is no rational solution of the equation $ax^2+bx+c = 0$? (Karakaş & Aliyev, 2003b:75)

Problem 16. Let $a,b,c \in IR$ and a+b+c<0. If the polynomial $p(x)=ax^2+bx+c$ has no root then find the sign of c? (Karakaş & Aliyev, 2003a:45)

Problem 17. For how many (a,b,c) positive integer triples does the equality $(2a+b)(2b+a)=2^c$ hold? (IX. National Mathematics Olympiad)

Among the 22 participants, 15 were female and 7 were male. All of the participants graduated from Anatolian Teacher Lycee in different cities of Turkey. Students need to be successful in an exam to be admitted to this type of secondary school. Participants had similar education before their undergraduate education, also they were admitted to the university on the basis of their scores in the University Entrance Exam.

The grade points average (GPA, out of 4) and gender of participants were as follows:

Table 1.

GPA	Participants (female)	Participants (male)
2 – 2,49	S10, S12, S15, S22	S1, S2, S9, S18, S19
2,5 – 2,99	S6, S13, S14, S16, S17, S20, S21	S3, S8
3 – 3,49	S7, S11	-
3,5 – 3,99	S4, S5	-

DATA SOURCES

The following tables give details of data collection sources and a classification of the problems used in the study.

Table 2.

Date	Methods of data collection	Participants
2006–2007 academic year	Classroom Observation	22 prospective teachers
	Prospective Teachers' Journals	22 prospective teachers
	Semi-structured Interviews	6 prospective teachers

Table 3. Classification of problem types

The types of the problems	Sub-groups of the problems	Numbers of the problems
I. Group: Open ended situations	I-A: Problems which might have better solutions	Problems 1, 3, 8, 9
	I-B: Problems which haven't got any specific solution	Problems 5, 6

Table 3. (Continued)

II. Group: Problems in which students were asked to find out more than one solutions	II-A: Geometry problems	Problems 14, 15, 16
	II-B: Algebraic problems	Problems 13, 17, 18, 19, 20, 21

A SAMPLE PROBLEM AND SOLUTIONS

Problem

Assume that the following assertion holds for a set M⊂Q:

c) If a and b are the members of M then a+b and ab are the members of M.
d) For every r∈Q, only the one of the following assertions is true.

   r∈M, -r∈M, r=0.

So what can you say about the set M? This problem was formed from the following proof problem but instead of explicitly revealing the identity of M, it was concealed to bring ambiguity into the problem.

"If a set M holds the following conditions then show that $M = Q^+$:

a) If a and b are the members of M then a+b and ab are the members of M.
b) For every r∈Q, only the one of the following assertions is true.

   r∈M, -r∈M, r=0."

S9's Solution for the Problem

S9's solution for the problem doesn't depend on mathematical accuracy. It is an intuitive solution. S9 began his solution with the idea that either $M \subset Q^+ \cup \{0\}$ or $M \subset Q^- \cup \{0\}$ and he mentioned the second condition given in the problem as a reason to his inference. Since he based on that product of two negative rational number is positive he concluded $M \not\subset Q^-$ and $M \subset Q^+ \cup \{0\}$. Then he wrote r∈M ⟹ -r∉M, r≠0 ⟹ M={0} or 0∉M. (He wrote a wrong statement {0}∉M, but it he probably meant 0∉M.) S9 investigated the case 0∉M and he determined $M=Q^+$. So he concluded that M={0} or $M=Q^+$. But in fact 0 can't be an element of M, so M≠{0}. In the last part of his solution, S9 deduce that M is infinite because of the elements a, 2a, ..., a^2, $2a^2$, ...a^3, $2a^3$,... belong to M for 0≠a∈M. However, this is true only if M has an element a. Therefore it is necessary that to see M≠∅, but S9 overlooked this detail. S9's solution doesn't depend on mathematical accuracy. He didn't write his solution in detail. It seemed that S9 used the second condition for determining the sets which might be M and then he used the first condition for justification of his idea.

S9's Journal

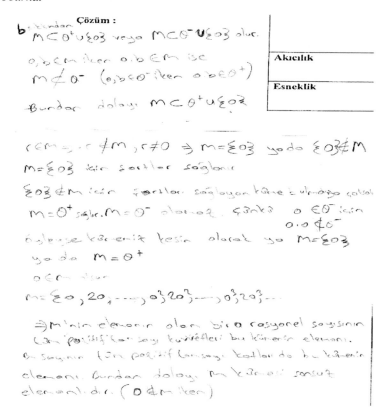

S5's Solution to the Problem

S5's solution is quite detailed. She progressed with small and certain steps in trying to prove every idea. It seemed she was concerned with mathematical accuracy. Also she sometimes chose long ways for her analysis. S5 began her solution by examining the properties of addition and multiplication on the set M with the aim of determining whether (M,+) and (M,.) are groups. She inferred from the second condition that 0 doesn't belong to M, so (M,+) isn't a group. She also added there is no inverse element in M for addition. She proved that 1 is in M by examining the special cases -1, 2 and their multiplication -2. Then she realized that -1 doesn't belong to M otherwise multiplying an element with -1 is always equal to the inverse element. S5 stated (M,.) is a group. But while she was proving the inverse element is in the set she made a logical mistake.

When she was examining some special integers she understood that negative numbers don't belong to M. She stated this idea with "$-k \notin M$ for $k \in Q^+$" and tried to prove it. It seemed that S5 restricted her own thinking with natural numbers because she used induction to prove her idea. So, she actually proved that the natural numbers were a subset of M (IN⊆ M), but she wrote M=Q⁺. On the other hand she also used a long and complex way for proving k∈M while k-1∈M.

S5 wrote in her journal about her thinking process which summarizes her solution in the following:

"I looked for what I can see. First groups and rings come to my mind because we are learning these in Abstract Mathematics these days. I think that is because the more you deal with something the more you see it. I look to define a one-to-one and onto function on this set. I examine which elements belong to this set, but I didn't think that I find this conclusion. While I was checking the operation I realized and tried a proof. I saw it is true…I can't improve any other idea."

S4's Solution for the Problem

S4 wrote about her solution which revealed her strategy:

"at first I thought how can such a set be formed. But instead of forming the set I examined which subsets of Q satisfy these conditions. In fact, at first I thought of the set M= Q^+. But, since it is easier to try a simpler set, I tried to show that the set M={0} satisfies these conditions. The union of these set $Q^+ \cup${0} is larger, I studied this set. I saw the set Q doesn't hold the given conditions. So I tried to show that we cannot form such a set. With the same idea I attempt to show M isn't like a set and {$r_1,r_2 \in Q, r_1+r_2=0$ }. Also I thought of the other subset of Q. After all that I saw the largest set M is $Q^+ \cup${0}."

Like S9, S4 thought that the set {0} satisfied the given conditions, but unlike S9 she explained this idea expressing the closure property of this set with respect to addition and multiplication. But the idea M={0} is incorrect, because $0 \notin M$.

S4 secondly examined the set $Q^+ \cup$ {0}. She chose M= $Q^+ \cup$ {0} and then she wrote in her journal "r>0 $\Rightarrow$ r∈M, r<0 $\Rightarrow$ -r∈M, r= 0 $\Rightarrow$ ±r∈M propositions hold for all r∈Q". But she missed that r= 0 $\Rightarrow$ ±r∈M is in contradiction with the second condition. On the other hand she tried to examine in detail whether $Q^+ \cup$ {0} holds the first condition. She looked into the cases r_1, r_2>0; r_1>0, r_2<0; r_1=0, r_2>0 with this in mind. She didn't point out the set which contain r_1 and r_2 but it is understood that these elements are in Q. S4 saw that all cases hold the first condition for the set $Q^+ \cup$ {0}. She made a similar analysis for the set $Q^- \cup$ {0}. She examined whether the cases r_1=r_2=0, r_1=0, $r_2 \in M$, $r_1 \neq 0 \neq r_2 \in M$ hold the first condition and she saw the last cases do not hold. S4 studied with some other subset of Q. With this aim, she defined a set as {r_1, $r_2 \in Q$: r_1+r_2=0} and then checked if it satisfied the first condition. But this set isn't well defined. After this analysis S4 explained why M doesn't equal Q. S4 finally asked herself whether a subset N of Q^+ satisfies the given conditions. She researched this question's answer by examining a special subset of Q. She chose a set N as [1/2, ∞) and cited N⊂Q but this is incorrect because this interval cannot be a subset of Q. S4 showed that N doesn't satisfy both given conditions by examining special values. Finally she concluded that M may be {0}, Q^+ or $Q^+ \cup$ {0}.

Excerpt from S4's Journal [solution has been translated/described above]

S4's and S9's solutions are similar in terms of examining the sets {0}, $Q^+ \cup$ {0}, $Q^- \cup$ {0} but differ from S9, S4 examined other sets as candidates for the set M. However S4's solution has more detail than S9's. Also S4's analysis is more formal than S9's. Both solutions do not depend on mathematical accuracy. Both S9 and S4 used the second condition for determining the sets which might be the set M and then they checked if the sets chosen hold the first condition. S5's solution is different than the others.

Çözüm: $(\mu \subset \mathbb{Q} \text{ ve } \mu \neq \emptyset)$

$\mu = \{q \in \mathbb{Q} : q = \frac{a}{b}, a = 0, b \neq 0 \}$

kümesi verilen şartları sağlar

* $a = 0$, $b = 1$ için $q = \frac{0}{1} \in \mu$
olduğundan $\mu \neq \emptyset$

* Tanımdan $\mu \subset \mathbb{Q}$

* $q_1, q_2 \in \mu$ olsun. $q_1 = \frac{0}{b}$, $q_2 = \frac{0}{c}$, $b, c \neq 0$

$\Rightarrow q_1 + q_2 = \frac{0}{b} + \frac{0}{c} = \frac{0}{bc} \in \mu$ $(bc \neq 0)$

$q_1 \cdot q_2 = \frac{0}{b} \cdot \frac{0}{c} = \frac{0}{bc} \in \mu$ $(bc \neq 0)$

Böylece (a) ... sağlanır. (b) ... asikve $q = 0$

Kısaca $\mu = \{0 \in \mathbb{Q}\}$ kümesi ... bir adımdır.

$\mu \subset \mathbb{Q}$ ve verilen şartlar sağlanırsa önce

$\forall r \in \mathbb{Q}$ için $r \in \mu$ olma şartı sağlansın.

0 zaman $\forall r_1, r_2 \in \mathbb{Q}$ için $r_1 + r_2, r_1 r_2 \in \mu$
olmalı $r_1 + r_2 = p$, $r_1 r_2 = q$ o.s. $p, q \in \mu$ var

$\Rightarrow \mu = \mathbb{Q}^+ \cup \{0\}$ ... ?

$\Rightarrow$ O halde $\forall r \in \mathbb{Q}$ için
$r > 0 \Rightarrow r \in \mu$
$r < 0 \Rightarrow -r \in \mu$
$r = 0 \Rightarrow \pm r \in \mu$.

... $r_1, r_2 > 0$ olsun. $r_1 + r_2 > 0$ $r_1 r_2 > 0$
olacağından $r_1 + r_2, r_1 r_2 \in \mu$ olur.

$r_1 > 0$, $r_2 < 0$ olsun $r_1 \in \mu$, $-r_2 \in \mu$ olur.

$\Rightarrow r_1 > 0$, $-r_2 > 0 \Rightarrow r_1 + (-r_2) > 0$ ve $r_1 \cdot (-r_2) > 0$

Benzer şekilde $r_1 < 0$ ve $r_2 > 0$ ... de sağlanır.

$r_1 < 0$, $r_2 > 0 \Rightarrow r_1 r_2 \in \mu$ olduğu

$r_1 + r_2 = i_r$, $r_1 r_2 = 0 \in$ olur.

Benzer şekilde diğer durumlar gösterilebilir.
(Aslında $\mu = \mathbb{Q}^+$ ... de yeterli olur.)

		— Şekil çizme
Akıcılık		
Esneklik		— Şartları sağlayan ... — Şartları ... "
	Düşünme Süreçleri	

Düşünme Süreçleri

— İlk önce böyle bir kümeyi nasıl oluşturabilirim diye düşündüm. Fakat kümeyi inşa etmek yerine $\mathbb{Q}$'nun alt kümelerine bakıp bu şartları hangileri sağlar diye inceledim. Aslında önce $\mu = \mathbb{Q}^+$ ... kümesi üzerinde düşündüm. Fakat bunda daha basit bir küme üzerinde çalışması kolay olur diye $\mu = \{0\}$ kümesinin bu şartları sağladığını göstermeye çalıştım. Daha sonra $\mathbb{Q}^+ \cup \{0\}$ biçimindeki kümesinin daha geniş kapsamlı olmasıyla bu küme üzerinde çalıştım. $\mathbb{Q}^-$ kümesinin sağlamadığını grup verilen şartları sağlamadığını göstererek böyle bir kümeye ... edemeyeceğimiz göstermeye çalıştım. Benzer düşünce ile verilen μ kümesinin $\{r_1, r_2 \in \mathbb{Q}, r_1 + r_2 = 0\}$ ... bir küme olarak tanımlayamayacağımı göstermeye çalıştım. Aynı şekilde $\mathbb{Q}$'nun diğer alt kümeleri üzerinde durdum. Sonra olarak ... μ'nin ... geniş ifadesi ... $\mu = \mathbb{Q}^+ \cup \{0\}$ olduğunu gördüm.

DATA ANALYSIS AND RESULTS

Grounded theory analysis methods were used in data analysis. In the following tables for each problem, the total numbers of the ideas produced by prospective teachers, the numbers of the categories (variety) of the ideas, and the numbers of the original ideas were presented. The analysis of the journals were made according to the problem types. In group I problems, basic ideas were analysed in terms of fluency, flexibility, and originality. In group II problems, the solutions formed by basic ideas, were analysed in terms of fluency, flexibility, and originality. All solutions were classified according to their similarities.

Table 1. The number of ideas, categories of ideas and original ideas produced by pre-service teachers for problems in group I-A
(fluency, flexibility and originality)

	Problem 1a			Problem 1b			Problem 3			Problem 7			Problem 8		
	I	*C*	*O*	*I*	*C*	*O*	*I*	*C*	*O*	*I*	*C*	*O*	*I*	*C*	*O*
S1	N	N	N	N	N	N	9	2	2	6	3	6	3	2	2
S2	7	2	2	19	3	4	7	3	-	3	2	1	5	3	2
S3	6	3	1	5	2	1	2	2	-	N	N	N	8	2	2
S4	13	4	8	2	2	-	13	3	8	8	1	4	9	3	5
S5	9	3	1	3	2	3	33	4	25	30	4	21	26	4	20
S6	9	3	-	16	2	5	15	3	5	5	2	-	2	1	1
S7	12	3	7	10	2	6	21	2	8	2	1	-	6	1	3
S8	4	3	3	5	3	2	1	1	-	4	3	2	2	2	1
S9	8	2	1	6	2	5	1	1	-	7	2	3	5	3	-
S10	5	1	1	2	2	-	7	3	-	7	2	1	7	3	2
S11	1	1	-	2	1	1	8	2	-	10	2	-	5	2	-
S12	6	3	2	10	2	1	4	2	-	0	0	-	2	1	-
S13	1	1	-	0	0	-	11	2	-	14	3	4	3	2	-
S14	5	2	-	3	2	-	12	3	4	4	2	1	5	1	1
S15	6	3	-	2	1	-	6	2	3	2	1	-	N	N	N
S16	1	1	-	0	0		3	1	-	3	1	-	2	1	-
S17	8	3	2	2	2	1	10	3	1	6	2	1	1	1	-
S18	N	N	N	N	N	N	N	N	N	N	N	N	N	N	N
S19	8	1	7	5	2	-	N	N	N	N	N	N	4	1	1
S20	7	3	-	9	2	-	10	3	4	4	2	1	3	3	-
S21	2	1	-	5	3	-	7	2	-	3	2	-	5	2	1
S22	16	2	12	0	0	-	11	3	-	7	2	4	4	2	-

N: No data
I: the number of ideas (fluency)
C: the number of categories of ideas (flexibility)
O: the number of original ideas (originality)

Table 2. The number of ideas, categories of ideas and original ideas produced by pre-service teachers for problems in group I-B
(fluency, flexibility and originality)

	Problem 5			Problem 6		
	I	*C*	*O*	*I*	*C*	*O*
S1	16	4	8	15	6	5
S2	10	6	2	11	6	6
S3	4	3	-	8	4	1
S4	16	5	6	29	9	9

Table 2. (Continued)

S5	10	5	2	**28**	8	**13**
S6	12	4	1	14	6	2
S7	11	**6**	3	11	5	1
S8	**14**	5	-	15	5	5
S9	4	3	-	6	4	1
S10	6	3	1	8	4	2
S11	12	5	2	11	7	1
S12	5	2	4	10	6	2
S13	12	5	-	12	6	1
S14	**13**	**6**	3	**20**	**9**	2
S15	10	**6**	1	14	6	4
S16	12	5	2	11	5	4
S17	8	5	-	14	6	2
S18	10	3	-	5	4	1
S19	10	5	1	6	4	-
S20	**13**	4	1	11	3	5
S21	8	5	-	11	5	4
S22	6	4	1	9	2	5

N: No data
I: the number of ideas (fluency)
C: the number of categories of ideas (flexibility)
O: the number of original ideas (originality)

Table 3. The number of solutions, categories of solutions and original solutions produced by pre-service teachers for problems in group II-A (fluency, flexibility and originality)

	Problem 10				Problem 11				Problem 12			
	E	S	C	O	E	S	C	O	E	S	C	O
S1	4	4	1	-	4	3	2	-	4	2	1	-
S2	5	4	3	-	2	1	1	-	3	1	1	-
S3	5	5	4	2	1	1	1	1	3	1	1	-
S4	N	N	N	N	N	N	N	N	1	1	1	-
S5	6	6	2	-	7	7	3	2	6	5	2	1
S6	8	7	3	-	N	N	N	N	6	5	2	1
S7	8	8	3	-	3	3	2	-	2	1	1	-
S8	2	2	2	-	3	3	3	1	2	1	1	-
S9	3	3	3	-	5	5	4	3	2	0	0	-
S10	4	4	2	-	4	4	1	-	4	4	1	-
S11	6	6	3	-	2	2	2	-	1	1	1	-
S12	N	N	N	N	N	N	N	N	4	2	1	-
S13	4	4	4	-	3	2	2	-	2	2	1	-
S14	N	N	N	-	N	N	N	N	5	4	1	-
S15	5	4	2	-	3	3	2	-	N	N	N	N
S16	3	3	2	-	3	2	2	-	4	4	1	-

Table 3. (Continued)

S17	4	2	2	-	4	3	1	-	N	N	N	N
S18	3	3	3	-	2	2	1	-	2	2	1	-
S19	5	5	2	-	5	4	2	-	3	2	1	-
S20	6	5	2	1	5	5	3	1	1	1	1	-
S21	3	3	3	1	3	3	1	-	4	3	2	1
S22	3	3	2	-	4	2	1	-	1	1	1	1

N: No data

E: The number of solution enterprises

S: The number of true solutions (Fluency)

C: The number of categories of true solutions (Flexibility)

O: The number of true original solutions (Originality)

Table 4. The number of solutions, categories of solutions and original solutions produced by pre-service teachers for problems in group II-B (fluency, flexibility and originality)

	Problem 9				Problem 13				Problem 14				Problem 15				Problem 16				Problem 17			
	E	S	C	O	E	S	C	O	E	S	C	O	E	S	C	O	E	S	C	O	E	S	C	O
S1	5	1	1	-	1	-	-	-	1	-	-	-	2	2	2	-	1	-	-	-	1	-	1	-
S2	2	2	2	-	1	-	-	1	N	N	N	-	3	3	3	-	1	1	1	-	N	N	N	2
S3	3	1	1	-	1	-	-	-	N	N	N	-	3	-	-	-	1	-	-	-	-	-	-	-
S4	5	2	1	-	-	-	-	-	2	1	1	-	3	3	3	-	2	1	1	-	2	1	1	-
S5	3	2	2	-	2	2	2	1	4	3	-	-	4	4	4	1	3	1	-	-	2	1	1	-
S6	4	2	1	-	-	-	-	-	-	-	-	-	3	3	3	-	2	1	-	-	N	N	N	-
S7	4	1	1	-	2	-	-	-	2	-	-	-	3	-	-	-	3	1	-	-	N	N	N	-
S8	2	1	1	-	-	-	-	-	2	-	-	-	2	2	-	-	-	-	-	1	2	1	1	1
S9	2	1	1	-	2	-	-	-	2	-	-	-	2	2	2	-	1	-	-	-	-	-	-	-
S10	3	1	1	-	-	-	-	-	N	N	N	N	-	-	-	-	2	-	-	-	1	-	-	-
S11	2	1	1	-	N	N	N	-	2	1	1	-	3	2	2	-	1	-	-	-	N	N	N	-
S12	N	N	N	-	2	-	-	-	3	2	1	-	3	-	-	-	3	-	-	-	N	N	N	-
S13	3	2	1	-	2	-	-	-	2	-	-	-	2	-	-	-	2	-	-	-	2	-	2	-
S14	5	3	2	-	-	-	-	-	3	3	2	1	2	-	-	-	3	-	-	-	N	N	N	-
S15	3	1	1	-	3	-	-	-	3	3	2	-	3	2	-	-	3	N	N	N	-	-	-	-
S16	2	1	1	-	N	N	N	-	-	-	-	-	2	2	1	-	-	-	-	-	2	1	1	-
S17	3	2	2	-	-	-	-	-	-	-	-	-	3	2	2	-	N	N	N	-	-	-	-	-
S18	2	2	1	-	N	N	N	-	-	-	-	-	2	1	1	-	1	-	-	-	-	-	-	-
S19	2	1	1	-	N	N	N	-	2	-	-	-	1	-	-	-	-	-	-	-	-	1	1	-
S20	4	3	1	-	N	N	N	-	3	2	1	-	5	-	-	-	2	1	-	-	-	-	-	-
S21	2	1	1	-	1	-	-	-	1	-	-	-	1	1	-	-	1	-	-	-	-	-	-	-
S22	N	N	N	-	-	-	-	-	-	-	-	-	2	1	1	-	1	-	-	-	2	-	-	-

N: No data   E: The number of solution enterprises;   S: The number of true solutions (Fluency)
C: The number of categories of true solutions (Flexibility);   O: The number of true original solutions (Originality)

FINDINGS AND DISCUSSION

The results of this study pointed out a numbers of issues related to mathematical creativity. The prospective teachers exhibited different problem solving behaviors and various problem-solving strategies to the different mathematical problems. In general, the findings indicate that

1. Prospective teachers encountered difficulties due to the kind of the strategies they developed and ways in which these strategies were used in the process of problem-solving.
2. Creative thinking skills in terms of fluency, flexibility and originality, mainly seemed to depend on personality and extraneous factors. None of these factors can affect creative thinking skills by themselves.
3. There seems to be a relationship between creative thinking skills.

The analysis of data indicated students problem solving fell into three dominant categories;
– Preferences (strategies) in finding solutions,
– Intuitive thinking,
– Logical thinking,

A fine grained analysis of each of these categories indicated the following characteristics of each category

Preferences (strategies) in finding solutions consisted of:

    a. Trying out special values in problem solving,
    b. Trying out special cases in problem solving,
    c. Looking for examples,
    d. Producing simple ideas,
    e. Algorithmic solutions,
    f. Attempts at formal proof,
    g. Looking for relations,
    h. Looking for patterns.

Intuitive thinking consisted of

    a. Intuition about finding alternative solutions
    b. Intuition about guessing the result of a problem

The characteristics of intuitive thinking were:
– Avoiding Algorithmic operations,
– Dislike of writing,
– Taking risks in solving the problems,
– Using the figures and the graphs in solving algebratic problems.

Logical Thinking

The characteristics of logical thinking were:
– Not avoiding Algorithmic operations,
– Continuing to solve a problems in a pre-determined path,
– Not taking risks in solving the problems,
– Not avoiding the writing of their thinking in detail.

DISCUSSION

Difficulties

The difficulties encountered by the prospective teachers were analysed to reveal the following properties:

a. Making logical mistakes
b. Making mistakes in operations
c. Fixation on operations
d. Not analysing the given data properly
e. Not developing an appropriate strategy
f. Restricting their thinking
g. Choosing the symbols and models which made thinking difficult
h. Making preferences which made thinking difficult
i. Fixation on a solution which was already known
j. Fixation on a solution which was found first
k. Relaxation due to finding out a solution.

Creative Thinking Skills

Creative thinking skills of the prospective teachers in terms of fluency, flexibility and originality, mainly seemed to depend on some personal and extraneous factors.

Personal factors included
− Having self-confidence,
− Motivated in problem solving,
− Having a will and persistence in solving the problems,
− Being selective in problems to solve.

The findings point out that these personal characteristics might positively or negatively affect creative thinking skills as well as each other.

Personal Choices

Some prospective teachers preferred some creative thinking skills over others. For example: Some preferred originality to fluency. Some preferred flexibility to fluency. These choices might affect their creative thinking skills negatively. In this study, prospective teachers who did not like writing and considered writing similar solutions unnecessary, found less solutions and ideas than the others. In addition characteristics such as: fixation on a solution which was already known, fixation on a solution which is known by all, and easily giving up solving the problems, might also prevent creative thinking skills.

Logical and İntuitive Thinking

Prospective teachers who preferred logical thinking produced small ideas from analysing the parts. Whereas, prospective teachers who preferred intuitive thinking did not give importance to small ideas due to their endeavor to see the whole. This situation might be interpreted as one in which logical thinking produced ideas more fluently than intuitive thinking. Prospective teachers who exhibited intuitive thinking also had a tendency towards flexible thinking more than prospective teachers who used logical thinking.

Other Affective Factors

In this study, some prospective teachers stated that they could not concentrate on the problem due to their lack of confidence. This lack of concentration might be regarded as an obstacle in producing solutions and ideas fluently, flexibly, and originally.

Differences between Uses of Strategies

Prospective teachers used different strategies in solving the problems. It was found that the use of these strategies varied from problem to problem. Moreover, for the same problem the use of a similar strategy varied from person to person. The strategy preferences led prospective teachers towards an easy way or difficult ways of thinking. This situation led prospective teachers towards not finding out the solution or spending more energy to find out the solution. This result is not related to the success or failure of the strategies, rather it is related to the effective use of the strategies.

The strategy of producing simple ideas is important in divergent thinking. This strategy led prospective teachers to produce original ideas. The strategy of producing simple ideas help to find out alternative solutions in the process of understanding the problem or to overcome the difficulties faced in solving the problems. Therefore, this strategy might positively affect thinking fluently and flexibly.

Prospective teachers who had difficulty in thinking in general terms, used the strategies such as trying out special values and cases in problem solving. These strategies helped them to create new ideas and positively affected thinking fluently and flexibly. The strategy of making algorithmic solutions was one of the most preferred strategies, however it did not seem to be effective in finding out original solutions or ideas. In order to find more creative solutions, it might be better to be flexible in selecting the strategies, and to use more than one strategy, rather than using just one strategy.

CONCLUSIONS

The findings of this study show that the examination system in Turkey seemed to effect prospective teachers' problem solving behavior as they had a goal (outcome) oriented problem solving behavior. Prospective teachers who had a goal (outcome) oriented problem solving behavior, had fixation on the solution which was already known, and relaxed due to finding out a solution, then had difficulty in finding out multiple solutions. This situation led prospective teachers to prefer to reach the result rather than trying to find out alternative solutions. Therefore, it seems that goal (outcome) oriented problem solving behavior prevented them to produce creative (fluent, flexible, and original) solutions. In this study, during the process of data collection, prospective teachers were encouraged to find out different solutions, this seemed to effect their problem solving behaviors. This encouragement seems to lead prospective teachers to have an endevour to find out different solutions. Therefore, it might be said that in order to develop creative thinking skills, encouragement in finding out different solutions is important.

In this study, even in the same problem types, differences were found in prospective teachers' thinking performances in terms of fluency, flexibility, and originality. In other words, creative thinking skills varied depending on the problems, the types of the problems and also on the subject area (geometry or algebra).

This situation implies that it is not possible to make generalizations about creative thinking skills depending on the problem situations.

Are there relationships between creative thinking components?

In this study, fluent thinking produced related, and increased the variety of these ideas, therefore leading to flexible thinking. In this case, fluent thinking feeds flexible thinking. However, some prospective teachers did not consider thinking fluently, rather, they tried to think flexibly or tried to find out original solutions.

This study contributes to the field by examining mathematical creativity in prospective secondary teachers through a detailed qualitative study within a classroom setting that attempted to make the constructs from the literature operational, in particular the constructs of fluency, flexibility and originality. As opposed to the study by Sriraman (2004) in which the Gestalt model was made operational, in this study an attempt was made to study mathematical creativity through Guilford's model and implement creative problem solving explicitly with the prospective teachers.

NOTES

[1] Even though 21 problems were planned in the study, only 17 were implementable due to time constraints.

REFERENCES

Baki, A., (2006). *Kuramdan Uygulamaya Matematik Eğitimi*. Trabzon: Derya Kitabevi.

Barbeau, E. & Taylor, P. (Eds.). (2009). *Challenging mathematics in and beyond the classroom. The 16th ICMI Study* (Vol. 12). Springer Science and Business.

Craft, A. (2003). The limits to creativity in education: Dilemmas for the educator. *British Journal of Educational Studies, 51*(2), 113–127.

Craft, A. (2002). *Creativity in the early years: A lifewide foundation*. London: Continuum.

Erickson, M. J., & Flowers, J. (1999). *Principles of mathematical problem solving*. New Jersey, NJ: Prentice Hall.

Guilford, J. P. (1959). Traits of creativity. In H. H. Anderson (Ed.), *Creativity and its cultivation* (pp. 142–161). New York: Harper & Brothers Publishers.

Guilford, J. P. (1962). Factors that aid and hinder creativity. *Teachers College Record, 63*(5), 380–392.

Hekimoglu, S., (2004). Conducting a teaching experiment with a gifted student. *The Journal of Secondary Gifted Education, XVI*(1), 14–19.

Houtz, J. C. (1994). Creative problem solving in the classroom: Contribution of four psychological approaches. In M. A. Runco (Ed.), *The creativity research handbook* (Vol. 1, pp. 153–173). Cresskill, NJ: Hampton Press.

Imai, T., (2000). The influence of overcoming fixation in mathematics towards divergent thinking in open-ended mathematics problems on Japanese Junior High School Students. *International Mathematics Education Science and Technology, Sayı, 31*(2), 187–193.

Karakaş, H. İ., & Aliyev, İ., (2003a). *Analiz ve cebirde ilginç olimpiyat problemleri ve çözümleri.* Ankara: TÜBİTAK Yayınları.

Karakaş, H. İ., & Aliyev, İ., (2003b). *Sayılar teorisinde ilginç olimpiyat problemleri ve çözümleri.* Ankara: TÜBİTAK Yayınları.

Leikin, R. (2009). Bridging the gap. In R. Leikin, A. Berman, & B. Koichu (Eds.), *Creativity in mathematics and the education of gifted students* (pp. 385–411). The Netherlands: Sense Publishers.

Posamentier, A. S., & Krulik, S., (1998). *Problem-solving strategies for efficient and elegant solutions.* California, CA: Corwin Press, Inc.

Posamentier, A. S., & Salkind, C. T. (1988). *Challenging problems in geometry.* Canada: Dale Seymour Publication.

Sriraman, B. (2004). The characteristics of mathematical creativity. *The Mathematics Educator, 14*(1), 19–34.

Sriraman, B. (2005). Are mathematical giftedness and mathematical creativity synonyms? A theoretical analysis of constructs. *Journal of Secondary Gifted Education, 17*(1), 20–36.

Weisberg, R. W. (1988). Problem solving and creativity. In R. J. Sternberg (Ed.), *The nature of creativity: Contemporary psychological perspectives* (pp. 148–176). New York: Cambridge University Press.

Weisberg, R. W. (1992). *Creativity: Beyond the myth of genius.* New York: W.H. Freeman and Company.

Yasemin Kiymaz
Ahi Evran Universitesi
Turkey

Bharath Sriraman
Dept of Mathematical Sciences
The University of Montana
USA

Kyeong Hwa Lee
Seoul National University
Korea
khmath@snu.ac.kr

HAAVOLD PER ØYSTEIN

13. WHAT CHARACTERISES HIGH ACHIEVING STUDENTS' MATHEMATICAL REASONING?

INTRODUCTION

This study investigates high achieving students' mathematical reasoning when given an unfamiliar trigonometric equation. The findings indicate that the students' way of thinking is strongly linked with imitative reasoning and only when they received some form of guidance, were they able to display flexible and creative mathematical reasoning.

Research Question

The purpose of this study is to investigate the reasoning that high achieving students' in upper secondary school display when they meet an unfamiliar trigonometric equation. The underlying motivation for the study, is the relationship between the socially constructed "high achievements" in school mathematics and the theoretical concept of "mathematical competence". For the purpose of this study, the author proposes that high achieving students are students who consistently get grades five and six in upper secondary school mathematics. But are high achieving students also mathematically competent students? Are the two terms synonymous? Research by Lithner (see for instance 2000, 2003 and 2008) indicate that even high achieving students make use of superficial reasoning when given an unfamiliar mathematical task. Niss & Jensen (2002) dissect mathematical competency into eight, distinct and clearly recognizable competencies: thinking mathematically, posing and solving mathematical problems, modelling mathematically, reasoning mathematically, representing mathematical entities, handling mathematical symbols and formalisms, communicating in, with and about mathematics and making use of aids and tools. Other frameworks, e.g. NCTM (2000) define mathematical competence similarly. However, mathematical cognitive activity is incredibly complex. Every investigation of mathematical understanding will have to be in some ways simplified (Niss, 1999). So although this study is motivated by the possible discrepancy between high achievements and the term mathematical competency in upper secondary school mathematics, the aim here is to capture some key aspects of high achieving students' reasoning structure when working with a mathematical problem. Not to give a complete description of high achieving students' mathematical understanding and mathematical thinking vis-à-vis certain mathematical concepts.

B. Sriraman and K.H. Lee (eds.), The Elements of Creativity and Giftedness in Mathematics, 193–215.
© *2011 Sense Publishers. All rights reserved.*

In this study, the author hopes to qualitatively characterise the mathematical reasoning of three high achieving students when they meet a mathematical problem and the following two research questions will be investigated:

- Is it true that high achieving students display superficial reasoning when given an unfamiliar trigonometric equation?
- What characterises the students' mathematical reasoning when given an unfamiliar trigonometric equation?

Hiebert (2003) argues that students learn what they are given an opportunity to learn. If there is a lack of focus on mathematical reasoning, mathematical thinking and problem solving in the students' learning environment, it is the author's contention that it may not be unrealistic to expect even high achieving students in some situations to focus on surface and not structural features of mathematical problems. Trends in International Mathematics and Science Study, TIMSS, Advanced 2008 (Mullis et al., 2009) and the PISA + study (Kirsti Klette et al., 2008) show that there is a lack of focus on problem solving and mathematical reasoning in both upper and lower secondary school in Norway. Students are rarely asked to explain their answers and communicate mathematical arguments to others. Instead, the primary activities in the classroom are direct instruction from the teacher and students working on problems on their own. Furthermore, the problems the students are working with are, according to Klette et al. (ibid), not stimulating problem solving skills. If students learn what they are given an opportunity to learn, do even high achieving students resort to superficial reasoning when given an unfamiliar mathematical task? Or are they able to, in many ways in spite of their learning milieu, identify and focus on the structural features of the problems and display mathematically correct reasoning? The first research questions sets out to determine whether or not there are high achieving students who actually do display superficial mathematical reasoning in upper secondary school. Once this has been answered, a more thorough investigation of the mathematical reasoning displayed is needed. The second research question looks more closely at the quality of the mathematical reasoning displayed by the students when they meet an unfamiliar task, to see if there are certain characteristics that are associated with the students' mathematical reasoning.

Literature Review

Algorithms are a key component of mathematics. They can not only serve as the basis for mathematical understanding, but they can also relieve the cognitive demands of complicated calculations. Even professional mathematicians use algorithms and fixed procedures when dealing with routine calculations. However, algorithms and procedures are just one small part of mathematics. Halmos (1980) states that problem solving is the heart of mathematics which in many ways is supported by Freudenthal (1991) who claims that mathematics is an activity of discovering and organizing of content and form. In a learning environment, algorithms and procedures need to be supplemented with other aspects of mathematics such as problem solving activities and deductive proofs. A narrow focus on algorithms and routine tasks can limit the students' ability to use mathematics. McNeal (1995) and Kamii & Dominick (1997) argues that students when working with algorithms, tend to focus on remembering each step in the algorithm and not the underlying mathematical structures. Pesek & Kirshner (2000) states that instrumental instruction can interfere with later relational learning. Furthermore, not only can a narrow focus on algorithms and skill to some degree hinder learning of mathematics, but the mathematics curricula in most countries emphasize problem solving on its own as an important aspect of mathematics. The NCTM Standards states that reasoning and problem solving are key components of mathematics and we find similar statements in the Norwegian mathematics syllabus (KD, 2006).

Traditional mathematics teaching emphasizes procedures, computation and algorithms. There is little attention to developing conceptual ideas, mathematical reasoning and problem solving activities. The result is that students' mathematical knowledge is without much depth and conceptual understanding (Hiebert, 2003). These findings are also seen in Selden et al.'s (1994) study where students with grades A and B struggle with non routine problems. Selden et al. concluded that the students possessed a sufficient knowledge base of calculus skill and that the students' problem solving difficulties was often not caused by a lack of basic resources. Instead, they say, traditional teaching does not prepare students for the use of calculus creatively. Lithner (2003) and Schoenfeld (1985) show how many of the students, even high achieving students, try to solve problems using superficial reasoning. A possible hypothesis which could explain this phenomenon is seen in Cox (1994), where the author argues that first year students in universities are able to get good grades by focusing on certain topics at a superficial level, rather than develop a deep understanding. It is important at this stage to clarify that it is not the author's claim or intention to argue that high achieving students are not capable of becoming mathematically competent students or that high achieving students in general are not mathematical competent students. However, there are certain indications that students can get good grades in school, in spite of certain shortcomings vis-à-vis the concept of mathematical competence as defined by Niss and Jensen (2002) and NCTM standards.

Much research within mathematics education has focused on learning difficulties regarding mathematical understanding and in a broader sense, my research question are part of a greater, more fundamental issue in mathematics education. Skemp (1976) defined this issue as the dichotomy between relational understanding and instrumental understanding. Instrumental understanding consists of a number of fixed and specific plans or strategies for solving specific tasks. The students lack an overall understanding of the relationship between the individual stages and the final goal of the exercise. To learn a new way to solve a particular branch of problems, as a *"way to get there"*, the learner is dependent on external guidance. Relational understanding, on the other hand, is defined as: *"[it] consists of building up a conceptual structure from which its possessor can produce and unlimited number of plans for getting from any starting point within his schema to any finishing point."* (ibid). The knowledge and understanding becomes the goal in itself, not necessarily successfully solving a particular problem. The plans are no longer fixed and immediately tied to a particular class of problems. Others, such as Ausubel (1962) and Hiebert & Lefevre (1986) outlines similar dichotomies: meaningful vs. rote learning and conceptual vs. procedural knowledge respectively. Relational understanding, meaningful learning and conceptual knowledge are all characterised by the fact that new knowledge is related and connected to other existing schemas.

A related issue in dealing with difficulties in mathematical understanding is students' tendency to view mathematics almost exclusively as a collection of processes or procedures. Evidence suggests that the flexibility to view objects as both a process and a concept is vital to future success (Gray & Tall, 1991). This cognitive conflict is similarly described via versatile and adaptable mathematical knowledge within the context of algebra (Sfard & Linchevski, 1994). Versatile knowledge is being able to view mathematical expressions in many different ways. Adaptable knowledge is being able to view a mathematical expression in an appropriate way. Versatility refers to the different ways of solving a problem and how each of those strategies are carried out. Adaptability refers to choosing the most appropriate strategy for the problem at hand. Sfard & Linchevski states that both versatility and adaptability is necessary to fully succeed in algebra. The extensive procedural focus on mathematics is characterised as a reduction of complexity of mathematical concepts, processes and mathematical thinking. Research shows that students, teachers, textbook writers etc, in order to satisfy tough curriculum goals focus on algorithmic thinking and not deep mathematical reasoning (Lithner, 2005).

CONCEPTUAL FRAMEWORK

In the field of mathematics education, the term mathematical reasoning is often used without an explicit definition, under the assumption that there is a universal agreement on its meaning (Yackel & Hanna, 2003). Lithner (2006) claims that reasoning is often implicitly seen as a process characterised by a high deductive-logical quality, frequently in connection with formal mathematical proofs. However, in this study the students are in upper secondary school and such a strict definition of reasoning is not appropriate. Thus, a more inclusive definition of the term reasoning is used in this study. In Merriam-Webster's online dictionary, reasoning is defined, among other, as "the drawing of inferences through the use of reason". Reason is then defined as "a statement offered in explanation or justification". So mathematical reasoning is, for the purpose of this study, the line of thought adopted to produce assertions and reach conclusions in task solving (ibid). Or, the arguments produced to convince one self and/or others of the truth of an assertion. A line of thought might be mathematically incorrect or flawed, as long as it makes some kind of sense to the reasoner itself.

Harel (2008) defines mathematical activity as a triad of concepts: mental act, way of understanding and way of thinking:

> "A person's statements and actions may signify cognitive products of a mental act carried out by the person. Such a product is the person's way of understanding associated with that mental act. Repeated observations of one's way

of understanding may reveal that they share a common cognitive characteristic. Such a characteristic is referred to as a way of thinking associated with that mental act".

Mental acts are basic elements of human cognition, such as interpreting, inferring, proving, generalizing etc. Although mathematical reasoning involves numerous mental acts, in this study mathematical reasoning itself is a mental act. It is the cognitive process of convincing oneself and/or others of the truth of an assertion.

In this study, the author intends to investigate what characterises high achieving students' mathematical reasoning. By looking at the students' arguments, solutions and written work, a pattern characterising their work could appear. Characteristics of their way of understanding might give some insight into their way of thinking. There is an important difference between behaviour and cognition. This dichotomy between way of thinking and way of understanding, is also seen in Lithner's (2006) view of reasoning as both a thinking process and the product of that process. The product of the thinking processes, the way of understanding, we can observe as behaviour, but whatever inferences we make regarding the underlying cognitive processes, will still be, to some degree, speculative. In this study, mathematical reasoning is a mental act and the purpose is to investigate the students' way of thinking. This is done by looking more closely at the students' way of understanding.

To further investigate the mental act of mathematical reasoning and the characteristics of the students' way of understanding, the author have chosen a framework by Lithner (2006) that allows me to qualitatively classify and assess specific aspects of the students' mathematical reasoning. The framework is built up using specific mathematical examples and well defined concepts describing mathematical reasoning. It is based on empirical data and it describes mathematical reasoning in general and is not tied up to a particular set of problems or themes. Here, two main classes of reasoning are defined: creative reasoning and imitative reasoning:

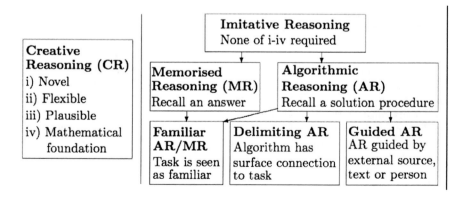

Figure 1. Creative and imitative reasoning (Lithner, 2008).

CREATIVE REASONING

The basic idea of creative reasoning, or creative mathematically founded reasoning as it is also referred to in the framework, is the creation of new and reasonably well-founded task solutions. Not necessarily geniality or superior thinking. For the reasoning to be called creative reasoning, two conditions must be met (Bergqvist, 2007):
- The reasoning sequence must be new to the reasoner (novelty)
- The reasoning sequence must contain strategy choices and/or implementations supported by arguments that motivates why the conclusions are true or plausible (plausibility), and are anchored in intrinsic mathematical properties of the components involved in the reasoning (mathematical foundation).

The definition of creative reasoning is very similar to creativity in general. Sternberg & Lubart (1999) define creativity as the ability to produce original and useful work. Sriraman (2009) raises the objection that many mathematicians would object to the criteria of usefulness, as a lot of work in mathematics do not have immediate implications for the "real world". However, in this study, the term usefulness is seen as a correct solution of a mathematics task. The mathematical reasoning is plausible and based on intrinsic mathematical properties. Not whether or not it has implications or uses in the "real world". Creative reasoning is therefore a subset of the general term creativity and the terms novel and plausible are analogous to original and useful. Furthermore, the originality and novelty of the mathematical reasoning, is relative to the reasoner. What might be trivial routine for a mathematics professor, could be an original and novel solution to a problem for an upper secondary mathematics student. The reasoning sequence must be new to the reasoner, not necessarily new to the rest of the mathematics community.

Creative reasoning does not imply strict logical deductive reasoning. Even though it is normal to distinguish a proof from a guess vis-a-vis mathematical reasoning (Polya, 1954). The value of the reasoning of a proof is based on its correctness or logical rigour. Students however, unlike mathematicians, engineers, economists etc, can afford to guess, take chances and not always give the correct answer to every problem or exercise. Creative reasoning therefore distinguishes a guess from a more reasonable guess, and not a guess from a proof. To determine whether or not a sequence of reasoning is creative mathematically founded, the following criteria must be fulfilled: novelty, flexibility, plausibility and a sound mathematical foundation.

Novelty refers to the fact that a new, to the reasoner, sequence of reasoning is created or a forgotten sequence is re-created. If an answer or solution is imitated, it is not considered to be creative mathematically founded reasoning. Second, the reasoning must be flexible. This implies the ability to utilize different approaches and adaptations to the specific problem. The student is not fixed on one specific strategy choice or sequence of reasoning that hinders progress. Plausibility means that there are arguments supporting the strategy choice and explains why the conclusions are true or plausible. Last, the arguments are based on intrinsic mathematical properties; the arguments are based on a sound mathematical foundation.

The arguments used to show that an answer to a problem or exercise is correct can be based on sound mathematical properties or less sound mathematical properties. However, before sound and less sound mathematical properties can be defined we need to establish the mathematical components which we deal with when solving problems. The framework defines the following components relevant for solving mathematics exercises and problems: Objects are the things that one is doing something with. This could be numbers, functions, variables etc. Transformations is what is being done to the objects. For instance adding to real numbers. Last, is the concept which is a central mathematical idea built on a set of objects and transformations (e.g. the function concept). These components have certain mathematical properties and the framework separates intrinsic and superficial properties.

An intrinsic mathematical property of an exercise is a property that is relevant for how you solve the exercise. This means that an intrinsic mathematical property is central to a particular context and in a particular problem. A surface property, on the other hand, has little or no relevance for how a given exercise can be solved. In each task, there are potentially numerous both intrinsic and surface properties. The relevancy of a mathematical property depends on the context. For instance, in deciding if or is larger, the size of the numbers is a surface property, while the quotient captures the intrinsic property (Lithner, 2008). Another example is naive empiricism (Schoenfeld, 1985) in an attempt to bisect angles. The visual appearance of angles is a surface property, while the formal congruency of the triangles in the construction is the intrinsic property.

IMITATIVE REASONING

Imitative reasoning is a term that describes several different types of reasoning which are based on previous experiences, but without any attempts at originality. This means that students try to solve problems and exercises by copying textbook examples, earlier task solutions or through remembering certain algorithms. Imitative reasoning is in many cases a superficial sequence of reasoning, not grounded on intrinsic mathematical properties, but rather on surface properties. The students chose their strategy for solving the problems on superficial properties they recognize from earlier experiences and not on intrinsic mathematical properties. From empirical research, imitative reasoning has been classified further into subcategories, where the two main categories are memorized reasoning and algorithmic reasoning.

Memorized Reasoning

Memorized reasoning is determined by two conditions: first, the strategy choice is founded on recalling a complete answer by memory. Second, implementing said strategy choice consists only of writing it down. For instance, remembering each step of a proof and writing it down is memorized reasoning. Of course, a common mistake when employing memorized reasoning is that the different parts of a solution can be written down in the wrong order since the parts do not depend on each other and the reasoning is not based on intrinsic properties.

Algorithmic Reasoning

An algorithm is a set of instructions or procedures that will solve a particular type of problem. For instance, the chain rule for finding the derivative of a composite function.

Algorithmic reasoning is determined by two conditions: first, the strategy choice is founded on recalling an algorithm that will guarantee that a correct solution can be reached. Second, implementing the strategy consists of trivial transformations. The formula for solving a quadratic equation is an example that illustrates the difference between algorithmic reasoning and memorized reasoning. In the latter case the exact same equation and corresponding solution would be written down from memory. In the former case the algorithm, or formula, would be applied to this specific equation. The student would not recall the entire solution to the equation, but rather remember the algorithm and know that it would give a solution.

Algorithmic reasoning is a reliable method for solving problems when the student knows exactly what to do and why the chosen algorithm is appropriate. Even professional mathematicians use algorithms when solving routine problems. The use of algorithmic reasoning in itself is not an indication of a lack of understanding as it saves time and reduces the risk of miscalculations. The key here is the mathematical properties on which the algorithmic reasoning is based on. In many cases students use algorithmic reasoning in problematic situations, which indicates that it is based on superficial and not intrinsic mathematical properties.

METHODS

Procedures

The empirical data was collected from three clinical task based interviews. In each interview, the students were given a specific trigonometric task designed by the author and asked to solve it while they were "thinking aloud". Each interview lasted for approximately 30 minutes. Before each interview, a short, informal conversation between the student and the author took place. The objective of the short, informal conversation was to create a more comfortable environment and situation for the student. At the start of the interview, the following monologue, recommended by Ericsson & Simon (1993) was given by the researcher in order to initiate the student's think aloud talk:

> "Tell me EVERYTHING you are thinking from the time you first see the question until you give an answer. I would like you to talk aloud CONSTANTLY from the time I present each problem until you have given your final answer to the question. I don't want you to try to plan out what to say or try to explain to me what are you saying. Just act as if you are alone in the room speaking to yourself. It is most important that you keep talking. If you are silent for any long period of time I will ask you to talk (p. 378)."

The interview was separated into two parts. The first 10–15 minutes, the author stayed silent and only reminded the subjects to keep talking if they stayed silent for extended periods of time. If the students struggled with the task given and showed signs of giving up, the author gave them a similar, but simpler task and asked them if they could solve the new task. After working for a few minutes on the new task, the author then asked them if they now could go back and solve the original task. The final 15 minutes of the interview, was less structured and the author asked more direct questions. Trying to get the students to justify and explain what they were doing and why they were doing it.

Participants

Three students in grade 13 who are all taking an advanced mathematics course in a local upper secondary school were selected for this study. However, it was not the author who selected the students to be interviewed. Instead, the mathematics teacher who was teaching the advanced mathematics course was asked to select 2–4 students which she deemed to be high achieving. The author wanted the teacher to select the students for the study, as this would, in a more general sense, give access to students who the Norwegian educational system classifies as high achieving students. The author had no other criteria set forth to the teacher, other than that the students had to be considered consistent high achievers in mathematics. The author did not ask the teacher to select what she would call typical or atypical high achieving students. There were two reasons for this. First, the author wanted to see which students the teacher, when given few restrictions, would classify as high achieving students. Second, it might have been difficult to find high achieving students if there were several restrictions.

Tasks

The task given to the students, was the trigonometric equation in which the students were asked to find a:

$$\sin x + \cos x = a$$

The task was chosen for several reasons. First, the students in grade 13 are quite familiar with trigonometric equations. In the textbook, there is a large section devoted entirely to trigonometric functions and a subsection which focus specifically on the equation. It would therefore be reasonable to expect high achieving students to have the necessary domain knowledge to solve the trigonometric equation. Second, the task is designed in such a way that it can be solved in a multitude of ways. Third, compared to the tasks given in the textbook and tasks given by the teacher to the class, the task is unusual. Not only because the answer is an interval and not a single value, but also because it contains both the variable x and the parameter a. Furthermore, in the textbooks, c is given as an integer. In the task in the study, c is an unknown parameter. This presumably creates a problematic situation for the students. They have the necessary domain knowledge to solve the problem, but may not know of any immediately available procedures or algorithms that will solve it. This opens up for both flexible and creative reasoning when trying to solve the equation. In this article, the terms problem, task and equation will be used interchangeably about the trigonometric equation the students' tried to solve during the interview.

If the students looked like they were struggling with the first task, a prompt was given. This is also a trigonometric equation, but less complex. Here as well, the students were asked to find a:

$$\sin x = a$$

This task was designed with two considerations in mind. First, the task is significantly easier than the original task. There are fewer components in the task and, as such, it might be easier to notice the structural aspects of the task than in the first task given. So the prompt was designed in order to help the students by reducing the complexity of the tasks. Second, it also allowed the author to see if the students were able to generalize their reasoning from the simpler task to the more complex task.

ANALYSIS

The data material consisted of the transcribed interviews and the written work the students produced during the interview. The interviews were transcribed by the author. As the research questions in this study deals with characterizing students' mathematical reasoning, the transcriptions were primarily focused on verbal and written mathematical communication. Such as arguments, guesses, assertions, conjectures etc directly related to mathematics which were produced in written or oral form during the interview. Although other aspects such as body language, type of interaction between the author and the student, tone of voice etc obviously play an important part in the students' behaviour and may say something about the students' mathematical reasoning in general, in this study the focus is the students' mathematical argumentation and justification. The explicit mathematical reasoning they display when they meet an unfamiliar mathematical problem.

The analysis consisted of two parts; first, identification of each reasoning sequence and then classification of each reasoning sequence according to the framework:

1. Lithner (2008) proposes that a reasoning structure is carried out in four parts. A task is met, a strategy choice is made, the strategy is implemented and a conclusion is obtained. To identify separate reasoning sequences, the strategy choice and conclusion of each reasoning sequence was identified in the transcripts. Strategy choice is seen in a wide sense here. Strategy ranges from local procedures to general approaches and choice includes recall, choose, construct, discover, guess etc. A conclusion is reached after the strategy has been implemented. The conclusion is simply the product of the implementation of a certain strategy and it can be both incorrect and/or incomplete. For each student, there might be one or several attempts at solving the task.

2. After the individual sequences was identified, each reasoning sequence was then classified according to the framework presented earlier. This was accomplished by first classifying the reasoning sequence as either creative reasoning or imitative reasoning. If the reasoning sequence was classified as imitative reasoning, further analysis is carried out to determine whether the reasoning sequence is algorithmic or memorized.

METHODOLOGICAL ISSUES

Validity

Regardless of which epistemological position one takes it is widely accepted that there is a need for some form of measurement of validity in qualitative research (Ritchie & Lewis, 2003). For the purpose of this particular study, a pragmatical and practical view of validity will be adopted. Research, both quantitative and qualitative, is a human experience prone to the same mistakes as every other human activity.

The primary concern in this study, is internal validity, which relates to the extent the research correctly map or document the phenomenon in question (Hammersley, 1990). Is the author really investigating what the author claims to be investigating? In this study, this question is related to whether or not the author is able during the interview, and in the following analysis, to characterize the students' mathematical reasoning. Every interview will have epistemological conflict between the need for complete or rich data and the need for minimizing interference (Clement, 2000). As a compromise, the interview session in this study consisted of two parts. During the first part, the students were asked to think aloud while they tried to solve a trigono-metric equation. The students talked freely with little or no intervention from the author. In the second part, the author engaged more actively in the interview and probed further, in order to get the students to explain in greater detail their mathematical reasoning. The structure of the interview was designed in order to provide valid and rich data, respectively.

Reliability

Reliability describes the replicability and the consistency of results. Hammersley (1992) refers to reliability as: "...the degree of consistency with which instances are assigned to the same category by different observers or by the same observer on different occasions." Although qualitative researchers, whether they are constructivists or positivists, do not calculate interrater reliability (Ballan, 2001), other steps can be taken to improve reliability. In this article, both the collection and analysis of the data was carried out by the author. To improve reliability, extensive excerpts from the interviews, which the analysis is based on, are given. The methods used to gather and analyze the data are also explained in detail.

RESULTS

Here, several examples of individual reasoning sequences will be given and analyzed at two points during the interview session: when they first begin working on the problem and when they are given the prompt and solve the problem. For each episode, a description of what the student was doing will be given. Then the reasoning structure will be outlined and commented on. Each of the reasoning sequences can be said to be the students' way of understanding and the recurring characteristics of their way of understanding, says something about the students' way of thinking.

Attacking the Problem

An interesting aspect of students' mathematical reasoning, is how they first attack a problem. How do the students approach a new problem when they are not given any specific instructions regarding how the problem is to be solved. Here, a description and interpretation of what the students first did when they saw the problem are given.

– Alf

Description

[The author gives Alf the task.]

Alf: "Ok, so here we have cosine and sine and we need to get this into a regular cosine function. Let's see. [Looks in his textbook for about 15 seconds]. I don't remember which chapter this was. Yes. Now I remember. It was about harmonic equations. Let's see. Ok. I see this is a sine and cosine function that can be transformed into a tangent function. Sin x divided by cos x. [Does some calculations on his work sheet]. Same as tan x. Plus one equals *a*. So that is tan x plus one equals *a*. That is what I was supposed to find?"

Author: "You can find a numerical value for *a* in the task".

Alf: "I can? But then I need to find tangent *a x*, I need to invert it. I can't find *x*. How can I find a numerical value if I have two variables? I have two unknowns. [Alf is quiet for 10 seconds]. Let's see. If I am going to find *a*, I need to find *x* first. But that makes no sense."

Interpretation

Alf's first reasoning sequence when he begins working on the problem is quite clear:

1. Strategy choice: divide each term by cos x and use that $\tan x = \dfrac{\sin x}{\cos x}$ to simplify the equation. Then, invert both sides of the equation and find *x*.
2. Strategy implementation: Alf divides each term on the left side of the equation by cos x. However, he forgets to divide the term on the right side by cos x.
3. Conclusion: The equation 1 + tanx = a can not be solved.

The procedure Alf first chose, transforming an equation with a sine and a cosine term into an equation with a tangent term, is, as he said, mentioned several times in the students' textbook. Both in the form of worked examples and as similar tasks. Alf recognizes the general structure of the equation and assumes it can be solved as the tasks and examples he has seen in the textbook. The argument he presents, is that he has seen this type of equation several times in the textbook. It is a familiar algorithm. So, it is reasonable to conclude that Alf's first attempt at solving the task is imitative in nature and, more specifically, algorithmic reasoning.

The mistake Alf made implementing the strategy, was apparently a minor and insignificant, as he corrected it later during the interview without the author pointing it out. It is also not unreasonable to expect that Alf would have drawn the same conclusion even if he had implemented the strategy correctly. This is seen when he states that he can't find a number if he has two variables. The two variables or unknowns are x and a. Even if he had implemented the strategy correctly, he would have ended up with what Alf calls "two variables".

– Anna

Description

[The author gives Anna the task.]

Anna: [Reads the task instructions and is quiet for a few seconds]. "Ok, I need to find some connection between sine and cosine, but i don't remember the formulas by heart. [Anna looks in her textbook for about 15 seconds]. Ok, if I divide each term by cos x, then I might end up with tan x here on the first part. [She proceeds to divide each term in the equation with cos x, writes down the answer on paper.] So I have one and a divided by cos x. That doesn't help me much."

Author: "Why not?"

Anna: "I think I have two unknowns here. Both tangent and cosine. [Anna is quiet for the next 15 seconds.]

Interpretation

Anna's first reasoning sequence is similar to Alf's first reasoning sequence:

1. Strategy choice: divide each term by cos x and use that $\tan x = \dfrac{\sin x}{\cos x}$ to simplify the equation. Then, invert both sides of the equation and find x.
2. Strategy implementation: divides each term on both sides of the equation by cos x.
3. Conclusion: the equation $1 + \tan x = \dfrac{a}{\cos x}$ can not be solved.

Anna's first attempt at solving the task is, as Alf's first attempt, algorithmic reasoning. She doesn't remember the procedure in full, but after looking in her textbook for a few seconds she remembers it and applies it to the task. She quickly concludes, however, that the procedure didn't solve the task and she has to start over. The only significant difference in Alf's and Anna's reasoning structure, is that Anna implements the strategy correctly. However, the conclusion is, as Alf's conclusion, that the resulting equation can not be solved, as she says she has two unknowns there. Presumably, both Anna and Alf wanted to invert both sides of the equation and find a numerical value for x. This is how the procedure is described in the textbook.

– Hege

Description

[The author gives Hege the task.]

Hege: "I don't remember this. It's been a while since we were working on this. Sine x plus cosine x equals [uniteligeble], we two unknowns here. I need to somehow combine sine x and cosine x into one expression. I don't remember anything of this." [She start looking through her textbook. She is quiet for about 30 seconds.]

Author: "What are you looking for?"

Hege: "I don't know. I need to find some formula to combine cosine x and sine x. [She looks in her textbook for the next minute, then puts it down.] It wasn't there. I'm trying to find some formulas for the sum. But I can't do it when I don't know what x is."

Author: "What are you supposed to find here?"

Hege: "An unknown, but I don't know how to do it."

Interpretation

Hege's reasoning structure is less clear than the previous two. She looks for a trigonometric identity or procedure in the textbook that can transform the given task into an equation with just one trigonometric expression, but says she didn't find what she was looking for. Although she quickly gives up, the reasoning structure can be formulated as following:

1. Strategy choice: simplify the equation by finding a formula or procedure that can combine two trigonometric expressions into one trigonometric equation.
2. Strategy implementation: look for a formula or procedure in the textbook.
3. Conclusion: an appropriate formula or procedure was not found and the task can not be solved.

Based on the description of Hege's first attempt at solving the equation, it is difficult to know exactly what procedure or formula she is looking for. If the author were to speculate, it seems she vaguely remembers a procedure or formula that can transform this equation from having two trigonometric terms into an equation with just one trigonometric term. Even though Hege's attempt at solving the equation is neither as sophisticated nor as fruitful as the other two students' attempts, it is similar in nature. As Anna and Alf, Hege's first attempt is clearly algorithmic reasoning as she looks for a specific procedure or formula that can help her solve the equation. The main difference between Hege and the other two students, is that Hege does not remember or know the exact procedure.

The Prompt and Solution

Another interest of the author, which would shed some light on the students' mathematical reasoning, was their behaviour when given the prompt. The purpose of the prompt was two fold. First, it served as an implicit hint. It gave some insight into how the original equation could be solved. Second, the author wanted to see how the students generalized the properties of the prompt to the original equation.

– Alf

Description

[The author gives Alf the prompt.]

Alf: "Ok. This is the sine graph. I can just draw it." [Alf draws the graph of the sine function on a piece of paper and is quiet for about 15 seconds]

Author: "Can you say something about a?"

Alf: "a is an interval. It's between -1 and 1." [Alf writes down $a = \langle -1,1 \rangle$ next to the sine graph.]

Author: "so if you now go back to the original problem..."

Alf: "ok, but the tangent function is completely different. It goes like this." [Alf draws the graph of the tangent function next to the graph of the sine function.]

Author: "What if you look at the original equation."

Alf: [Alf is quiet for 10 seconds]. "I can transform it into a sine function and then find what a can be. As an intervall. It is dependent, but it must be within some range. It can. Wait a minute. A must be a function of [unintelligible] oscillation with sine. I can see that now. [Alf does some calculations on the piece of paper]. Then we have a squared plus b squared. This is it. C is the square root of two. Then we have to find the others as well. That means. But c is also one. So that is easy. It is the square root of two multiplied by sine x. Plus b over a. Which is one. Plus d, which we don't have to find, because that is just the equilibrium position which is zero. So d equals zero. [Alf continues to write down his solution on the piece of paper]. Ok, since the peak amplitude is the square root of two, that means a is between the square root of two and minus the square root of two."

Author: "Why is that?"

Alf: Because I made it into a sine function. Which means I have a graph that represents a here."

Interpretation

When given the prompt, Alf immediately says that this is the sine function and that a must be between -1 and 1. After a bit of guidance, he identifies the original equation of being similar in nature to the prompt. He knows that a is an interval in both cases. The generalization from the simpler to the more complex case is mathematically correct and he identified the structural similarities of the two equations. He furthermore shows a flexible understanding of the equation when he says that it is a function. The problem given is no longer just an equation with two variables, as Alf stated earlier, but a is a function of x as well now. This allows him to calculate the range of the function. The reasoning structure as he solves the equation is as following:

1. Strategy choice: The equation is also a function. The left side of the equation can be transformed into a sine function using $a \sin kx + b \cos kx = A \sin(kx + c)$. Find a by finding the range of the function.

2. Strategy implementation: Alf calculates $A = \sqrt{a^2 + b^2} = \sqrt{2}$, $k = 1$ and, wrongly, that $c = \dfrac{a}{b} = 1$. He concludes that the equilibrium position is zero. Giving him that $\sin x + \cos x = \sqrt{2} \sin(x + 1)$. The peak amplitude is $\sqrt{2}$, so $a = \left[-\sqrt{2}, \sqrt{2} \right]$.

3. Conclusion: A is an interval between minus the square root of two and the square root of two.

Even though Alf made a minor mistake in calculating c, this reasoning structure is to some degree creative in nature. The calculations Alf carried out were algorithmic and procedural, but looking at the equation as a function and evaluating its range is flexible, plausible and based on mathematical properties. Three of the four criteria needed for the reasoning to be classified as creative. The last of the criteria, novelty, is more difficult to evaluate. The author can not claim with certainty that the reasoning sequence was new to Alf, but the fact that he needed to see the prompt to make the necessary connections and initiate this reasoning sequence, indicate that it could be novel. Either as entirely new to the reasoner or as rediscovering a forgotten reasoning sequence.

An important point that needs to made, is that it was only after seeing the prompt Alf discovered the structural properties of the original equation necessary to apply his strategy choice. It was only after seeing the simpler equation he noticed that a had to be an interval and that he could look at the original equation as a function. From there, he could apply a familiar procedure in order to find the function's range. When Alf first began working on the equation, he didn't seem to investigate more closely the nature of a or what he was asked to find. Instead, he just looked at the equation, applied a familiar procedure and concluded it could not be solved as the equation contained two variables. The author finds it reasonable to conclude that Alf first focused on the surface properties of the equation and only after seeing the prompt, did he focus more closely on the structural features of the equation.

– **Anna**

Description

[The author gives Anna the prompt.]

Anna: [Quiet for 20 seconds]. "I have two unknowns. If it had been a number instead, for example two [pointing to a], then I could just say that x is sine inverted of two"

Author: "Ok".

Anna: "But I wouldn't get anything. Not now anyway."
Author: "Why not?"
Anna: "Because sine can not be greater than one. [Quiet for 5 seconds]. I am very uncertain about this. When I have two unknowns."
Author: "What is a? Is it an integer?"
Anna: "It can be many. A is a variable, right?" [Quiet for 15 seconds].
Author: "Remember to keep talking."
Anna: "I don't know. It's all very difficult now."
Author: "You said a could be many. What can a be?"
Anna: "It can be between one and minus one. I don't think I can find a more accurate answer than that."
Author: "What if you look at the original equation?"
Anna: "[Quiet for 10 seconds]. Yes, I don't know. It's been a while since we worked on this. Secondly, when there are so many unknowns. I don't know. What am I supposed to find here? Is it a number, is it an interval is it an expression."
Author: "What did you find in the other task?"
Anna: "That a had to be between one and minus one."
Author: "What is that?"
Anna: "It is an interval. [quiet for a few seconds]. Ok, it is exactly the same task. There is an interval here as well. Only difference is that here we have sine x plus cosine x and here it is just sine x. So if I can use this way of solving this, then I get. But then I get one and minus one."
Author: "It's the same interval in both equations?"
Anna: "Yes, it must be. If sine x plus cosine x, then both of them can be one. So one plus one equals two. But they can't be one simultaneously. If we look at the unit circle, [draws the unit cirlce] if cosine x is one, then sine x is zero. So maybe what I found is correct after all."
Author: "You could see if it is correct."
Anna: "Ok, if I try 40 degrees. [makes the necessary calculations on a calculator]. Ok, that is not right. I got 1.41. [Quiet for 25 seconds]. I must have mis-understood. [She picks up the calculator]. If I put it in here. If i put in y eqauls sine x plus cosine x. And set x from zero to ten and y from minus two to two. [She plots the graph of the function on the calculator]. If I find the maximum and the minimum, that will tell me how high and low a can be. Ok, so I get that maximum is 1.4 and the minimum is minus 1.4."
Author: "Have you now found a?"
Anna: "Yes."

Interpretation

It is clear from the transcript that when Anna is given the prompt, there are a two features of the problem that confuse her. The first is, as she mentions, the two un-knowns or variables. There is both an x and an a in the equation. It seems obvious that she is not used to working with a single equation with more than one variable. She expresses her frustration as she doesn't know what to do or how to solve an equation with two variables. The second frustration, is seen when she asks what she is supposed to find. It seems she is uncertain of the properties of a. This is also seen when she asks if a is a number, an interval or an expression. On a more general basis, the frustration stems from not knowing how to solve the equation and not knowing what the solution is supposed to look like. However, with a little guidance from the author, she correctly answers that a is an interval between one and minus one.

The uncertainty regarding a is also seen when she tries to generalize her findings in the simpler equation to the original equation. Even though she found that a had to be between one and minus one in the simpler equation, she asks the author if a is supposed to be an interval, an integer or an expression. However, after the author asks what she found out when given the prompt, she correctly concludes that a must be an interval in the original equation as well. She then says that the interval in the original equation is also one to minus one, but she quickly corrects herself. First saying that the interval must be from two to minus two. Then, referencing the unit circle, she goes back to her original answer and says the interval is one to minus one. She doesn't offer any justification for chosing a 40 degree angle as an example or why she think calculating one example could verify her solution. It may be possible that by looking at the unit circle, she, explicitly or implicitly, concluded that the sum sine x plus cosine x would be greater near a 45 degree angle. When she sees that the answer is greater than one, but less than two, it seems she understands that the upper limit of the interval is somewhere between one and two. As Alf, Anna was now able to treat the equation as a function. Where a was a function of x. The reasoning structure that enable her to solve the equation is as following:

1. Strategy choice: The equation is also a function. The function can be plotted on the calculator. Finding the maximum and the minimum of the function will give the interval of a.
2. Strategy implementation: Plot $y = \sin x + \cos x$ on the calculator. The maxima is 1.4 and the minima is -1.4.
3. Conclusion: $a = [-1.4,\ 1.4]$

Although Anna needed some help from the author to solve the equation, there are some indications of creativity in her reasoning process. As Alf, her reasoning is flexible as she is able to view the equation as a function and find the interval by calculating the maxima and minima of the function. Here, two connections were necessary. First, she had to look at a as a function of x and consequently plot the left side of the equation on her calculator. Second, she needed to make the connection between finding a and finding the maxima and minima of the function. The reasoning sequence is flexible, it is based on mathematical properties and plausible. The author can not say with certainty that the reasoning sequence is new to Anna, but later in the interview she expresses that looking at the equation as a function was unusual; especially since a was a function of x and not y as a function of x. This might indicate that the reasoning sequence is indeed new, or rediscovered, to Anna.

As such, the reasoning sequence does fulfil all the criteria of creative reasoning, but at the same time she experienced several difficulties and needed help from the author to solve the equation.

– Hege

Description

Hege's reaction and work when given the prompt was very similar to what Anna did. Therefore, only a quick summary of her work will be given here. Hege needed some help from the author identifying the interval of a in the prompt. When she tried to generalize the results from the prompt and back to the original equation, she first expressed that the interval of a was from one to minus one in the original equation as well. She then reconsidered and concluded that the interval was from two to minus two. However, she quickly corrected herself, saying that cosine and sine couldn't both be one simultaneously. Hege quickly concluded that the interval of a had to be between one and minus one. Trying to verify her conclusion, she chose $x = \frac{\pi}{3}$ and found that a = 1.36 Afterwards, she said that the upper limit of a had to be greater than one, but less than two. She then became quiet for some time and the author asked her what she was thinking:

Hege: I'm trying to think. If I... [quiet for 10 seconds]. I have to maximize this. If I insert two pi. No, that's not right. No, I don't know how to do it. [Quiet for 15 seconds].

Author: Can you do it graphically?

Hege: Yes, you can. But you will find y instead of a.

She then proceeds to plot the graph of $y = \sin x + \cos x$ on her calculator. She finds the maxima and minima of the function.

Hege: The maximum and minimum of the graph is...eh...1.4 and minus 1.4. [quiet for 15 seconds]

Author: What does that tell you about a?

Hege: Doesn't it say a is between minus 1.4 and 1.4?

Author: Is that your answer?

Hege: I don't know when the equation is solved!

Interpretation

As Anna, Hege solved the equation by looking at I as a function, plotting the graph and finding the maxima and minima of the function using her calculator. The reasoning sequence is therefore:

1. Strategy choice: The equation is also a function. The function can be plotted on the calculator. Finding the maximum and the minimum of the function will give the interval of a.

2. Strategy implementation: Plots $y = \sin x + \cos x$ on the calculator. Find the maxima and minima of the function by using the tools available on the graphical calculator. The maxima is 1.4 and the minima is -1.4.
3. Conclusion: $a = \left[-1.4,\ 1.4\right]$

Like Anna, Hege realized that in order to find the interval of a, she had to, first, find the maximum value of the left side of the equation. However, unlike Anna, she did not view the equation also as a function. Only when the author asked her if she could find the maxima graphically, did she make the necessary internal connection. She was now able to treat the equation as a function. This is seen when she says that solving the problem graphically will give her the values for y and not a. It is reasonable to conclude that Hege's understanding of the function concept is not flexible. So the well known procedures and algorithms for finding the maxima and minima of a function are not applicable in this situation, where the right side of the equal sign is a and not y. Hege was not able to solve the equation without significant help from the author and although she found the interval of y of the function $y = \sin x + \cos x$, she was not immediately able to transfer this information to the case of a.

DISCUSSION

The purpose of the study was to investigate the mathematical reasoning of high achieving students in upper secondary school. Two research questions were formulated in the introduction and in this section, the author will try to answer both. When the students were first given the equation, all three attempted algorithmic reasoning. The students in varying ways attempted to find an algorithm or formula that would solve the equation. Algorithmic reasoning, when applied correctly, can reduce the cognitive load of solving mathematical problems. However, in this case, all three students attempted to use or find algorithms and/or formulas that were not helpful for solving the equation. A plausible explanation is that the students did not consider the intrinsic properties of the equation, but focused instead on the surface appearance. On the surface, the equation looked like equations they had met earlier in the textbook. The equations in the textbook could be solved using the formulas and algorithms Anna and Alf utilized, while Hege presumably looked for a similar algorithm or formula. This is seen in Hege's statements, where she said that she didn't remember how to solve the equation. The answer to the first research question, is therefore that in this case the high achieving students did display superficial reasoning when given an unfamiliar trigonometric equation.

The students' behaviour when they first approached the equation, also reveal that imitative reasoning is a strong characteristic of their mathematical reasoning. All three students' first strategy choice was to somehow simplify the equation using some standardized procedure or formula. Based on the students' behaviour, it became clear quite early on that they were not able to solve the equation on their own. After Alf was given the prompt, he quickly realized a had to be an interval in both the easier equation and in the original equation. He then solved the equation by looking at it as a function. Anna and Hege also solved the equation by looking it as a function, but unlike Alf they needed significant help from the author during the interview to make the necessary connection. However, regardless of the guidance from the author during the interview, all three students were able to view the equation as a function. This allowed them to solve the equation using simple calculations. The problem was that they did not make this connection without explicit or implicit guidance. Alf needed the prompt and Anna and Hege needed explicit guidance from the author during the interview. The ability to view the equation in multiple ways indicated versatility, but not necessarily adaptability (Sfard & Linchevski, 1994) as the students needed help to view the equation as a function.

Based on the observations made in this study, it is the author's claim that the students possess the necessary domain knowledge to solve the equation. The students' were, for all intents and purposes, able to make the necessary connections and calculations to solve the equation on their own. The problem was a more general and structural behavioural pattern. When the students first began working on the equation, they immediately began looking for a formula, algorithm or procedure that would let them solve the equation. Later in the interview, all three students were able to focus on the intrinsic properties of the equation and solve it, but only with explicit or implicit help from the author. As defined earlier in the article, the students' behaviour, arguments and written product is the basis for their way of understanding. By looking at the students' way of understanding, it may be possible to say something about their way of thinking. Based on the observations in this study, the author contends that it is plausible to suggest that the students' way of thinking vis-à-vis mathematical reasoning is characterised by an expectation that mathematical problems can be solved using a familiar procedure or algorithm.

The findings of this study reinforce earlier findings, which have indicated that even high achieving students display superficial reasoning when faced with a mathematical problem (Selden et al., 1994, Lithner, 2000 & Schoenfeld, 1985). Although the results are not generalizeable to all high achieving students, the three cases presented in this study do generate other questions. In particular, why do the students in this study display superficial reasoning? Why isn't their way of thinking, when given an unfamiliar equation, more flexible and creative? Hiebert (2003) argues that students learn what they are given an opportunity to learn. A possible explanatory hypothesis, is that the three students in this study have gotten good grades in school mathematics by focusing on memorizing and applying algorithms and procedures. They are simply a result of their learning milieu, which rewards imitative reasoning and not creative reasoning. However, the framework and methods used in this study can not give an answer to these questions. Future studies in which high achieving students' learning milieu is investigated is needed.

REFERENCES

Ausubel, D. (1962). A subsumption theory of meaningful verbal learning and retention. *The Journal of General Psychology, 66*, 213–244.

Bergqvist, E. (2007). Types of reasoning required in university exams in mathematics. *Journal of Mathematical Behavior, 26*, 348–370.

Clement, J. (2000). Analysis of clinical interviews: Foundation and model viability. In *Handbook of research design in mathematics and science education*. New Jersey, NJ: Lawrence Erlbaum.

Cox, W. (1994). Strategic learning in a level mathematics? *Teaching Mathematics and its Applications, 13*, 11–21.

Ericsson, K., & Simon, H. (1993). *Protocol analysis: Verbal reports as data*. Cambridge: MIT Press.

Franklin, C. S., & Ballan, M. (2001) Reliability and validity in qualitative research. In *The handbook of social work research methods*. Sage Publications Inc.

Freudenthal, H. (1991). *Revisiting mathematics education: China lectures*. Dordrecht, Boston: Kluwer Academic Publishers.

Gray, E., & Tall, D. (1991). Duality, ambiguity and fexibility in successful mathematical thinking. *Proceedings of PME, 15*(2), 72–79.

Halmos, P. (1980). The heart of mathematics. *American Mathematical Monthly, 87*(7), 519–524.

Hammersley, M. (1990). *Reading ethnographic research: A critical guide*. London: Longmans.

Harel, G. (2008). What is mathematics? a pedagogical answer to a philosophical question. In R. Gold & R. Simons (Eds.), *Current issues in the philosophy of mathematics from the perspective of mathematicians*.

Hiebert, J. (2003). What research says about the NCTM standards. In *A research companion to principles and standards for school mathematics*. Reston, VA: National Council of Teachers of Mathematics

Hiebert, J., & Lefevre, P. (1986). Conceptual and procedural knowledge in mathematics: An introductory analysis. In J. Hiebert (Ed.), *Conceptual and procedural knowledge: The case of mathematics* (pp. 1–27). Hillsdale, NJ: Lawrence Erlbaum Associates.

Kamii, C., & Dominick, A. (1997). To teach or not to teach algorithms. *Journal of Mathematical Behavior, 16*, 51–61.

Klette, K., Lie, S., Ødegaard, M., Øystein Anmarkrud, Arnesen, N., Bergem, O. K., et al. (2008). *Pisa+: Lærings og undervisningsstrategier i skolen technical report*. ILS, UiO.

Lithner, J. (2000). Mathematical reasoning in task solving. *Educational Studies in Mathematics, 41*(2), 165–190.

Lithner, J. (2003). Students' mathematical reasoning in university textbook exercises. *Educational Studies in Mathematics, 52*, 29–55.

Lithner, J. (2005). A framework for analysing qualities of mathematical reasoning: Version 3. In *Research reports in mathematics education* (p. 3). Department of Mathematics, Umea University.

Lithner, J. (2006). *A framework for analysing creative and imitative mathematical reasoning*. Umea: Department of Mathematics, Umea University.

Lithner, J. (2008). A research framework for creative and imitative reasoning. *Educational Studies in Mathematics, 67*, 255–276.

McNeal, B. (1995). Learning not to think in a textbookbased mathematics class. *Journal of Mathematical Behavior, 14*, 18–32.

Mullis, I., Martin, M., Robitaille, D., & Foy, P. (2009). *TIMSS advanced 2008 international report: Findings from IEA's study of achievement in advanced mathematics and physics in the final year of secondary school*. Chestnut Hill, MA: TIMSS & PIRLS International Study Center, Boston College.

NCTM. (2000). *Principles and standards for school mathematics*. Reston, VA: National Council of Teachers of Mathematics.

Niss, M. (1999). Aspects of the nature and state of research in mathematics education. *Educational studies in mathematics, 40*, 1–24.

Niss, M., & Jensen, T. H. (2002). *Kompetencer og matematiklrring. Ideer og inspiration til udvikling af matematikundervisning i Danmark Utdannelelsesstyrelsens temahefteserie nr 18- 2002*. Undervisningsministeriet.

KD. (2006). *Kunnskapsløftet*. Oslo: Utdanningsdirektoratet/Norwegian directorate for education and training. Retrieved August 30, 2010, from http://www.udir.no/grep

Pesek, D., & Kirshner, D. (2000). Interference of instrumental instruction in subsequent relational learning. *Journal for Research in Mathematics Educational Action Research, 31*, 524–540.

Polya, G. (1954). *Mathematics and plausible reasoning*. Princeton, NJ: Princeton University Press.

Ritchie, J., & Lewis, J. (2003). *Qualitative research practice.* Sage Publications Ltd.

Schoenfeld, A. (1985). *Mathematical problem solving.* Orlando, FL: Academic Press.

Selden, J., Selden, A., & Mason, A. (1994). Even good calculus students can't solve nonroutine problems. In J. Kaput & E. Dubinsky (Eds.), *Research issues in undergraduate mathematics learning.* Washington, DC: Mathematical Association of America.

Sfard, A., & Linchevski, L. (1994). The gains and the pitfalls of reifcation the case of algebra. *Educational Studies in Mathematics, 26,* 191–228.

Silverman, D. (2006). *Interpreting qualitative data.* Sage Publications Ltd.

Skemp, R. R. (1976). Relational understanding and instrumental understanding. *Mathematics Teaching, 77,* 20–26.

Sriraman, B. (2009). The characteristics of mathematical creativity. *ZDM, 41*(1), 19–34.

Sternberg, R., & Lubart, T. (1999). The concept of creativity: Prospects and paradigms. In *Handbook of creativity.* Cambridge University Press.

Yackel, E., & Hanna, G. (2003). Reasoning and proof. In J. Kilpatrick, G. Martin, & Schifter, D (Eds.), *A research companion to principles and standards for school mathematics.* Reston, VA: National Council of Teachers of Mathematics.

Haavold Per Øystein
University of Tromso
Norway

KHAYRIAH MASSARWE, IGOR VERNER,
AND DAOUD BSHOUTY

14. FOSTERING CREATIVITY THROUGH GEOMETRICAL AND CULTURAL INQUIRY INTO ORNAMENTS

INTRODUCTION

This paper discusses pathways of creativity and focuses on the one which goes through practice in creation and analysis of useful and mathematically meaningful artifacts. We followed the pathway in the workshop "Geometry of Ornaments" conducted in 2008–2009 in one of the Israeli Arab teacher colleges. Ornaments are treated as geometric patterns of cultural value composed of basic units repeated under different transformations. The workshop involved prospective teachers in practice of construction and analysis of geometric ornaments from different cultures as well as in teaching geometry in this context to middle school pupils. In the follow-up, we observed creative performances demonstrated in innovative works of some of the students. Their creativity was expressed in constructing new stylized ornaments, discerning interesting geometrical problems related to these ornaments and finding different approaches to solve them. The students became aware of ornaments not only as decorations, but also as interesting geometrical objects.

The need for people capable to develop creative mathematical solutions for problems of the modern technologically oriented world is constantly increasing. Efforts made in different countries to foster and nurture mathematical creativity in students, have been presented at the Discussion Group 9 "Promoting creativity for all students in mathematics education" of the 11th International Congress on Mathematics Education (Mexico, 2008) and at other meetings. Educators reached the point that efforts ought to shift from concentrating on potential mathematicians, towards addressing every student as "a unique creative individual whose cultivation of his/her 'inner self' is fostered by the education system" (D'Ambrosio, 2007).

This social trend induces extending the educational research on mathematical creativity towards a broader view of factors influencing the development of creative thinking. Traditional studies of mathematical creativity concentrate on inspirations, problem solving processes and outcomes within mathematics (Mann, 2006) while practice indicates that these factors should also take into consideration the cultural context (D'Ambrosio, 1985; Bishop, 1988).

Sriraman (2004) points to incompleteness of traditional definitions of mathematical creativity. He calls to "interpret the characteristics of mathematical creativity" using a broader view based on contemporary approaches to the study of creativity developed

B. Sriraman and K.H. Lee (eds.), The Elements of Creativity and Giftedness in Mathematics, 217–230.
© 2011 Sense Publishers. All rights reserved.

by psychologists. In particular he relies on the approaches systematically observed by Sternberg (1999). One of these approaches specifically addresses the cultural aspect of creativity. It emphasizes the vitality of the cultural and social environment in developing individual creativity, defining directions of creative work, and accumulating creative products in cultural heritage.

The important role of the cultural context in the development of mathematical creativity has been repeatedly noticed at the Fifth International Conference "Creativity in Mathematics and the Education of Gifted Students" that took place in Haifa in 2008:
- Understanding pupils' cultural diversity is essential for teaching and fostering their creativity (Milgram, 2008).
- To foster creativity, teaching should be adapted to specific needs of different ethnic and cultural groups (Nevo, 2008).
- Ignoring social and cultural factors can suppress educational outcomes of gifted students (Subotnik, 2008).

A focused open discussion of the subject took place at the post-conference workshop "Intercultural Aspects of Creativity: Challenges and Barriers". The participants worked in discussion groups. The authors of this paper took part in the group *Using artifacts of local culture in stimulating creativity*". The discussion was fruitful and helped the participants to find and coordinate directions for further studies. In particular, the group discussed different existing pathways of creativity in the cultural context. Each of the participants pointed to a pathway of her/his special interest. This paper is an extended version of our paper (Massarwe, Verner and Bshouty, 2010). It briefly introduces the pathways of creativity discussed in the group and presents our study of one of the pathways related to studying geometry through the multicultural inquiry into ethnomathematics.

CREATIVITY PATHWAYS

The discussion in our international group, including mathematicians and educators from Hungary, Israel, Mexico, Turkey and U.S.A., indicated that the participants had different perceptions of mathematical creativity and different opinions on how to develop it. These differences are in line with different conceptions of creativity existing in the literature (Sriraman, 2004; Treffinger et al., 2002).

When trying to form a general view, we concluded that there is a need to consider different pathways of creative endeavor based on mathematical and constructive activities with artifacts. The pathways point to different creative learning processes stemming from different cultural contexts. Three pathways were discerned. The first one comes from the intellectual challenge of understanding the World, the human self, and the Universe. This led to creative thinking that was developed along the road of mathematical modeling of natural phenomena.

The second pathway is the historical development of creators in different fields. The history gives many examples showing that the needs that emerged through the progress of nations posed situations that demanded creative solutions. This made societies seek ways for fostering creativity among their people. A remarkable example of development of creators in the Ottoman Empire was presented at the Workshop by Batdal (2009). The Enderun (the Palace School) was established in Istanbul as a free-boarding school for gifted students from religious minorities (Millet) which were recruited throughout the country (see: http://en.wikipedia.org/ wiki/Enderun_School). The aim was to educate talented people to govern the culturally diverse and continuously spreading empire. Most of the leading commanders, civil servants, as well as artists, poets and musicians were educated in the Enderun.

The third pathway is imposed by the cultural development of societies, including the development of languages, religions, arts, trade, cultural exchange, typography, etc.

The progress in this pathway comes from the development of spiritual, emotional and social perceptions and the aspiration to express them in visual symbolic form (Verner and Bshouty, 2008).

In this paper we focus our attention on the third pathway. Historically, communities lived in different surroundings and developed creative solutions that answered their materialistic and spiritual needs. The communities accumulated their experiences and in due time synthesized the knowledge into theories. The process of theorization was deeply rooted in the ethno-cultural tradition of the communities (Prediger, 2004). The learning effort and creativity of people involved in this process were directed to conceive past experience in order to tackle contemporary problems. The diversity of theories developed in different communities urged a multi-cultural dialogue for knowledge exchange that led to the development of universal theories of mathematics, sciences, technology, art, religion, etc.

The trend of universalization, being so important for the progress of civilization, led to a movement which swept mathematical education into a cultural-free one. The fruits of this trend included the unification of mathematical symbols, axioms, and curricula. The negative tendency that accompanied this progress was the detachment of mathematics from the students' world.

MATHEMATICS EDUCATION IN CULTURAL CONTEXT

Educators notice that teaching mathematics as a culture-free subject is one of the reasons behind the decline of students' motivation and their difficulties in mathematics study (Bishop, 1988; Presmeg, 1998). In order to bridge the gap between the universal mathematics and the student world, a new movement in mathematics education calls for teaching mathematics in a cultural context relevant to the student - ethnomathematics education (Bishop, 1988). Studies in ethnomathematics education indicated its contribution to mathematical achievement and creativity of learners from different ethnic groups in addition to providing them with equal opportunity in mathematics education (Presmeg, 1998; Gerdes, 2005).

We emphasize yet an additional contribution of ethnomathematics education, an opportunity to expose students in the mathematics class to cultures other than their own. This is especially important in the modern world, where societies are becoming multicultural and globally connected. While mathematical learning is supported by the context of a student's own culture, the multicultural context brings additional benefits. In particular, through constructive and inquiry activities in multicultural ethnomathematics, students develop capabilities of holistic and divergent thinking which underlie creativity (Gibson, Folley and Park, 2009).

Geometry lies in the heart of culture and ethnomathematics (Gerdes, 2005). Compass and straightedge were basic constructive instruments by which people solved practical problems, accumulating their experiences in their cultural heritage. To answer their spiritual needs, people created geometric symbols, representing their beliefs and feelings. Most notably, ideas, beliefs, and feelings were expressed by elaborated ornaments. Ornaments are geometric patterns of cultural value composed of basic units repeated under different transformations. Different cultures developed unique collections of creative artistic ornaments that are in the core of their heritage. For example, in Hindu cultural tradition, creative geometric ornaments, Rangoli, are widely constructed outdoors, using colored rice with bare hands. Mathematical ideas embedded in fifteenth century Islamic ornaments (complex girih tiles) were reconsidered five centuries later by Penrose to create quasi-crystalline patterns, consequently leading to the discovery of quasi-crystals showing spatial five-fold symmetry (Lu and Steinhardt, 2007; Darvas, 2007, p. 67).

EDUCATIONAL FRAMEWORK

The study presented in this paper is part of the Technion project "Teaching Geometry in Cultural Context". The project goal is to develop an approach to teaching geometry through involving the students in the multicultural inquiry into ethnomathematics. This way we strive to foster students' motivation to learn geometry, develop their geometrical thinking, and arouse awareness of cultural identity and appreciation of other cultures. In the framework of this project we develop courses and workshops which focus on creative practice of geometrical construction and analysis of ornaments. The participants are prospective and in-service teachers and students in Israel's Jewish and Arab high schools. They study geometry through mathematical analysis and construction of geometrical ornaments, and inquiry of their cultural symbolic meaning.

The following advantages of practice with ornaments can be noted:
- Geometric ornaments are a rich source of creative applications of geometry.
- Ornaments are part of the world cultural heritage, created in folk art and crafts throughout the history of nations (El-Said, 1993).
- For peoples of the Middle East, ornaments traditionally served a means to express spiritual believes related to their cultural and religious identity.
- From our experiments, practice in analysis of ornaments and their construction can attract pupils and students and serve an effective way for teaching geometry with applications.

Our project is growing as a tree-like multi-case study: the case study of the Technion course "Teaching Geometry in Cultural Context" represents the stem of the tree; the branches are case studies in which courses and workshops for different groups of learners are developed, implemented, and evaluated. This paper presents one "branch" - the workshop "Geometry of Ornaments" conducted in 2008–2009 in one of the Israeli Arab teacher colleges. The 10 hours workshop was part of the teaching practice course. In the workshop teacher students were exposed to the importance of integrating the cultural aspect in learning and teaching geometry. The follow-up data in the case study were collected through observations, interviews, videotapes and consideration of students' performances.

The students inquired ornaments from their culture and other cultures, analyzed geometrical properties of ornaments and constructed them. They developed instructional units and lesson plans and practiced teaching geometry in the context of ornaments to middle school pupils. The workshop assignments included the following:
– Draw a given Islamic ornament by compass and straightedge.
– Solve geometrical problems examining properties of ornaments, posed by the teacher.
– Suggest geometrical problems of your own related to the discussed ornaments.
– Choose an ornament from your own culture or other cultures, construct and analyze it (open task).

The students found these assignments completely new and, in the beginning, were anxious about the scope of the tasks that they were asked to perform. Soon after deepening in the subject, they became more and more creative. The students selected for the open task ornaments not only from their Islamic culture, but also Hindu ornaments (Rangoli) and others. They looked into the historical source of the ornaments and the symbolic meaning of their geometrical patterns. Their motivation arose with the advancement of the inquiry.

When studying the experiential learning process that took place in the workshop, we observed numerous examples of impressive students' progress in creative performance. This is in line with Sternberg's inference that "when creative students are taught and their achievements are then assessed in a way that values their creative abilities, their academic performance improves" (Sternberg, 1999, p. 9). When considering learning activities of the students as creative, we confronted them with the four categories of creativity used for the evaluation of creative thinking (Torrance, 1974): fluency - generating a number of relevant solutions; flexibility – tackling the problem from different perspectives; originality – implementing novel ideas; and elaboration – examining modifications of the problem and the solution. As the learning activities in the workshop were not conventional for geometry studies, we believe that examples of creative performance can be of interest to the reader and thus we present some of them.

EXAMPLES OF CREATIVE ACTIVITIES

Example 1

A typical basic unit of Islamic ornaments (see Figure 1A) was presented to a group of second year students majoring in mathematics education at an Arab academic college. The open assignments given to the students were:
– To construct the basic unit by compass and straightedge
– To find implementations of the basic unit in ornaments from Islamic art and architecture

- To create an original ornament from the constructed basic unit
- To analyze the properties of basic unit and its construction through formulating and solving geometrical problems.

The main steps of the students' construction of the basic unit are presented in Figure 1 (B-D).

The students took the assignment of finding ornaments that implement the basic unit, as a challenging inquiry. They searched web sites and books on Islamic art and architecture, looked over the ornaments in the mosques in their own and neighboring villages. They presented ornaments constructed using the basic unit, such as in Figure 2A. The students also found ornaments in which their basic units are similar to the original one, such as those shown in Figures 2B and 2C.

The students disclosed that the basic units of both ornaments, shown in Figures 2A and 2B, have octagonal rotational symmetry. However with the evident similarity of the two ornaments, certain elements of their basic units are different. Thus, the following problem arose: what change in the construction of the first basic unit should be made in order to build the second basic unit? The first solution was suggested to follow the same steps shown in Figures 1B and 1C, and then make a different final step as shown in Figure 3A.

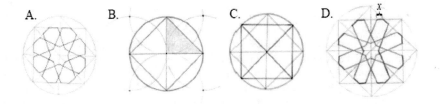

Figure 1. A. The basic unit; B-D. Construction steps.

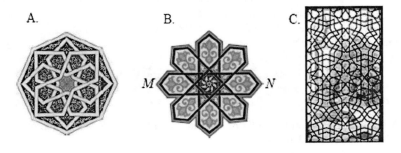

Figure 2. Islamic ornaments: A. Composed of the basic unit;
B-C. Based on similar units.

Analysis of the construction steps of the two basic units indicated that at the final steps of their construction, shown in Figure 1D and Figure 3A, the segments designated by x can be chosen of arbitrary length, without changing the shapes. It was also observed that in the second ornament (Figure 2B) the angles at the tips of the bar MN are obtuse, while in the constructed basic unit (Figure 3A) the angles are right ones. Therefore, an improved procedure was proposed which uses two parameters x and y, where y regulates the angles at M and N (see Figure 3B).

This example presents typical inquiry activities with ornaments in the course. In these activities the students generated and examined several relevant solutions of the original and modified ornaments. We believe that these activities relate to creative thinking, specifically in the categories of fluency and elaboration (Torrance, 1974).

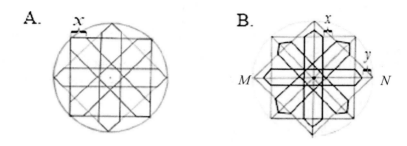

Figure 3. Construction of the varied basic unit.

Example 2

Figure 4A presents a detail of the ornament shown in Figure 2C. The detail provoked additional discussion and inquiry. In this case the basic unit consists of five bars (not of four as for previous cases). The students observed a regular decagon and a pentagon and wondered: How can we construct a regular decagon or a pentagon?

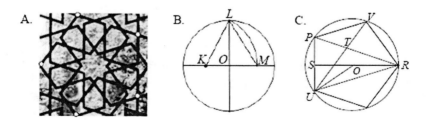

Figure 4. A. Decagonal ornament detail; B. Construction procedure;
C. Regular pentagon.

MASSARWE ET AL

Searching the web indicated that the problem of constructing a regular pentagon has been solved in a variety of ways, since ancient Greek till recently. Modern descriptive geometry textbooks propose the following procedure for constructing a regular pentagon (see Figure 4B):
- In the circle with center O and radius r draw two perpendicular diameters
- Determine point K so that $KO = r/2$
- Draw a circular arc (LM) with center K and radius KL
- The length of the side of regular pentagon inscribed in the circle equals $|LM|$.

The textbooks did not provide a proof of this result. The students, feeling themselves as constructors of ornaments questioned the correctness of this procedure and initiated the discussion of how to prove it. With our guidance, the students perceived a method of geometrical proof which was unfamiliar to them. The method consists of three steps. Firstly, to calculate the length of LM as determined by the procedure for a circle of radius 1. Secondly, to calculate the length of a side of a regular pentagon inscribed in a circle of radius 1. The final step is to show that both results are equal.

We believe that the elementary geometric proof presented below is in place. Let $r = 1$. The length of constructed segment $|LM|$ can be calculated as follows:

$$|KL| = \sqrt{|KO|^2 + |OL|^2} = \frac{\sqrt{5}}{2}, \quad |OM| = |KM| - |KO| = \frac{\sqrt{5}-1}{2}$$

$$|LM| = \sqrt{|LO|^2 + |OM|^2} = \frac{\sqrt{10 - 2\cdot\sqrt{5}}}{2}$$

We will show that $|LM|$ equals to the length of the pentagon's side. In the regular pentagon shown in Figure 4C, each angle equals $180° - 360°/5 = 108°$. By elementary computation we have that

$$\angle VPR = \angle PRU = 36°, \quad \angle PTU = \angle TPU = 72°,$$
$$\angle UPR = \angle PUR = 72°.$$

Therefore, the triangles $\triangle PRU$ and $\triangle PUT$ are similar. Denote $RU = RP = y$, $UP = RT = x$, and $OS = z$. Then, by similarity

$$\frac{RU}{UP} = \frac{UP}{PT} \quad i.e. \quad \frac{y}{x} = \frac{x}{y-x} \quad \Rightarrow \quad y = \frac{1+\sqrt{5}}{2}x.$$

224

The ΔRSU is a right angle triangle, therefore $(1+z)^2 = y^2 - (x/2)^2$.
Substituting y, we get

$$(1+z)^2 = \left(\frac{1+\sqrt{5}}{2}\right)^2 x^2 - \frac{x^2}{4} \quad \Longrightarrow \quad z = \frac{\sqrt{5+2\sqrt{5}}}{2} x - 1$$

Next, the ΔOSU is also a right angle triangle, and therefore $z^2 + (x/2)^2 = 1$.
Substituting z from the above equation we get

$$\left(\frac{\sqrt{5+2\sqrt{5}}}{2} x - 1\right)^2 + \left(\frac{x}{2}\right)^2 = 1.$$

Solving for x we get that the side of the pentagon is

$$x = \frac{4 \cdot \sqrt{5+2\sqrt{5}}}{6+2\sqrt{5}}$$

To complete the proof, the prospective teachers were instructed to use elementary algebra and show that $x = |LM|$. For a circle with radius r, using dilation, one sees that the same procedure works.

The problem of constructing a regular pentagon in the course was unintended; it arose in the context of the decagonal ornament brought by one of the students. The inquiry into this problem was useful, as it exposed students to new geometrical and algebraic ideas and presented a new perspective of a geometrical proof, as a way to justify a practical construction procedure. We believe that this inquiry fostered students' creative geometrical thinking, specifically related to the flexibility category.

Example 3

This is an example of implementing novel ideas by two of the students interested in computers. It should be noted that geometric transformations and computer graphics technologies were not taught in the course. Nevertheless, the students, on their own (in addition to drawing by compass and straightedge), constructed basic units and created different ornaments using computer graphics. One student created two ornaments using MS Office Word tools while applying two different geometric translations (Figure 5A). The other student studied the CorelDRAW program and used it to construct and design the basic unit and create the ornament shown in Figure 5B. We consider this performance as a manifestation of students' creativity related to the originality category.

A.   **B.**

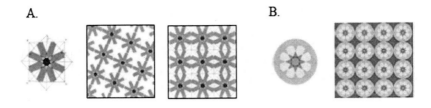

Figure 5. Basic units and ornaments created using computer graphics.

WORKSHOP DATA COLLECTION AND ANALYSIS

Together with observation of geometrical and construction activities with ornaments we collected and analyzed data on students' attitudes towards learning geometry in cultural context and their reflections on the workshop experience. In our study the group of second year college students, participated in the workshop (N=28), was divided into an experimental and control subgroups (N=14). The experimental group was taught by one of the authors (Massarwe), while the control group was taught by a teacher not involved in the study.

The experimental group went through the activities described above, while the control group dealt with disciplinary activities solely. At the end of the workshop, the authors organized a seminar in the Department of Education in Technology and Science, Technion. In this seminar the students from the experimental group gave Powerpoint presentations of their work to students of the control group and to us. The presentations were followed by discussions concentrated on creative aspects of their work.

A pre-course and post-course questionnaires tested students' experience in and attitudes towards learning and teaching geometry in cultural context before and after the workshop. Students' answers related to different aspects of creativity are summarized below.

Experience of Learning Mathematics with Applications

As indicated by the pre-course questionnaire, only 21% of the students had experience of learning mathematics with applications. In spite of this lack of experience, all the students believed that learning with applications can significantly contribute to understanding geometry.

Experience of Learning Geometry in Cultural Context

Absolute majority of the students (93%) before the course studied geometry with no connection to cultural context. Only 28% mentioned that at school they were exposed to visual symbols and geometrical patterns used in their culture.

Experience of Connecting Geometry with Culture and Art

All the students reported that before the course, they were not exposed to connections of geometry with culture and art. After the course, the students of the experimental group answered that the course helped them to recognize the universality of geometry (93%) and its beauty (100%). After the workshop, all the students reported that they were surprised of the important role that geometry plays in culture and art.

Geometrical View of Visual Patterns

All the students of the experimental group pointed out that due to the workshop they became more attentive to ornaments in their environment and interested in their symbolism. All the students of the control group that they became interested in ornaments and their geometrical properties.

Curiosity and Pride in Own Cultural Heritage

Already before the course, absolute majority of the students were curious to see examples of the use of geometry in their own culture (93%) and other cultures (86%). After the course all the students noted that this experience aroused feeling of pride in their cultural heritage.

Interest, Motivation and Readiness to Teach Geometry in Cultural Context

After the workshop all the students in the experimental group reported that they acquired skills needed for teaching geometry in cultural context. Their self-confidence was based on real experience of lessons given to middle school pupils. The students also mentioned that activities with ornaments aroused pupils' interest and involvement in their lessons.

Self-directed Inquiry

All of the students in the experimental group reported that the course gave them an opportunity for self-directed inquiry. They expressed intent to deepen knowledge in the geometry of ornaments.

The Impact of the Technion Seminar

All of the students in the control group said that the seminar presentations enriched their knowledge, were interesting and aroused their pride in their own culture. They were impressed by the fascinating connection between geometry and culture and inspired to learn and teach geometry with applications. The workshop helped them to understand the universality of geometry, its important role in culture and to recognize complex geometrical patterns as compositions of basic geometrical figures. The teacher of the control group attended the seminar and found the presentations very interesting. He expressed interest to participate in the project.

Summarizing the data analysis in this section, it presents indications that involving students in geometrical and cultural inquiry evokes among them emotional feelings, beliefs and attitudes that facilitate their self-directed learning and creativity. Mathematical activities in cultural context contribute to the formation of affective structures "essential for developing mathematical inventiveness"; these structures are mathematical intimacy, integrity and identity (Goldin, 2008).

The inspiring and personally meaningful cultural context serves an application channel for mathematical intimacy, through which the student becomes engaged in geometry studies. Mathematical integrity, i.e. commitment to truth and understanding in doing mathematics, is stimulated in the cultural context of ornaments by two main factors: (a) by student's aspiration to understand and construct complex visual patterns as combinations of basic geometric objects; and (b) by student's desire to solve a real culturally meaningful problem. Mathematical identity in our approach is formatted together with cultural identity through the integration of mathematical inquiry and cultural inquiry into the student's own culture and other cultures.

DISCUSSION AND CONCLUSION

The 2008 International Workshop "Intercultural Aspects of Creativity: Challenges and Barriers" demonstrated (1) consensus in appreciation of the importance of cultural context in the development of mathematical creativity, and (2) diversity in perception of approaches to integrating cultural context in mathematics education. Through brainstorming at our Workshop discussion group, we realized that in order to discern the ways in which teaching in cultural context can contribute to the development of mathematical creativity, we need to observe examples of its manifestation in the course of historical development. Moreover, by observing these examples we perceive principal pathways of creativity development that can be adapted in mathematics education. Three pathways were identified by our group:

1) Educating creators to become leaders serving society's development.
2) Involving learners in scientific research towards understanding the World, the human self, and the Universe.
3) Involving learners in practical activities of creating culturally meaningful artifacts by which they express their spiritual, emotional and social perceptions in visual symbolic form.

These empirically derived pathways of creativity development correlate with the factors proposed by Sternberg (2003, p. 107): intelligence, knowledge, thinking styles, personality, motivation, and environment. Each pathway leans on certain factors:

- The first pathway of creativity development (educating creators) focuses on personality and thinking styles of students who are potential mathematicians.
- The second pathway emphasizes the role of intelligence and scientific knowledge in the development of mathematical creativity.
- The third pathway concentrates on the motivation and environment factors which are driven by practice in creating culturally meaningful artifacts.

This paper explores the third pathway of creativity development. Prospective teachers in one Arab college were involved in analysis and construction of ornaments and in teaching geometry in this context to middle school pupils in the framework of the workshop "Teaching Geometry in Cultural Context". Follow-up of the learning activities indicated that students' motivation and desire to make a deep inquiry in both mathematical and cultural aspects of ornaments increased through the workshop. The students verified this conclusion saying that the more they inquired the geometrical properties and cultural meaning of ornaments; they became more active and interested in the subject. We observed creative performances demonstrated in innovative works of some of the students. This is expressed in constructing new conventionalized ornaments, discerning interesting geometrical problems related to these ornaments and finding different approaches to solve these problems.

Most of all, a conceptual change in the perception of geometry happened. The students became aware of ornaments in their environment, seeing them not only as decorations, but as culturally meaningful geometrical patterns possessing interesting geometric transformations and symmetries.

ACKNOWLEDGEMENT

This research is partially supported by the Ministry of Science and Technology, Israel. The authors thank Yusuf Avci, Gulsah Batdal, Gyorgy Dravas, Ildiko Judit Pelczer and Mark Saul for inspiring discussion of the subject at the Workshop discussion group.

REFERENCES

Batdal, G. (2008). *History of the gifted education and developing creativity in Turkey.* Retrieved August 23, 2009, from International Workshop and Research Project: Intercultural Aspects of Creativity: Challenges and Barriers Web site: http://construct.haifa.ac.il/~rozal/templeton/Gulsah%20BATDAL-%20Templeton%20workshop.pdf

Bishop, A. J. (1988). Mathematics education in its cultural context. *Educational Studies in Mathematics, 19*(2), 179–191.

D'Ambrosio, P. (2007). Students feed monkeys for education: Using the Zhuangzi to communicate in a contemporary system of education. *KRITIKE Journal of Philosophy, 1*(2), 36–48. doi: http://www.kritike.org/journal/issue_2/d'ambrosio_december2007.pdf

D'Ambrosio, U. (1985). Ethnomathematics and its place in the history and pedagogy of mathematics. *For the Learning of Mathematics, 5*(1), 44–48.

Darvas, G. (2007). *Symmetry.* Basel: Birkhauser.

El-Said, I. (1993). *Islamic art and architecture. The system of geometric design.* In T. El-Bori & K. Critchlow (Eds.), Reading, UK: Garnet Publishing.

Gerdes, P. (2005). Ethnomathematics, geometry and educational experiences in Africa. *Africa Development, 30*(3), 48–65.

Gibson, C., Folley, B. S., & Park, S. (2009). Enhanced divergent thinking and creativity in musicians: A behavioral and near-infrared spectroscopy study. *Brain and Cognition, 69,* 162–169.

Goldin, G. (2008). The affective dimension of mathematical inventiveness. In *Proceedings of the international conference "Creativity in mathematics and the education of gifted students"* (pp. 3–14). Israel.

Lu, P. J., & Steinhardt, P. J. (2007). Decagonal and quasi-crystalline tilings in medieval Islamic architecture. *Science, 315,* 1106.

Mann, E. L. (2006). Creativity: The essence of mathematics. *Journal for the Education of the Gifted, 30*(2), 236–262.

Massarwe, K., Verner, I., & Bshouty, D. (2010). Pathways of creativity: Joyful learning of geometry through analysis and construction of ornaments. *Mediterranean Journal of Mathematics Education. Special Issue Intercultural Aspects of Creativity: Challenges and Barriers, 9*(2), 93–105.

Milgram, R. M. (2008). Talent loss: Causes and solutions. In *Proceedings of the international conference "Creativity in mathematics and the education of gifted students"* (pp. 15–20). Israel.

Nevo, B. (2008). Definitions (axioms), values, and empirical validation in the education of gifted children. *Proceedings of the international conference "Creativity in mathematics and the education of gifted students"* (pp. 21–28). Israel.

Prediger, S. (2004). Intercultural perspectives on mathematics learning – Developing a theoretical framework. *International Journal of Science and Mathematics Education, 2*(3), 377–406.

Presmeg, N. C. (1998). Ethnomathematics in teacher education. *Journal of Mathematics Teacher Education, 1*(3), 317–339.

Sriraman, B. (2004). The characteristics of mathematical creativity. *The Mathematics Educator, 14*(1), 19–34.

Sternberg, R. J. (2003). *Wisdom, intelligence, and creativity synthesized.* Cambridge, UK: Cambridge University Press.

Sternberg, R. J., & Lubart, T. I. (1999). The concept of creativity: Prospects and paradigms. In R. J. Sternberg (Ed.), *Handbook of creativity* (pp. 3–15). Cambridge, UK: Cambridge University Press.

Subotnik, R. F. (2008). The psychological dimensions of creativity in mathematics: Implications for gifted education policy. In *Proceedings of the international conference "Creativity in mathematics and the education of gifted students"* (pp. 35–48). Israel.

Torrance, E. P. (1974). *Torrance tests of creative thinking.* Bensenvill, IL: Scholastic Testing Service.

Treffinger, D. J., Young, G. C., Selby, E. C., & Shepardson, C. (2002). *Assessing creativity: A guide for educators.* Sarasota, FL: Center for Creative Learning. ERIC ED477675. Retrived September 16, 2009, from http://www.eric.ed.gov/ERICDocs/data/ericdocs2sql/content_storage_01/0000019b/80/1b/26/d4.pdf

Verner, I., & Bshouty, D. (2008). *Geometric applications in architecture: Problem solving, design, and multicultural education* [PowerPoint]. Haifa, Israel: International Workshop and Research Project: Intercultural Aspects of Creativity: Challenges and Barriers.

Khayriah Massarwe and Igor Verner
Department of Education in Technology and Science

Daoud Bshouty
Faculty of Mathematics
Technion – Israel Institute of Technology

Forthcoming Books in the Series

Being Creative Inside and Outside the Classroom (2011)
Authored by
James C. Kaufman, John Baer

The Roeper School - A Model for Holistic Development of High Ability (2011)
Edited by
Bharath Sriraman, Don Ambrose, Tracy L. Cross

Creatively Gifted Students Are Not Like Other Gifted Students: Research, Theory, and Practice (2012)
Edited by
Kyung Hee Kim, James C. Kaufman, John Baer, Bharath Sriraman, Lauren Skidmore

Creativity, Mathematics and Climbing: "Higher" Views of Embodiment (2012)
Authored by
Anne Birgitte Fyhn, Bharath Sriraman